D0504129

LORD COCKBURN: SELECTED LETTERS

LORD COCKBURN:
SELECTED LETTERS

Edited by
ALAN BELL

JOHN DONALD

First published in Great Britain in 2005 by
John Donald, an imprint of Birlinn Ltd
West Newington House
10 Newington Road
Edinburgh
EH9 1QS

www.birlinn.co.uk

ISBN 10: 0 85976 630 6
ISBN 13: 978 085976 630 2

British Library Cataloguing-in-Publication Data
A catalogue record for this book is available on request from the British Library

Typeset by Hewer Text (UK) Ltd, Edinburgh
Printed and bound in Great Britain by Creative Print and Design, Ebbw Vale, Wales

Contents

Abbreviations

Bic. Comm.	*Lord Cockburn: a bicentenary commemoration*, ed. Alan Bell, (1979)
BL	British Library
CJ	*Circuit Journeys, by Lord Cockburn* (1888, reprinted Edinburgh 1975)
ER	*The Edinburgh Review*
HWUA	Heriot Watt University Archives
Jeff.	*Life of Lord Jeffrey, with a selection from his Correspondence*, by Lord Cockburn (1852)
Jnl	*Journal of Henry Cockburn 1831–1854* (1874)
LAS	*Letters chiefly connected with the Affairs of Scotland, from Henry Cockburn*, ed. T.F. Kennedy (1874)
Mems	*Memorials of His Time*, ed. Karl Miller (Chicago and London 1974)
NLS	National Library of Scotland
SCJ	Senator of the College of Justice
SL	*Some Letters of Lord Cockburn*, ed. Harry A. Cockburn (1932)

Introduction

HENRY COCKBURN, when writing the biography of his close friend and fellow-judge Francis Jeffrey, remarked that 'the life of a man who, throughout the thirty years of his manhood, did little except by writing anonymous pamphlets (called Reviews) and by bamboozling Courts, is necessarily devoid of incidents'. The same could be applied in greater measure to Cockburn himself, because his 'pamphleteering', unlike Jeffrey's, did not involve being a busy founding editor of a celebrated Whig periodical – the *Edinburgh Review* – but merely contributing to it (anonymously) a few specialised articles on Scots law reform. Cockburn's special claim to fame lies not in the literary work published in journals, nor in the political achievements of a lifetime of Whig politics in opposition and then in triumph, but in a posthumous literary reputation still cherished in his native Edinburgh. This is founded on his *Memorials of His Time*, the recollections of his upbringing in Edinburgh and of his early days in that then small national college of legal practitioners, the Faculty of Advocates, the Bar of Scotland.

His executors had prepared his *Memorials* for publication in 1856, two years after their author's death. Other volumes followed later: the *Journal* in 1874, and the *Circuit Journeys*, diaries of his judicial progresses, in 1888. A Cockburn Association was founded in Edinburgh in 1875 as a very early Civic Trust, in memory of a doughty campaigner for the preservation of Old Edinburgh and for the dignified management of a new one. All this helped to confirm and extend the impression Henry Cockburn had given of himself in the *Memorials*, of a genial, sociable personality much concerned for the history and traditions of Edinburgh, who was at the same time fully appreciative of the changes needed for the city, and its nation, in a new age. There could be added to all this a general memory in legal circles of Cockburn as an advocate, a barrister who was 'a good hand for a jury' (the phrase is Walter Scott's), and as a sound but not exceptional judge in the Outer House of the Court of Session.

In addition to his autobiographical writings, which have always had a keen following, there remained another source, Cockburn's letters, which have survived in considerable quantities, though they have been little used, in the National Library of Scotland and elsewhere in Edinburgh. These confirm, and fill out in many biographical details, the impression of Cockburn as a congenial personality of well-deserved reputation in the Edinburgh of his day. It is this unpublished correspondence that forms the basis of the present selection.

The basic facts of Henry Cockburn's life can be set out here very simply, as he did those of Francis Jeffrey, and they will be expanded when annotating the letters of his maturity. He was born on 26 October 1779, the son of Archibald Cockburn of Cockpen (1738–1820), himself an advocate of the Scots Bar (admitted in 1762) who later became Sheriff of Midlothian (1765), Judge of Admiralty (1782) and finally a Baron of Exchequer (1790–1809). Henry's (to his family, Harry's) mother was Janet Rannie, daughter of David Rannie of Melville, whose elder sister Elizabeth was the first wife of Henry Dundas (created Viscount Melville in 1802); his career and domineering reputation are set out unforgettably in his nephew's *Memorials*. The young Cockburn attended the High School of Edinburgh, where he had an undistinguished career, and then at Edinburgh University, where he knew and was influenced by professors like the philosopher Dugald Stewart and other later luminaries of the Scottish Enlightenment.

At the university and in his early days at the Bar, he was a keen member of the Speculative Society, a literary and debating society of high standards founded in 1764, through which he was introduced to a circle of Whig lawyers which included the slightly older Francis Jeffrey (1775–1850). In 1802 Jeffrey had been one of the founders and the first editor of the *Edinburgh Review*, which soon became the leading liberal literary and political magazine of its day.

Cockburn was admitted to the Faculty of Advocates on 13 December 1800. In spite of his early conversion to the minority Whig party, which ran demonstratively against the strong Tory attachments of his father, and particularly his Melville uncle, he was appointed an Advocate-Depute in 1808 (resigning this appointment in 1810), and he practised with increasing success, especially as a defence counsel. On 18 March 1811 Cockburn married Elizabeth MacDowall, of Castle Semple, Lochwinnoch, Renfrewshire; they had eleven children, one of whom died in infancy (a list of them is given in the Appendix). In 1813 he acquired Bonaly, a property in the Pentland foothills just beyond Colinton. Here he much improved the originally simple buildings, and later considerably enlarged them. He laid out the grounds, and furnished himself with a rural retreat where he spent most of his vacations within easy reach of Edinburgh, where the Cockburn family lived at 14 Charlotte Square. He had become prominent in local dining clubs, including the Friday Club (which generally met on Saturdays), whose history he later wrote, and he was active as a social figure, particularly interested in the encouragement of the fine arts and local architectural improvements. Cockburn wrote a few (anonymous) articles for the *Edinburgh Review*, mainly on Scots law reform and related matters, and he collected a substantial library which justified his membership of the Bannatyne Club, an historical publishing fraternity responsible for some pioneering record publications.

Above all he showed himself keen in the cause of parliamentary reform, and became one of the organisers of increasingly prominent Whig meetings. In 1831 he was elected Rector of Glasgow University, at the time a politically sensitive post that he held for three successive years. In December 1830 Cockburn was an obvious choice to be Solicitor-General for Scotland in the Whig administration, in which Jeffrey took the senior appointment of Lord Advocate. Cockburn thus acted as link man in Edinburgh for the arrangement of political business, and he helped draft the parliamentary Reform Bill. On 5 November 1834 he was appointed to the Court of Session, and in 1837 was made also a criminal judge, a Lord of Justiciary, continuing in these roles for the rest of his life. In 1847, through no fault of his own, he ran into financial difficulties that were sorted out by careful management. He had to move from Charlotte Square to a new, smaller house at 2 Manor Place, but ensured that his various sons were adequately set up in life. He died at Bonaly, after a brief illness and on returning from one of the judicial circuits he greatly enjoyed, on 26 April 1854.

Such, in brief, is Henry Cockburn's career. Throughout it he maintained a number of correspondences, some with London friends such as the Edinburgh-trained lawyer John Richardson, who had become a parliamentary solicitor in London, some with correspondents in other parts of Scotland. The earliest letters in this volume, written during the opening years of the century, are clearly the rather self-conscious work of an essayist still in search of a suitable tempo as a correspondent. They have, it is true, a certain stylishness, but one that is better suited to the rostrum than to the page. At this stage Cockburn needs to relax a little as a letter-writer, leaving his classical intentions behind. Two of his correspondents of this early period, Charles Anderson and James Grahame, were clergymen, who had themselves been familiar with the essay-writing traditions of eighteenth-century Edinburgh debating societies. Even so, they may have been surprised by the stately periods that their jovial friend ventured at such length in his letters. It was a decade before Cockburn relaxed his own epistolary style to match the characteristically humorous, sometimes jocose, social manner for which he had become well known.

The social circles of the Whig opposition were generally easier in their civic life than the conservative Establishment of the period, often enviably so. Sir Walter Scott, though firmly opposed to the Whigs in a political way (and increasingly so as they became able to speak out and make their voices heard) had a high private regard for Cockburn and his friends, socially. A well-known passage in Scott's *Journal* (9 December 1826) recalls a dinner party given by John Archibald Murray and his Whig friends: 'capital good cheer and excellent wine – much laugh and fun'. The following morning (a Saturday) Scott felt the worse of the good measures of Burgundy and Champagne, but even though bilious enough to have had to call out the doctor, he was none the less appreciative of the company he had enjoyed:

> I do not know why it is that when I am with a party of my opposition friends the day is often merrier than when with our own set. Is it because they are cleverer? Jeffrey and Harry Cockburn are to be sure very extraordinary men, yet it is not owing to that entirely. I believe both parties meet with the feeling of something like novelty – we have not worn out our jests in daily contact. There is also a disposition on such occasions to be courteous and of course to be pleased. [*Journal* (1972), 250–1]

The political polarisation of Edinburgh was, it seems, much stronger in the Dundas-Melville circles of Cockburn's own family than when moderated by the traditional convivialities of the Bar.

Cockburn's period as Solicitor-General for Scotland – Autumn 1831 to Autumn 1834 – is deliberately under-represented in this volume. This is because he was necessarily preoccupied with governmental business, and a representative group of these documents would have distorted a general selection. The bulk of his official correspondence is well shown in his letters to the Scotch Whig MP, T. F. Kennedy of Dunure, who published a substantial volume of them in 1874 as *Letters chiefly connected with the Affairs of Scotland*. Even more importantly there survive in the National Library of Scotland (Adv. MSS. 9.1.8–11), 1,163 pages of foolscap transcription, by Cockburn's daughter Jane, of Lord Advocate Jeffrey's letters to his Solicitor-General, mainly from the period 1831–4. Cockburn's replies are not included, but he has characteristically annotated most pages, and the contents of his regular dispatches from Edinburgh can be inferred without difficulty.

Here his brief, lively comments on individuals are often equal to those in the *Memorials* and letters, and Cockburn's own habitual preoccupations, not all shared by Jeffrey, were never repressed by his official duties. In April 1833 the Lord Advocate wrote reprovingly: 'In such a crisis you cannot expect that we are to do anything about Salisbury Craigs, or paltry promotions'. Cockburn, more civically inclined, wrote unrepentantly, if later: 'No! What was any ministry, even this one, to the preservation of Salisbury Craggs?' [Adv. MSS. 9.1.9, f.156*v*.] A brief period in the management of Government business only served to emphasise Cockburn's impression of the inadequacies of the then House of Commons as a forum for the discussion of Scotch business. Thus on 5 June 1833 his note reads:

> There never was such an instance of the habitual ignorance and indifference of Government (all governments) to Scotch affairs as in this of patronage – a deep, vital and pressing question, kindred to others in the English and Irish churches, and in which one plain course was clearly pointed out by responsible and consulted Scotch advisers; yet because it was *as yet* merely Scotch, and conducted without turbulent agitation, it was impossible to get *any line whatever* adopted by ministers. This has long been the established system for managing this part of the empire. [Adv. MSS. 9.1.10, f.7]

Whatever his disillusionment with Westminster, his praise of Jeffrey's own role at the time of the Parliamentary, and later Municipal, reform discussions, was unstinted. When Burgh reform measures finally achieved a step forward, Cockburn wrote:

> Next to the reform of the representation, [this was] the most memorable, and important, necessary change in modern Scotland. No country was ever insulted and cursed by two greater abominations than our old system of representation and of municipal government. Jeffrey is greatly envied the honour of having had the knocking them both in his head. [*Ibid.*, f.57]

The other great event of early nineteenth-century national life in Scotland, the Disruption, also receives only incidental attention here. Cockburn was occasionally involved in matters ecclesiastical as a judge, and indeed as a friend of Thomas Chalmers, whom he admired for his achievement as a social reformer and mourned deeply after his dramatically sudden death in May 1847. But his own role in the ecclesiastical affairs of Scotland was only that of an observer – though no mere observer, as a substantial part of his *Journal* is devoted to the events of the Disruption period. Those pages show the extent of his own involvement as advocate, politician and judge. Their evidence is reviewed in a substantial essay by Iain F. Maciver, 'Cockburn and the

Church', in *Lord Cockburn: a Bicentenary Commemoration* 1779–1979 (1979). The legal background has recently been set out in Chapter 9 of David M. Walker, *A Legal History of Scotland,* vol. VI (The Nineteenth Century), 2001.

Cockburn's letters during his later years tend to be rather shorter, and certainly more clearly written (probably because of weakening eyesight) than those in early life. He found further opportunities for letter-writing while on judicial circuit. The *Circuit Journeys,* an attractive book published rather belatedly by his family in 1888, is the main result of these travels, but letters written during circuits also show him recording immediate impressions. The *Life of Lord Jeffrey, with a Selection from his Correspondence* (1852) had also concentrated his mind on literary work. Drawing as it did partly on Cockburn's own notebooks, the Jeffrey biography made him consider the fate of his own manuscript reminiscences, emphasising a nostalgic mood that is revealed in his later letters. The principal text, edited by his executors, became *Memorials of His Time* in 1856. Cockburn's grandson, Harry A. Cockburn, produced an illustrated edition of the *Memorials* in 1910, with some passages used in the *Life of Jeffrey* restored to their correct places; the Chicago University Press reprint of 1974 has been used in annotating this selection of letters. (Some very interesting fragments of the *Memorials* manuscript survive, and it is hoped that one day a new edition, incorporating these addenda, might be produced.)

The great majority of the letters printed here are previously unpublished. Most come from the manuscript collections of the National Library of Scotland, not least those numbered 'Dep.235'. These are the Cockburn family collection placed there by the late Frank Cockburn, with additions made by his widow, Margaret S. Cockburn. They generously gave me permission, many years ago, to make a selection for publication. This family collection, with further documents that by other routes have now found their way to the National Library, had been drawn on by Harry A. Cockburn for his *Letters of Lord Cockburn, with pages omitted from Memorials of His Time* (1932). H.A. Cockburn selected fifty of his ancestor's letters, but rarely gave complete texts: I have used eighteen of these, all of them now given entire. Extracts from the National Library's and other collections were used by Karl Miller in his *Cockburn's Millennium* (1975) and by the contributors to the *Bicentenary Commemoration* that I edited in 1979.

Cockburn wrote his letters at speed, with little attention to the niceties of punctuation. Commas, dashes and semi-colons are scattered unbalanced on the page, and produce paragraphs that sometimes cannot be read fluently. In this selection the punctuation has been standardised in a way that I hope improves the pace of the original text without the writer's haphazard orthography getting in the way.

In spelling, Cockburn had his quirks and preferences, most of which have been retained. He was much concerned with the future of the good *Scotch* tongue (and insistent on this spelling, which I have followed here). As he put it at the end of his life: 'Scot*s* is the affected pronunciation and spelling of a paltry, lisping, puppy Englishman. A *good* Caledonian calls himself a *Skotch-man*. Even the Suthrons don't call themselves Englisman. They keep their H but won't give us ours!' [Letter of 25 March 1854: WS Library] This and other shibboleths recur in his letters. 'Bonaily' as a pronunciation of 'Bonaly' seems now to be reckoned a lost cause; Cockburn himself, whose preference has to be duly noted, lost it as a spelling early on.

In a more general way, he noted with regret the decline of an upper-class Scotch vernacular ('among the gentry it is receding shockingly') and he was inclined to remark on a notable, if unfamiliar, usage. Mention of the cockchafer 'put me in mind of a very well made phrase of old Roby Craig's, anent a female friend of that structure. He used to call them "Nip-Doddles". Thus – 'Do ye ken Jenny Morison? – Lord! She's a fine lass! The best nip-doddle in the hail parish".' With such clear preferences in mind I have preserved, without special comment, distinctively Scotch spellings (and many of his personal spelling preferences that are also perhaps significant). An exception had to be made, however, for some surnames, where Cockburn himself was careless and inconsistent. His close friend and colleague Andrew Rutherfurd is generally recognised under that name, though Cockburn very frequently lapses into Rutherford. Similarly the (Wellwood) Moncr*eiff* family have all been given that spelling (as used today by their descendants), rather than the many variants that Cockburn used quite haphazardly.

I have been fortunate that several of Cockburn's principal correspondences, for example those with John Richardson and Andrew Rutherfurd and a substantial portion of his letters to Jeffrey, are in the custody of the National Library of Scotland. I am grateful to the Trustees for permission to publish letters in their possession, and particularly to the late William Park and James Ritchie, successive Keepers of Manuscripts, for their early encouragement of the project. As already mentioned, the late Frank and Margaret Cockburn placed their family collection of numerous letters and other documents in the National Library for the use of scholars, and I must thank them, posthumously, for their encouragement.

Among private owners of letters printed here I am grateful to Mrs Annis Frackleton and Mr Harry More Gordon, and also to several other owners and institutions (including the National Archives of Scotland) who have allowed me to consult documents not published here. I am grateful for permissions to the authorities of the British Library; the Cockburn Association; the Houghton Library, Harvard University; the Henry E. Huntington Library, San Marino CA; New College Library, University of Edinburgh; New College Archives, University of Oxford; the Royal Scottish Academy; and the library of the Society of Writers to H.M. Signet. I have accumulated many debts to friends in Edinburgh who have waited very patiently for the eventual publication of this book, among them Dr Iain Brown of the National Library of Scotland and his former colleague Mr Iain Maciver. Finally, many thanks to Professor Karl Miller. In 1975, in the preface to *Cockburn's Millennium*, he mentioned his hope that, having transcribed Cockburn's letters, I would go on to edit them. Thirty years later, I have at last found time to rise to Professor Miller's challenge, and I hope that he will not be disappointed by the result of a suggestion he made many years ago.

Edinburgh, January 2005   Alan Bell

THE LETTERS

To Charles Anderson[1]
NLS 3546.1

36 George's Street, Edinburgh, 5 July 1803

My Dear Anderson

The Season is at length approaching in which, if it be not inconvenient for you, John[2] and I propose to disturb the solitude of your academic lucubrations and exhibit to you, on the banks of Loch Caterine, the fields of the Peripatetic school – a sect to which both of us have been long, and I am afraid too devotedly, attached. The pure and pious parish of Gask is to be polluted by the presence of two vile pettyfoggers, who after feeding as fully as they can (poorly enough however – Lord knows) in town upon the follies and vices of men, retire to the country to create game for their winter's pursuit – our poverty if not our will. Believe me neither of us have got fat upon it.

The Session rises upon Saturday next, the 9th of July. We intend to remain in town a week after this millennium, and to set forth (each being his own sumpter mule[3]) on the Monday se'ennight following – being the 18th of the month. We shall be that night at the scenes of Michael Bruce's infancy;[4] and next morning shall lay the town of Perth under contribution for a breakfast. Now the path by which the pilgrims are to sojourn to Gask being unknown to them, what if you should imitate the antique custom of coming forth, tho' it should even be the length of Perth, and blessing your guests? The Salutation Inn would be an ominous place to meet at.

Where we are to go after leaving you, we shall determine when that inhuman hour comes. Only we have greatly, very greatly, abridged our

---

1 Charles Anderson (1778–1829), an Edinburgh graduate, was ordained to Gask, Perthshire, 1802, presented to Closeburn, Dumfriesshire, 1814. He m.1820 Elizabeth Hathorn Macmillan (d.1827) and had two sons.
2 For John Richardson, see 24 Jan 1806 below.
3 Pack-horse.
4 Kinnesswood, Lochleven, Fife.

intended tour. From an extravagant folio work, it has shrunk into a moderate duodecimo – well suited for the pocket. Your must therefore write me, giving your criticisms on the prospectus of it I have now submitted to you. Only I must positively insist that if our approach to the priory of Gask be in the least – remember now in the very least – inconvenient to you, you are to say so with the frankness that ought invariably to be used between friends. Nothing but the certainty that we are not disturbing you can make the very short visit we shall be able to pay you agreeable either to us or to you.

You owe me eight shillings – having made me subscribe a long while ago to something written by a Mrs Grant[1] which she calls poems – and which you assured me it would not be infamy, as I now perceive it to be, to have my name affixed to. [Next] time that Apollo chuses to impregnate this Lady with a Highlander, may I not be brought in for a share of the expence of delivering her monster and taking him from the filthy sheets of his mother.

Simpson[2] has thrust himself into the management of a trial for murder here on Monday next. And no doubt will make an harrangue which will not only bring the prisoner but the council to justice – both will infallibly be knockt in the head for ever and for ever – Amen.

Yours Sincerely
Henry Cockburn

Write soon.

[*Addressed*:] Revd Mr Anderson, Gask, by Perth

To Charles Anderson
NLS 3546.5

Caroline Park, 5 October 1803, 1 morning

My Dear Anderson

I had perfectly forgotten that fate, which presides even over the tossing up of a halfpenny, had destined me to write you a letter about the beginning of October, when a few days ago, being at Roslin with John, as we were admiring the woods already changing to the venerable appearance of the castle which fronts them, John remarked how fine those of Dunkeld would be. The very sound made me start. I recollected you and my promise, and resolved *quam primum* to fulfil it. Well then John must be right. I should delight to see the

1 Mrs Anne Grant, of Laggan, Invernessshire.
2 James Simpson (1780–1853); adv.1801.

Dunkeld woods just now. And notwithstanding the assiduity [with] which I keep up the show of study, I dare say that if Providence had not planted so very scanty a quantity of the root of all evil in me, I should have gone forth to Dunkeld. Indeed of that precious root for which all men toil so much in vain I have not got by nature a single shoot; and my system of mental husbandry is so extremely wretched, and the soil so peculiarly poor, and exposed to so many months of fallow, that I am afraid I shall never be able to bring the roots which others give me to any height. What 'a wise provision of nature' it is, that in this case, by means of what is called a 'Prophetic eye of taste', while 'I plant the seedling', I can 'already sit under its branches and enjoy the coolness' (I had almost said with more truth the coldness) 'of the shade'.

There is nothing new here – except by the bye what Christison would call a 'fac' – in the literary world. Thos. Campbell is to be married.[1] 'Tam the hermit sighed, till woman smiled.' Her name is Sinclair – from Liverpool – know nothing about her. No money. This step I take to be more poetical than prudent. It will burden Pegasus with a wife and family – and we all know he is heavily loaded enough already. However it may have two great advantages – it will make Thos. more steady and laborious; second, by making him less 'Peace-enamoured', it may preserve his health – tho' neither of these are quite certain as to Poets.

By the bye another very curious Fac is this. We have often disputed about Brougham's poetical taste.[2] Now I have lately heard him seriously, coolly, candidly declare, in Company, that excepting in *Comus* and *perhaps Allegro*, Milton was not more poetical – possessed of more genius – than Pope!!! Declared himself, without any affectation, insensible to the merits – supposed merits I mean – of *Paradise Lost*. This being said in such a way as to convince me that it was true, settles the point, and turns Brougham out with those who Beattie declares for not liking music ought to 'Sneak with the scoundrel *Fox*, and Grunt' (which Brougham is very apt to do) 'with glutton swine'. These are all the philosophical facts in this part of the world that are new; tell me how many you have discovered equally important in Gask.

Anderson, I am very glad that your letters to me will not be – from your situation can not be – filled with anything but what relates to yourself. This will please me most, and will make you write oftner. It is an excellent subject –

1 Campbell (1777–1844) married Matilda Sinclair (d.1828) on 10 October.
2 Henry Brougham (1778–1868); adv.1800, barrister 1808; MP 1810; Lord Chancellor 1832–4. An originator of and contributor to the *Edinburgh Review*. Known in Parliament House circles as 'The Evil'.

full of humour, useful, inexhaustible, not indecent. I could say a great deal upon it. Particularly in the way of advice upon its new situation – could tell you how it may be affected by its removal from Society, books, disputes, and all those things which repel the mildew of the mind, Indolence. But this being a long subject, and a delicate one, I shall not handle it except in a separate letter, not even without permission. Write soon and believe me

Yours very Sleepily

H. Cockburn

[*Addressed:*] Revd Charles Anderson, Gask, by Perth

To Charles Anderson
NLS 3546.7

36 George Street, 15 November 1803

My Dear Anderson

I have just got into my own room from the first meeting of the Spec. Society;[1] and never has self-humbled guilt been more deeply mortified than I have been, upon entering for another – I believe now, the last – time, a place where I might have done so much good, and have done so little. Brougham, Horner, Jeffrey and others, who from their exertions there will not only be looked up to during their lives, but perhaps have the circumstances of their youth enquired into when they are gone, were all absent; and I was left with ten or twelve insignificants, of whom (I may without vanity pay myself the melancholy compliment) I was perhaps the only one who recollected the past with unmingled anguish. Every object in the room brought back – alas! only to my fancy, the reality is gone for ever – the exertions which their good sense and energy prompted some to make for their improvement; while I was encouraging instead of shaking off the natural lethargy of the faculties, and never descrying the day in which the few liberal feelings my folly should leave me were to be recognised only by their condemnation of my Indolence.

No doubt it is sometimes possible to stretch a little beyond the ordinary term those golden years which, when employed as nature intends and the Society does not always hinder, render youth the Augustan period of life. But it is no more than possible. Let us idly dream away a single year, and habits

1 For the Society, founded in 1764, see *Mems*, 25, and 67–70 for a rosily nostalgic account. Cockburn had been elected in November 1799 and now went into 'extraordinary' membership; he remained a staunch defender of its privileges.

creep upon us which for ever after torture us like an incubus, wishing but unable to recover them. Whether it is a blessing or a curse, that without being aware of it, looking no farer than the next moment, we are silently fixing the destiny of our lives? How easily might I have perceived that of all those who have enjoyed the most pleasing, tho' the most perishing, of all reputations, that of liberalysing the practical details of life, no one could be more encouragingly situated than myself. My time all my own – health, books, independance, nay a knott of acquaintance of undoubtedly superior talents to carry me along with them! But rivalship cannot prompt those who have no emulation. And henceforth I am never, even in the very humble sphere of professional exertion, to be distinguished as one of the leaders of the passing file. Yet I may be frequently stung to the heart by being mentioned as one of the youthful associates of those whose early diligence shall be rewarded by a larger than ordinary share of the public attention.

If I had never wished to have extended my views beyond the ambition of a practical drudge, I might have been unaffected by the gradual withdrawing of my former prospects. But in a commonplace book,[1] which I have long made a practice of keeping, in this humiliating record of my weaknesses, this map of my mind to which I often turn when I wish to examine any place I have passed in my progress, I found tonight sentences like the following, which relate to a far-gone period – I believe the commencement of the Academical Society:[2]

'At this moment I remember (may it never be forgotten!) the enthusiasm of virtue, fame and science, which during the walks I regularly took two or three years ago in the Summer evenings, used to encourage and animate my severest study. I then thought every labour despicable, in comparison of the bright prospects with which I fondly believed it was possible they could be succeeded.

'I may hope again to recall those enthusiastic, those poetical evenings which the prospects of science first opened upon me, swelled my breast in extacy. At this moment I recollect the emotions which then filled my eyes with tears. I have before me the favourite spots where I stood: the sun setting behind the Ochills; all the fools (as I thought them) who would otherwise have disturbed my walk, gazing on the Volunteers on the Links; a solitary blackbird hymning to the evening star; my own mind expanded and warmed by my morning's and forenoon's study; filled with the regret that I had lost so much of the

1 HC advised Anderson in a further letter (6 December 1803): 'if you wish to solace the decline of your life by feeling over again the emotions of your youth, you will immediately begin to keep' a commonplace book.
2 The Academical 'rose in 1796 and, after a short though very active life, died of decline about 1816' (*Mems, 25*).

earlier part of my life, which if properly employed might (as I thought) have enabled me to transmit a name to posterity.

'Now that I have rescued again from everlasting oblivion the enthusiasm of my youthful ardours, may I never lose it.'

Even so long ago as when these were written, you will perceive I began to blame myself for what I now so deeply – tell me if not irrecoverably – repent of. I am able to pick out, of a very old date: 'These prospects have since been both contracted and darkened.' And: 'Yet altho' these superior emotions will be for ever hallowed in my recollection, I am also sure that neither the attainments nor the celebrity of which they are the proofs that I painted, will ever be acquired.'

This peep which I give you in confidence into my mind may – to a second person – perhaps appear absurd. These sentances however are the records of liberal designs, which a fatal littleness of mind has prevented from being executed; and which – for they are scarcely revived even by a wish, were it not for this memorial they once dictated – I should not have remembered had ever existed.

How much of all this, my dear Anderson, may apply to you, I cannot guess. Little did I think when I jocularly proposed to lecture you about your present situation, that I should have to illustrate my lesson by so unfortunate an example. Beware lest you be following it.

Break the truth with Indolence, else you may wake, look for your mind, and not find it. Fame and even knowledge may be easily resigned; but without the energy of a living mind, happiness is dull; with the consciousness of having lost it, life is despicable. What sublimer delight can a man enjoy, than that of watching, like God taking care of the world, the progress of his own mind! What can debase him more than the belief that the most common and obvious weakness has made him lose all that he admires in others?

I know very well that the short-lived regret with which perhaps every man at one time looks back upon the great schemes of improvement which his boyish philosophy gives rise to, is very just[ly] accompanied by a smile at their romantic nature. But believe me, where these schemes are reasonable, still more if partly realized, their failure – when it proceeded from folly, instead of casting, as it is generally imagined to do, a pensive but not unpleasing twilight over his future life – draws a settled gloom upon it, wh[ich] even the business of the world can scarcely dispel.

Yours ever
H. Cockburn

P.S. From very obvious reasons you will perceive the propriety of concealing this letter from every mortal – and I entreat you to write to me soon.

H. C.

To Charles Anderson
NLS 3546.12

36 George Street, Edinburgh, 24 January 1806

My Dear Anderson

I believe it was agreed on when we parted that our correspondence should be renewed by you. Yet I cannot delay telling you that you have lost Richardson,[1] I may almost say for ever. He has gone to settle as a sollicitor in London. His late profession here is so overstocked that it is just possible for any person with the utmost patience and activity who has nothing to trust to but his own merits to succeed. No opening ever appears but a son, a cousin, a nephew or some other connection is instantly set to close the breach. By this means the business is so locked up that even in the most favourable circumstances it is a miracle if a new and unconnected candidate is not obliged to repent too late that he ever engaged in so unequal and illiberal a contest.

From the total want of relations, John has the misfortune to be committed from his infancy to the world at large; and tho' he has left this (not his native place) with the blessing of more genuine friends, and a more varied and extensive acquaintance than any one ever procured for himself by the simple influence of his own worth, yet that esteem which constitutes so much of happiness has very little effect on success in business. But by removing to London all this operates in his favour; and he is instantly in a situation where the value of his manners will be felt, and his other personal qualities secure to him the reward from which they were excluded by the vulgar monopoly here.

Accordingly he was promised such support and from such hands as would have made it highly imprudent to remain here, where after sacrificing other ten of his most valuable years he might still have had to look foreward with regret and anxiety. He was aware that in leaving Edinr and his society here, he quit[t]ed a situation sufficient to grattify all the wishes of rational ambition. But the privation was in some measure lessened by the warm introduction he obtained to some of the best little circles in London.

Thus we have lost Richardson. We may see him occasion[al]ly if we go up

1 John Richardson (1780–1864), son of a farmer in Gilmerton; his mother, Hope Gifford, was a niece of Principal William Robertson. He was apprenticed WS 1796, but moved to London, setting up in Parliamentary practice. His business flourished, latterly as Richardson, Loch & McLaurin. For more than 30 years he discharged the London duties of Crown Agent for Scotland. Richardson moved in literary circles, e.g. as a friend of Scott, Campbell and Crabbe; his London address in Fludyer Street, Westminster, became a calling place for Edinburgh friends. See *Mems*, 174–5.

in Spring, and I trust he will generally be down here a little in Autumn. But these are only occasional visits, and another God bless you will only make the winters close in the more heavily. As a friend whose worth, good sense, kindness, gentleness, and elegance, could always be depended on, we have lost him for ever. He resolved every day before he went to write to you; but was so hurried that he was obliged to devolve the melancholy task on me. He went in the mail last Tuesday, and I hope was in London this morning.

To tell you how deeply I regret and ever will regret his irrecoverable loss, is but to tell you what you and all who knew him must feel. I can scarcely believe that he is gone. The three last years spent in the company of such a friend (for he *was* a friend!) start before me like a dream, and leave this place where I have been all my life a solitary waste. I cannot look on the top of a single hill in the neighbourhood, without having some moments of genuine happiness recalled to my heart. I feel a want in every prospect of future life that rises before me, with scarcely a hope that it will ever be supplied. Such another may be found – but it is in vain to look for him.

How few survive the lessons of the shooll [*sic*] that made him. From the hour that he was born he was obliged to advance himself by his own personal qualities. In doing so he followed the biass of his heart directed by a sound head, and cultivated, at least acquired, all the excellencies that can engage a secure friendship. From the lowest and most helpless obscurity he has by his own genuine goodness alone created to himself a Society of men who never agreed in anything but in the sincerity of their love for him and their still sincerer regret at his departure. You knew him well. Tell me a single defect but what flowed from a source purer than the noblest virtues, the influence of his affections in blinding his judgement.

It is consolatory that there does not seem to be any reasonable doubt of his success in London. If a few years should give him a fixed independance, and enable him by marriage to supply the dreadful want of relatives, so that he might be sure of attention at least, whatever might be his fate, from the selfishness if it were nothing else, of those who are interested in him as a part of themselves, I shall learn to be happy in his removal to the metropolis. One pleasure nothing can ever take from us, I mean that of thinking on his virtues and endeavouring to imitate them.

Yours very Sincerely
Henry Cockburn

P.S. John's direction is No 16 Fludyer Street, Westminster, London.

[*Addressed*:] Revd Chas Anderson, Gask, by Perth

[*To John Richardson*]
NLS Dep.235(1) (*SL*, 9–10)

Niddrie, Sunday [3 July 1807]

Here I have been since yesterday – amidst all the beauty of earth, and all the goodness of heaven. Except Alice and Aunt Sidney, they are all off to Libberton, and I steal the silence that has ensued, with delight, to hold converse with you. Many thanks for your long and broad letter of yesterday. I have it not here, but can well remember its contents. God pity poor Classon. I hope it will not be as you fear. I rejoice that you have so many acquaintances among our patriotic senators, tho' I doubt if Sir George Warrender will be one of that meritorious band.[1] May either unanimity or faction soon cut short their legislative or party labours. Continue in the mean time to walk to Kensington, as that alas is the only way you can enjoy this divine weather, or prepare yourself and me for the enjoyment of the autumnal months that are almost in view.

The circuit is, no doubt, a cursed annoyance. And I am affraid that our scheme, of making an equestrian tour, will not do. Besides all other objections, we could in truth be little together, especially at night when 'his Lordship' must know that we were in the same inns with him. The Justice asked me, t'other day, to go with him, and I half promised. But there will probably be a long vacation of parliament, and the Mountains [*i.e.* Hills] being in town, our time will pass with less distraction than usual.

Why not cultivate your memory? It is the greatest of intellectual luxuries to have a treasure in store from which such draughts of nectar can be taken. It will be still more absurd in you, to allow business to make you give up your book of forms. What hinders you to bring all your material down here with you, and work nine hours a day? This will be an excuse to me to be busy also. If you can easily get me a Quintilian and an Ovid, I wish you would. I shall send you some money for that and another purpose by Bell, who leaves this on Thursday.

I look anxiously for your journal, of which, since you like that mode of epistolizing, I am sorry I did not keep one since I last wrote to you. But this was it, so far as I can remember. *Saturday*, went to Firth, found all well, glorious bathe in the Esk. *Sunday*, came in to the Club. Very pleasant – Pluffy,[2]

---

1 Sir George Warrender, 4th Bt, MP 1807–32.
2 John Playfair (1748–1819), Professor of Mathematics and Natural Philosophy, is presumably meant here. (*Mems*, 338).

Jef.,[1] Murray,[2] Jef's brother, Timotheus, Skiny, and Irving.[3] Pluf. asked kindly for you and resolved that we should be a club extraordinary when you come down. Came home muzzy with Champagne, and rose on *Monday* before 6. Dictated till 9. Read a process till 12. Went to a 'Sage consult' at Gillies'[4] at 12, about an Exchequer debate on a point of English law. I am never employed by His Majesty in such cases, and therefore saw no reason why I should not appear against him. At one I went to another consult at Blair's[5] about the Town Clerk of Elgin. One of the pursuers is an old good natured stammering schoolfellow of ours, Pat. Sellar.[6] At 3 came home and walked to Car[oline] Park with J. Brougham.[7] It was to settle a bet with Cooper who says he can fish any *man* ashore in spite, not of his teeth, but of his legs and arms, with a single hair. But it was too ventose for human natation. Came up by 9 and was busy till 12. *Tuesday*, rose at 6, dictated from 7 till 8. Went to the Court at 9 and staid till 3. All the entail cases were decided – after huge speeches. I gained, as indeed was very easy, my point. The Justice then delivered the opinion of the court in Glengarry's case. It was the best speech I ever heard the Justice, or any man on our bench, make. They fined the Savage in £2000. Dined alone – and drilled from 6 till 8 – was busy till 11.

Wednesday, rose at 6, and considered the Exchequer case till 9. Went to the House, and after some small matters there, went to the Excheq. and utterly pounded Skinny and the Ox Craigie[8] (who represented Clathick and Boyle there) with English law. Craigie instead of responding entreated for more time, which was granted. Dined alone, and studied a proof for debate next day, all night. A divine walk in the evening. On *Thursday*, rose at 6 and went on with the proof – went to the court, but Army did not get to the case. Heard Craigie make a beastly speech to the Exchequer – judgement in a few days.

---

1 Francis Jeffrey (1773–1850); adv. 1794. Elder son of George Jeffrey, Principal Clerk of Session. Educated High School, Glasgow and Edinburgh universities, and (briefly) Queen's College, Oxford. Editor of the *Edinburgh Review* from 1803. Married, 1801, Catherine (d.1805), daughter of Professor Charles Wilson, St Andrews; 1813, Charlotte, daughter of Charles Wilkes, New York, USA. Further developments in his career noted *passim*.
2 John Archibald Murray (1778–1859); adv. 1800. Second son of Alexander Murray, SCJ (as Lord Henderland). MP, Leith, 1835–7; knighted 1839, SCJ 1839.
3 Jeffrey's brother, John. William Erskine (1769–1822); adv. 1790, SCJ (as Lord Kinneder) 1822. Alexander Irving (1766–1832); adv. 1788, SCJ (as Lord Newton) 1826.
4 Adam Gillies (1766–1842); adv. 1787, SCJ 1811.
5 Probably Robert Blair of Avontoun, then Dean of Faculty.
6 Probably Patrick Sellar of Westfield, Moray, later factor to the Earl of Sutherland.
7 Henry Brougham's brother
8 Craigie (d.1834); adv, 1776. He became SCJ in 1811: 'a worthy heavy old lawyer', *Jnl*, I.59.

Took a coach and went to bathe – exquisite. Read all the evening D'Alembert *Sur la destruction des Jesuites.* A most profound and interresting account of the progress of a faction at first below contempt to power almost irresistible. Dined with Cranny,[1] Wm Clerk,[2] Murray, Gaffer Young, H. Erskine. Very pleasant till half past 12. Murray is always best by himself. He leaves this when the court rises to go to the west (English) circuit with Horner.

On *Friday,* rose at 6, and went (after working) to the Court at 9 – got a few little matters over and came away at 10. Dictated from half past 10 till 3 –took a coach and bathed – still more divine. Dined with H. Jardine, Lord Melville and clan.[3] Went to Hope Street and found the Mountains returned from Firth. They were sitting in a dark room, very melancholy – at leaving the country and the prospect of Gartsheugh. They are fools. Have no notion of comfort. Absurd about the town. Because it is called the Town, they must not go out one step – tho' within six minutes' walk they have scenes which what they call the country will strain in vain to rival. *Saturday* rose as usual at 6, and was in the House at 9 – waited for two causes till one – visited the Mountains, and came out here. Jacob, like a blockhead, has been in the house all this week. Oh that you were here. I forgot to mention Lady Hunter Blair, the best of old Lady's [*sic*].[4] She, Alice, Aunt Sidney, Maggy, Anne and Alicia Gordon are listening to a good sermon read by Maggy, 'On drawing near to God'; the blackbirds, the cascade, the honeysuckle and Laburnum – everything, the day, the season, and the place, do not invite us to draw near, they bring us into the very presence of God. But the discourse is finished and I perceive the hats getting on. Alice is taking the garden key from the accustomed drawer, the certain sign of a gossiping visit to old Lucky at the gate.

Monday night. Delightful evening and a long walk last night. Came away this morning by 6 – magnificent spectacle from Arthurius – was here by 8, and breakfasted and purified – I mean purified and breakfasted – by half past 9. Dictated from 10 till 12. Consulted first with John Burnet[5] and then with Ro. Craigie about Exchequer Law from half past 12 till 3; dictated till 4 – dined (with Ringan) in Hope Street – dictated from 6 till 7. Saw a white tea-inviting signal from the Hope Street window, which I accepted; returned soon and

1 George Cranstoun (1771–1850); adv. 1793. Dean of Faculty 1825; SCJ (as Lord Corehouse) 1826.
2 William Clerk (1771–1847); adv. 1792. Clerk of Jury Court, 1815.
3 Henry Jardine of Harwood (1766–1851); WS 1790. Knighted 1825. Henry Dundas (1742–1611), 1st Viscount Melville, cr. 1802.
4 Widow of Sir James Hunter Blair (1741–87); she, a sister of 10th Earl of Cassilis, d.1817.
5 John Burnet (1763–1810), adv. 1785. Judge of Admiralty, April 1810.

dictated till 9. I now write to you – before repeating my descent on the pavement of the Street of Hope. The Misses[1] are there more seriously, not offended, but mortified, than I ever before saw them; at your long silence.

I agree with you about the pain with which every person who can read old Cicero must learn his weakness of character. But it is a consolation that some people deny it. Don't miss – if you can hit – Laing's first Speech, which must astound the senators.[2] Peace with his sister Plenty preside in the Cannon! Never shall I forget my first day there. Could you not parody now – for I can't well – Shakespeare's line about 'seeking . . . in the Cannon's mouth'?

Tuesday morning – have only time to say Vale.

H. C.

[*Addressed*:] John Richardson Esqre, 5 Fludyer Street, London

To John Richardson
NLS Dep.235(1) [*SL* 9–10 (–)]
[1807]

On *Tuesday*, you see, after I last epistolised you, I dined with Jeffrey at Murray's, and we Speculated together. Jeffrey made a clever, ingenious, but wrong speech about moral and physical causes. Came home, and laved the visage and went to Cranny's. Huge party – of the usual kind. Did not stay half an hour; being up at 6 sleepifyed me, as much as the prospect of being so again next morning did. So on *Wednesday* in the links at half past 6 – Murray and the little Erskine (excellent little fish) breakfasted here. The Coffee pots are really inimitable luxuries – to say nothing of the pleasure of cooking the coffee. At 12 went to a consultation at Burnett's to settle his new paper maker Indictment. It was worse than the old one – if possible; and therefore, to exonerate myself, I made out one of my own accord, almost new, which I deposited with Nairne as a record of my own standing clear of Burnett's. Gillies was decided that Burnett was absurd and I triumphed over him. Dined alone, and read till 10; whisted at the Coopers' at night.

On *Thursday* quaffed coffee at 6 in the morning – and arrayed in gold and green, like a ripe Laburnum, I proceeded amidst east wind, snow below and

1 The Miss Hills ('Mountains' above) were the daughters (Isabella and Helen, and Barbara) of Lawrence Hill (1755–92), WS 1779, and his widow Christian, née Dreghorn (d.1830), who lived at Woodhall, Colinton.
2 Perhaps Malcolm Laing (1762–1818); adv. 1785. MP, Orkney, 1807–12.

sleet above, to muster my said undefeated warriors. Murray was colded and che[z] Bonar, so the small Institute and I went forth to Dalmahoy. We reached the scene of former glory between 10 and 11 – devilishly cold. Staid there till 3, and got home by 6. The mutton was richly embrowned and the plotty [*sc.* mulled wine] exhilerating and soporific. Erskine was obliged to be sent home in a coach. I dozed at the Coopers' till 12. Slept so tired and so much of the order of the *Sorbonne* that (by about two millions of degrees) it put me in mind of the night in which we lay – not slept – in the hay loft of Mrs McFarlane's at Row of Denan.

On *Friday,* indicted all forenoon. Dined with Dr Davidson[1] who deplored that I had given up even my religious *profession.* Haldane is making great noise by having become an Anabaptist.[2] He leads down his flock – every sheep so old as to be fit for immediate killing, not merely lambs – to Stockbridge to be washed every Sunday by scores. T'other day there were about 2000 Spectators; the glass stood at 30. Coventry said he would rather not be saved than immerse on such a day.

This morning (*Saturday)* I came here – but the weather was so dreadful that the aid of Mrs Smith was necessary. They are all well. John, at this moment, in the arm chair next to the Ladies' room, sound asleep. Miss Hill is in the opposite chair reading Julius Caesar, and admitting it is better than Miss Baillie.[3] Miss Helen is at the table opposite her, hemming a pillow slip. And Barbara is lowly seated at the string-bound stool, attempting to determine whether 37 pence be 3/6d or 3/7d.

And so you see the days and the weeks pass away ever the same. I am often surprised at the little variety within which happiness may be found. I cannot recollect any remarkable event that has diversified the last four months of my existance. To some, this would be the picture of misery. But I do not think so. Days in private life, as aeras in history, are generally made famous by pain. Where this is found not, satisfaction with a few familiar things seems to me to evince contentment, and not dulness – or rather to testify some power in one's own mind of creating a personal and conscious variety, which is not often seen by others – and sometimes not even observed by ourselves.

1 Thomas Davidson (formerly Randall) of Muirhouse (1742–1827), minister of the Tolbooth. HC's brother-in-law (who had in 1798 married as his second wife HC's eldest sister Elizabeth), and thus his senior by 37 years. They had a further daughter and four sons, the youngest of whom was father of Thomas Randall Davidson, Archbishop of Canterbury 1903–28.
2 James Alexander Haldane (1768–1851), an East India officer, now turned Baptist.
3 Joanna Baillie (1762–1851), the dramatist and poet.

Yet is it a pity, after all, that so many of our feelings – and so many occurrences in existance – are daily suffered to drop for ever into irrecoverable oblivion. We would be confounded by alarm if we were to be told that all we knew of the world and its history was to be taken from us in half an hour. Yet if Smith's maxim be true, which it certainly is, that a man is all the world to himself, why should we so easily and so perpetually part as we do with views and emotions which, at the time we are conscious of them, seem to us to be the only things worth living for? You have lived *nearly* thirty years – all this time your mind has been actively employed, and your heart warmly attached, to some things or other. Yet if you will sit cross legged at the fire half an hour, I suspect you will be able to make everything you can recollect, of past years, arise before you. Undoubtedly many delightful thoughts – many happy days and even months – hundreds of curious and long established opinions, strange anticipations and stranger resolutions, vain forebodings, and still interesting wishes, and millions of other things which you would give the world to be able to feel over again, are gone from your remembrance, completely and for ever.

I had this deeply and melancholy impressed upon me t'other day upon looking over an old commonplace book, which revived so many facts and strange old notions in me, notions that with all their absurdity I loved, that I began to lament that I had not kept a minute diary of all the memorabilia of all my days. Such a thing would, if right done, be very useful as well as amusing. I know no life in which there is anything in the least like a true account of the feelings of a boy. I delight to hear you talk of Dalkeith school, because then I see in another the simple and actual notions I have so often felt myself, and wondered if any body else did the same. Think what a curious volume you could make by just telling plainly what your prevailing feelings were for the six years you were under the beastly despotism of Bell.

It is incredible how ignorant people are of things like this. Till I was sixteen I never once could discover the most remote or fanciful possibility that reading of any kind could be either useful or pleasant. During all the time I was brutified at the High School, I was asked 'Have you no ambition?' 'Bless me! Do you not see Ogilvie above you?' 'You'll never do any good.' Alas! ambition, above, doing good, and such words were, to me, as chaff sown upon cristal. And then when I grew a little more ancient – God help me – what an eternal variety of prospects and opinions about futurity!

I saw t'other day my whole life, from about my sixteenth to my seventy-second year, laid regularly out, and what I supposed, and what I wished, should be its condition in every portion of that time, precisely marked. It is really a curious specimen of the mode in which youth views, and the minuteness with which it attends to, futurity. There is an absurdity about things now familiar to me – a romantic cast about philosophy and virtue, and an impatience of Hope in some things, and the very reverse in others – that to any body else would seem madness or silliness, but of which I would not lose the recollection, as I see the reality of the picture gradually filling up, for almost anything.

Now this brings me back to my position, that a life written with such minute fidelity to common nature would of all things be the most interresting to the writer, and the most useful to others. I am therefore sometimes half persuaded to record, e'er 'the glimmering landscape fade', the simple but real thoughts by the consciousness of which my past years and moments have been engaged. I wish you would employ some quiet evenings in the same pleasing occupation. Toil it is not – no more than it is to run thro' the rooms in old age where our younger years were spent, or walk over the fields of which every ridge reminds us of something, that we once would have been mortified if any body had told us there was ever to be any thing else in the world worth minding. It will occupy a little time [*rest missing*]

To James Grahame
NLS 3519.26

4 North Charlotte Street, 12 December 1808

My Dear Grahame[1]

Your nine months were delivered this day. The obstetrical operation was performed by a little black semi-gentleman, who it appears is a Methodist preacher in your county. He was in the mail, and having been getting up a new sett of psalms for his congregation has acquired a taste for poetry. Smelling something in his way in the coach, he fell upon it, opened your parcell, and read it all the way in to the great edification and amusement of the company. But it is safe now. My poor opinion you can always command, but at this busy season you cannot expect it before the end of the xmas holydays. I wish you would tell me exactly what you want. Is it minute criticism – line upon line – or only a general opinion? If the former, how do you wish the references to be marked – not I presume by polluting the blank pages of the pure copy sent.

1 James Grahame (1765–1811); adv. 1795, previously WS (1791), having been apprenticed to his cousin Laurence Hill. He was ordained curate of Shipton (Moyne), Gloucestershire in 1809. His *Sabbath* was published (at first anonymously, but soon acknowledged) in 1809. Shaldon did not materialise as a cure; he died, soon after moving to county Durham, as curate of Sedgefield.

If *Geraldine*[1] had been written by me, I should have held your opinions respecting it to be well founded, and been indifferent, as I could truly say it was almost the only verse I had written since I was fifteen. But the joke was taken. You have been censuring one of Shakespeare's best little pieces, modernised by Warton. This is the poem of which Shakespeare says in a letter to a cousin of Spencer's, a relation of Sir Henry Wotton's, 'Well beloved Sire – I send you one off my best litt. pieces ycleped The Holy Grove or Geraldine, composeed upon the sadde going awaye of yr nieece. Methinkes it bee on of the verry best of yr kind greetinge friends W.S.' You will see this letter in the third vol. p.201 of the last edition of Spencer's works. So you may criticise Geraldine as you please or dare, being Dick's own.

Your opinion about Combination is as ill founded as that about this little exquisite production. You may say what you like man, but it is *impossible* to defend a combination which is kept up by concussing me to join it. I won't send you the papers on this subject, because I wrote one of them which would convince you, and I like to keep you in ignorance that I may abuse you. '*Liberal decision*' forsooth! Pretend to tell me that the raving madness of Hermand, the drivelling dignity of Craig, and the distinguished animation of Cullen are to be set up against the sedate, candid, thinking wisdom of the composed and cautious Justice; or against the plain, consistant, intelligible good sense of Meadowbank, more judicious than accute, and fonder of truths than principles; or against the pure straight-going integrity of honest Armadale – despising interest in party, and party on the bench.[2] Nonsense Sir. But I see thro' it. If it had been a combination of stockingweavers, brewers, or English parsons agt Scotch ones – the devil a fear of you, no mercy for combiners then. But as you have a poem to sell – for which of course you have no objections to a good poetical price – you encourage a pretence for charging it high on account of the dearness of paper.

The Miss Hills are going in a day or two to Glasgow to visit their brother James. They have both been amazingly well all Summer. A delightful summer

1 On HC's teasing references to this poem, see Karl Miller, *Cockburn's Millennium* (1975) and his 'Cockburn, Nature and Romance', *Bic. Commem.* (1979), 125–6, etc.

2 George Fergusson (1743–1827), adv. 1765. SCJ (as Lord Hermand) 1799–1826.
William Craig (1745–1813); adv. 1768) SCJ, 1792.
Robert Cullen (1742–1810); adv. 1764 SCJ 1796.
Allan Maconochie (1748–1810); adv. 1773. SCJ (as Lord Meadowbank) 1796. (His son Alexander, Lord Meadowbank *secundus*, became SCJ 1819.)
Sir William Honeyman (1756–1825; adv. 1777). SCJ (as Lord Armadale) 1797–1811; baronet 1806.

it has been. Divine weather, good friends, good health – and utter idleness. The last pleasure has fled since our courts sat down. They are going on admirably; and what is a little unaccountable, with no apparent inconvenience to, or chance at present of splitting, the bar. But this is news which perhaps is indifferent to you. Since you are about fairly to get into the church, you have no cause to regret that it is so. It is indeed (the law I mean) a fighting life, and one which must be utterly nauseous where the heart is not reconcileable to it, or health precarious. Both of these objections to it combined in your case; and therefore, from the first moment it was mentioned, I was clear you should leave it. It is a little painful indeed to forego half acquired habits and dear earned experience; but the departure of these leaves a useful body of knowledge behind, and is greatly compensated by the variety of new occupation. I have no doubt that you will get soon comfortably established at Shaldon, and feeling your health improve will find new energies awakened, and new and better hopes to be grattified. Under the influence of these, you will look back on the years and employments of Edinr, with affection certainly, but not with regret. Or if a little of that should sometimes mingle with your recollections, I am sure it ought to be taken out of them, by the reflection of increased usefulness where you are. That your parishioners will be happy both in this world and in the next, on account of your coming amongst them, I cannot have a doubt; and with such a satisfaction as this, it is impossible you can ever wish the years that are to be for those that have been.

Do not complain of the distance. This never makes much difference; in correspondence none, in visiting little. Those who would go a hundred miles, would just as easily make up their [minds] to do more business and go four hundred. I hope to pay you a visit some of these days; in all probability in August if you be settled. At all events whenever and wherever you go, be assured that you carry with you my most affectionate wishes and remembrances – that if ever you come here you shall find the best room in your old house ready for you, and that whatever you want done in your absence in town you will always find me ready to do it – so long as I am alive.

Yours Sincerely
Henry Cockburn

I expect to hear from you about the minutiae of the expected opinion.

[*Addressed*:] James Grahame Esq, Warmanbie, by Annan

To John Richardson
NLS Dep 235(1) [*SL* 11–12 (–)]
                31 December 1808

No more of 1808. He is at his last gasp, and a very dull looking departure he is making as seen at least from this part of the world. His last hours have been dimmed by the slow and universal silent foggy rain, thro' which nothing distant is seen but a blunt streak or two of half melted snow upon the Pentlands. There seem to be no carts or cries in the street, no sounds in the house, no motion in the air. All nature is looking in silence on the deathbed of this year; or like the stillness that precedes and forebodes a Summer shower preparing to strike up into joy when the new one shall appear – as he is expected tomorrow.

But altho' this one be nearly gone, he has left us legacies, which will long retain him in, and endear him to, our memories. I cannot think of the many and various days of felicity which we enjoyed under his reign, without hoping that he will stand out in my recollection long after succeeding years are forgotten. During this year we have had no bad health; no misfortune; no interruption to any favourite or rational expectation. The tenour of our days had been attended to with all the blessings and steadiness that ever mark human life. We have had much delightful correspondence, been gradually advancing in the business (as it is called) of life, and extending and consolidating all the settled feelings and connections by which this great cable moors us to the world; and the three months of Autumn cannot be mentioned without overpowering us with remembrances of the best enjoyments of humanity. The very change produced by our friends moving to Woodhall[1] makes a memorable improvement in our lot within the last year. The seclusion, the vicinity, the health, the amusement, the secrecy of that paradise, has been enough to extend the odour, the warmth, and the beauty of Summer, over a Winter double the duration and double the gloominess of this one.

Could we but ensure ourselves that the months which are soon to approach were to bear as much enjoyment with them as those they succeed have done, how happy might we be! On this prospect to be sure, as on all our future prospects, there is a trembling uncertainty; but it is the tremour of hope and not of fear. Experience has been unusually kind to us – for I do not recollect one year in which she has not hitherto, by grattifying our hopes, told us ever after to make them good and reasonable, if we wished them still to be fulfilled. That ours are so yet, there is no doubt.

1 The Miss Hills, at Colinton.

God be praised that neither of us are ambitious, avaricious, or vain; but expect happiness from those simpler grattifications of affection, reading, and nature, which no fortune can withhold, and only one accident – the last one of our nature – break. We are entitled therefore to expect in 1809 a renewal of the satisfactions of 1808 if we live. And if we do not – why, but this is too serious a supposition – and if realised would require better consolation than now suggests itself. Till it be realised however, we are bound to show our grattitude to the preserver of all things, by enjoying that life which we hold. And therefore let thy heart be glad.

Be active – and don't let the days that are now passing away elapse without some record of the industry they were spent with. It is needless to day 'Cherish affection, nature, or such pleasures' – for they are now grown into habits, and even suppose they were not, they induce them by the immediate rewards they bring. But the acquired taste of useful well directed industry, tho' the most grateful and permanent of any, and that which enhances all the rest, has an unfortunate bitterness at first that dissuades most people from possessing themselves of it.

But be you my Dear John wiser, and work, and not only work but write, at your book. How delightful would the approaching autumn be both in its own hours and in succeeding ones, if it were to find you *seriously* employed in engaging or correcting the press. I have run on for so long that I have left no room for the little incidents of our own days which are more interesting to us than the great incidents of centuries and nations. The Mountains are perfectly well they say. I was at Car[oline] Park[1] last night, came up this morning, am going to Niddrie.[2]

If the additional keys make a *material* difference of price, Mrs Tod will as well want them; if not she wisely thinks she may as well take them. She calls £10.10 a *material* difference. So if they cost more than £10.10 don't get them; if less, do.

H. C.

[*Addressed:*] John Richardson Esq, 5 Fludyer Street, London

---

1 'Where my father's family lived for about thirty-five years, [it] must have been the finest place of its kind near Edinburgh. It . . . had an obvious air of stately nobility. . . . My father did it no good. He was agricultural, and sacrificed all he could to the farm.' (*Jal* ii. 143)
2 For Niddrie, the Wauchope seat below Arthur's Seat, see *Mems*, 15–16.

To John Richardson
NLS 3989.6

Woodhall, Sunday [11 June 1809]

Meant to have been at Noll yesterday, but the day was bad, and the occasion Sacramental within the parish of Libberton – and there is an awkward sort of inconsistancy to my taste in a preaching Saturday. So I herded with my clan at Belmount.[1] The Cooper, John,[2] John Tod and I went forth very like cits; a hackney coach with wives, maids and children going before – and the men walking cautiously with umbrellas behind. The fry of young and strong ones was so much increased at Belmont that the house was absolutely creeping with it. We all dined in the small, small room – which soon evinced, by grateful streams flowing down its walls, its sense of our presence; and then the large lamb-legs, and buttered sparagus, and huge turreen of broth, and hot gooseberry pye, and hot dumplings, and claggy cream, and currant wine, and ginger beer, and strong cheese, and porous radishes, and all curing and justifying dram, and clatter of knives, and want of plates, and roaring of children, and breaking of glasses, and the Ladies complaining of sickness – then up with the window, then a cough, then down with the window – and no ceremony (being friends), and so every one with his joke and his manual wit, and an awkward servant to crown the whole – you see our Saturday's family party.

Then we got *fine* in the Summer evening at sunset, and so went up to tea in the ten feet room, and sat two on a chair with the coarse cover slipt off for the occasion, with two hissing tea vases, and a hot fire to keep the coffee kettle warm, and crammed away at the fine country butter and country honey, and country bread, slaked with large flowered cups of tea with cream *from our own cow* – which when it was announced to be ready, we all flew to the table at once, some treading on the children, some spilling their tea upon them – then the mothers horrified, then a calm, then the gravel-crushing coach wheels heard, when we started up at the signal of departure. The shawls and bonnets being adjusted, and the due declarations being made of the pleasure given and received, the maids and children were put into one coach, when the ladies and gentlemen, being only eight in number, were nicely accommodated in another coach; thus we drove in – every one, it being Saturday and in a coach, joking his joke, and all seeming to think the day would be done if there was a moment's intermission. We landed at Tod's, and down we sat to whist, chess

1 At Murrayfield, but not the present Belmont, which dates from 1828.
2 Perhaps HC's brother John, the wine merchant.

and backgammon – and more gooseberry pyes and more cream and more ginger beer. At last it was announced by the fatigued Landlady to be Sunday, and we all went to our respective places of abode – and thus ended that mixture of all that is absurd and wise, refreshing and tiresome, curious and old, delightful yet rare, called a Ploy.

This morning I rose and walked out here before breakfast – and if God were to try it again he could not make a better morning. Pure, fresh-green; every village smoking for the peasants' family breakfast; the trees bursting into redoubled Spring; and the universal moisture ascending into sun-screening vapour. I never saw a more perfect village scene than Slateford; above the bridge, the smooth, broad stream, sailing under the very windows of the people-chosen parson, and regularly touched by the long branches of the waving willows, and reflecting the white breasts and loquacious heads of the delighted goslings; below the bridge the river dashing its foam from under the arch. At a quiet pool of it an old man washing his face, another sage walking round his own cabbages and looking at his own bees, with a long blue coat, and a red nightcap and a tall staff of a weeding hook; a number of children with their best cloaths (but one standing stark at the door enjoying the sun pulling loads of hathorn, and even the mother coming forth to help them, that the place might be fit for expected visitors and a youth twisting broom into a horse's man[e]; a number leaning over the bridge and spitting into the stream; the nymphs with their Sabbath day's cloathes half on cleaning the porridge pots, and the corbies swinging on the trees; these, and a thousand things which it is impossible not to see, but difficult to remember, made this a proper landscape for the first page of Grahame's best poem.

On knocking at the North door I found John with a blue eye and sanguinary lip, having had a giddy fit and tumbled in the night time – so you see that temperance and water which John has for months wisely and resolutely adhered to, won't always do. Miss Hill, who has not been very well, was better, and Miss Helen as you would wish her to be. After discussing two eggs etc., duchelled [?] till one – when, God preserve me!! – a carriage! Out swarmed Fletchers old, young, he and she.[1] Stayed an hour – the lady quiet, simple, goodnatured and kind – the gent. astonished at the trees and the water, delighted with Bonaparte's check, and deploring that Scotland was not a separate kingdom.

They are gone, and I resume. Your last I got yesterday. Be not dismayed at your literary idleness. No business man can be a regular obdurate student, except he be cursed with the ferreous intellect and adamantine frame of such a person as

---

1 Archibald Fletcher (1745–1828); adv. 1790, formerly WS, and his wife Eliza (d.1858).

Kames,[1] who used to sleep four hours – or five when he was luxurious. I call this a curse – because it infallibly makes its owner work for the beastly pleasure of working. The proper theory I think is to have business as the common object, and literature as the solace of life; business as the roast beef of the feast, but books as the des[s]ert or the society of it. But they cease to be so, when they are made into a task. It is not their matter that should be devoured and digested, but their spirit – and the spirit that loves them, that should be inhaled and prevail; and this may be done with very few, but favourite, draughts.

Therefore all visions of months of solitude and study are over with me. I used to indulge and did (at Car. Park) practise them, but then I was idle otherwise all the year round. But now, when I have luckily come to be pestered six or eight months every year, and very often feel the dull pressure of more than I can do, and must rise early and sit up late – and all at a work not always agreeable, idleness is as necessary as air to a man half suffocated. And you will observe that those men who in such circumstances have been accustomed to rescue their souls oftenest from such polluting labour, are both the best, the most useful, and the happiest. Therefore, except as a mere amusement, my reading is done; and burrying myself at Gask or any such place would be as absurd now as it was wise when the vow to do [it] was made. If this be the case – of course our not seeing each other, like a couple of virtuous philosophic fools, this or any other autumn, is out of the question. You would just waste the time bemoaning you were not in Scotland, and I in gossiping at town dinners at the Club and elsewhere, and both of us would feel with unavailing sorrow afterwards that life is too short and friendships too precarious from that cause, to justify anyone in delaying to enjoy the best pleasures, for ones comparatively worthless.

Therefore do you appear here *before* the 31st of July – and let the Pentlands again lift you to the noblest scenes and the most refreshing pleasures of this lower world. No more doubt upon this subject. As to the Circuit, you have not yet and positively answered my query. We may (*ni fallor*)[2] go to the West one together as before. Much to do – or indeed anything, except at wicked Glasgow – there never is. As you must be in Glasgow, this I presume is the only Circuit we *can* go together – for the South one and Arran, I doubt of. If we go to Ayr we must be always with Campbell, Bell, Shaws and others. Therefore will you go West? Say forth, say unconfined thy say.

I am glad to have got Alexander within your door. It must be useful to know such a man. Did Wed-or-burn make, as is said here, a very absurd

1 Henry Home (1696–1782); adv. 1723. SCJ (as Lord Kames) 1752.
2 'Unless I be deceived.'

appearance in the Lordly house?[1] You had better, if possible, leave one tooth to fix in your native mutton, but if it does plague you, you are very right to cast it away. Glad Horner has cast away the Carnatic [*sc.* Inida]. Never saw the dad in Edinr, and Leonard not often. Asked him often to breakfast, but could never come. How is your Duke of Roxburgh coming on? They treat you with great contempt here, saying he has no chance whatever.

Wednesday forenoon. I left Woodhall on Monday morning at 9, and wrought here all day. Murray and Keay dined with me, and we went to Mrs Siddons – where I am going tonight, and tomorrow, and next night. Tuesday (yesterday) wrought all day, dined alone, and perambulated in the evening. This morning Henning called. He is thriving in the bust line, and has made a large one of Mrs Siddons.[2] But there is a national want of good enamel, which obliged him to write to Tassie,[3] as a brother artist, for he does not otherwise know him, begging some of his which it seems he has, from being in London, the art to get good. Tassie sent word that he should have it, and that its price would be about £5. So Henning[4] called to say that he understood you wanted, last time you were here, some casts, and that the most convenient way of paying them (for him) would be for you (if you were so good, etc., etc.) to advance payment by giving Tassie £5. The real meaning of this obviously was a loan of that sum from you. As I rather like Henning's rise and himself, it was impossible to refuse so necessary an accommodation, and therefore said I was sure you would do so. Of this I am sure still, but as I don't see why you who have need of all your money should thus advance to Henning, and as I can more easily get casts here than you, I resolved to send the £5, which accordingly is enclosed. Be so good as to pay it to Tassie in Leicester Square. If he or C. Bell[5] can tell you where good enamel is [got] in London, it would be a great favour to reveal it to Henning.

No more time, it being past 2.

Adieu

H. C.

When do you set off?

[*Addressed*:] John Richardson Esq, 5 Fludyer Street, London [*Forwarded*:] Woodhall

1 James Wedderburn (1782–1822); adv. 1803. Solicitor-General 1816–22.
2 Sarah Siddons (1755–1831), the actress.
3 William Tassie (1777–1860), who had succeeded his uncle James (1735–95).
4 John Henning (1771–1851, modeller and sculptor.
5 Sir Charles Bell (1774–1842), the surgeon, who left Edinburgh for London 1804, and returned as professor of Surgery, 1836. Knighted 1829.

To James Grahame
NLS Acc.10,479

Woodhall, 18 September 1809

My Dear Grahame

As by this time you will have got into the practice of writting and delivering sermons with perfect ease, it will be no intrusion or disturbance to you to hear from your friends, and therefore I, at last, dare to write to you. Here we are all in the old way. A drizzly Edinr day, in which the doubt is not if it rains or fairs, but whether it be rain or mist; a very comfortable fire; Miss Hill on the one side labouring at the Italian; Miss Helen on the other, combating the Spanish. Richardson is off to call at Boneally[1] – and where should John be but upon the king's high way? We are all well; the Ladies of this mansion have had their share of headaches and colds this summer, which has been so wett as to make the existance or reappearance of the rainbow doubtful; but they are now quite well. Richardson has been here about six weeks, and will be for six more; he is fat and flourishing. The inhabitants of Boneally are well too. So are those at Firth, from whence we walked yesterday. In short – to have done at once with the bill of mortality – I know nobody that is ill.

And how are you, and Mrs Grahame, and your ox, and your ass, and your manservant, and your maidservant? I hope that the warm waters of Bath have boiled the rhumatism out of you, and the pulpit exertions clarified your breast from astma. How do you like it? Richardson and I are to pay you a visit – but it is like to be like thieves in the night. You are not to know of our approach till you descry us in a remote pew quizzing you, when you are demonstrating the propriety of supporting a rich church establishment, and praying the Lord to save the land from the abominations of Presbiterianism. They say you do not mean to take any tythes; but let me dissuade you from this – rather take them and give them to me.

We have all been looking eagerly for the Georgics[2] – which people take to be a poem complimentary of the family of our gracious sovereign. I forget to mention a subject which ought to come, but so far as I remember was not made to come, within it. This is what in Midlothian is called a milk[3] – what in other places is called I do not know, but the thing itself is the annual

1 Bonaly was then in the possession of Ninian Hill.
2 *British Georgics*, Edinburgh 1809.
3 See *Scottish National Dictionary* for this Lothian custom; HC's is probably as full a description as exists.

examination of a country scoll; when just before separating for the harvest, the children get on their best cloathes, their heads powdered with flour, ribbons round their necks, knotts on their shoes, and adorned with all the taste, and all the means, of rusticity, go forth in a fine morning, their hearts beating with the actual and strange arival of the great day – and sit down, boys and girls all mixed, to be examined before their parents, the people at large, and to be asked questions by the minister himself – perhaps even by the Laird, if the Laird have the sense to partake of such a feast; and this being done, come to the premiums of A.B.Cs pasted on new boards, of pictures, and even of printed books, received with half shame and half pride, but seen at home with acclamation, sagacious advice, and most pleasing and extravagant hope, and turned over and over again; and all read and remembered during the vacance at the back of every stook. But before parting, the swoln (and justly swoln) master being duly complimented, all the school must feed on curds and cream, grozzets, and other dainties of an undressed, true *fête champêtre*, to which it must proceed headed by the teacher, led by a fiddle and a bagpipe, and followed by all the village; and the party at last dispersed amid a calm evening to their own homes, scarcely sleeping from recollection of the glories of the day that has closed – and from anticipation of the open-field, autumnal, occupations which the coming morning is to begin. I have seen this fifty times at the school at the Grange near Hope Park – and I dare say so have you – and as it is a most pleasing and Scottish picture of rural life do you paint it, if it be not too late, for your month of July or August.

You must have a great deal of time now to poetise and read – for if one be well (which I trust Bath has made you) having a little to do always creates time for more. Besides what is more congenial to such thoughts than the visitations which a clergyman ought to make, and which therefore no doubt you do make, to the homes of his parishioners? But beware of doing too much – an error which many of the good poets of our day have fallen into; for example Scott and Southey, who have nearly outwritten themselves and the public too.

Having betaken yourself to the Gospel, I presume you have no interest in the Law, and therefore I had to recall to your quiet, perfumed parish the din and odour of the Outer House. The ghosts that flit or solemnly stalk along it are in every respect as they were – the building, inside and out, is so completely changed that you would not know it. No improvement has taken place which ought to make you regret having bidden it Adieu; or wish that your feet, instead of reposing on the hearths of the simple and the pious, should struggle to maintain a hard earned, precarious, and not more honorable place, which a peculiar disposition only can render valuable after it is got.

In point of usefulness too in a still way, I am sure you will have cause to congratulate yourself on the change; for the contrast is strange between a hard blackiron lawyer, if not a batchelor, wedded to his cook, advanced at the age of seventy to a bench which has only the advantage of making his income less, and his dotage more visible – and at last dying, with no question asked but who is to succeed him; and a clergyman whose life has been passed among occupations and people to which he has all along been connected by no tie but that of religion – a relation which strengthens while every other decays – and at last consigns his bones to the hallowed respect that becomes the death-given exaltation of his Soul. But, you see, as the source of all your taste for this true happiness is in Scotland you must occasionally come and inspire it again amidst the scenes and the friends that gave it you.

If you were to stay where you are long, you would become a mere Englishman; a fellow that called the country of Wallace, Miss Hill, and Burns, 'that part of Great Britain called Scotland', forsooth! – when our forefathers used more justly to style the South, when they had overrun it, 'that part of Scotland called England'. So you must make up your mind and arrangements to reinhale your native breezes sometime or other next year. To say nothing of better offers, the one which I made to you before, of laying open all the rooms of your old mansion in Charlotte Street to you, is hereby repeated.

Edinr, man, is very like what it was. Solitude in Summer, and riott in Winter; the wise enjoying in growing rapture the views of the blue Firth, the well placed hills, and the romantic town, and the unworthy drawling up to put on thin and rhumatic breeches when the decent part of the family is in bed, and hastening away to large literary stupid dinner-crammed parties at supper, talking about *the* Review and *Scott* – and all saying in the morning that this life is nonsense, but all repeating it, till God in pity prolongs the days so much that candle light is absurd, and it is made fashionable to go to the country.

But here comes John Hill from the town where he has been without the least necessity, except for the strange pleasure men take in voluntarily putting themselves into situations where they must be taken notice of – for John is piteously telling the woeful state of the roads, and how often he was wett, and how far he has walked; and one person is getting John porter, and one advising instant shifting, and some abusing him – and so John is of more importance than if he had just sat at home.

So far I had got before dinner. It is now after it. Glorious maccaroni; it would do you good if you could come and eat it. Can you not tythe any in your parish? There being a want of butter here t'other night, Richardson and I could not be kept off a fine *skep* of bees whose labours we had been enjoying, and approving of, very much, during the Summer – and a finer smeak[1] you never saw. All dead in a minute – and the comb not touched. We did it according to your Georgic upon smeaking – and it is true to a line. But there comes tea – and I feel the smell of the said honey.

Tea being over, I resume. Hermand, in his most delicious circuits, fully makes up for the death of old Eskgrove.[2] He is really bringing them into repute. Had you seen him walking in his sleep in the Black Bull at Glasgow, making dice out of a turnip at Cairndow, attempting to clear his way with a bayonet at Jedburgh, giving a history of the Spanish war in a sentence at Dumfries – for sheep-stealing – to show the aggravation of interfering with the improvement of wool, kissing Lord Cullen at Inverary, etc., you would ever after have followed in his train. But there come cards. Lost everything.

Yet he is a good fellow, Hermand, only deranged. Blair's[3] court is an admirable one. He is as calm, clear, and steady as the sun in the Meridian, does the whole business himself, and does it admirably. The Justice has able men with him, but from want of one decidedly superior his court is unruly, violent, impertinent, absurd, and unpleasant. Blair's is like the cave where the winds sleep, eternal calmness; the Justice's, like the cave where they combat – the moment you set your nose or ear in, your hat is blown off, and you are harried about topsy turvy, till some delivering blast throws you beyond the uproar. But here comes supper. Excellent maccaroni again – and all are gone to bed.

The glories of this place encrease by use. The Miss Hills could not have contrived a better one for their purpose. Retired, sheltered, dry, and beautiful at all hours and seasons. Even the uniform sound of the river below, that lulls every chamber at this still and solemn hour, imparts a character of sequestered peacefulness, which is invaluable. But the paper is done, and nothing but – with the sincerity that is due – to be a God bless you.

H. Cockburn

[*Addressed*:] Revd James Grahame, Shipton Vicarage, by Tetbury, Gloucestershire

1 Hive-smoking, as in the *Georgics*; a skep, as elsewhere, is a basketwork hive.
2 Sir David Rae (1724–1804); adv. 1751. SCJ (as Lord Eskgrove) 1792; Lord Justice-Clerk 1789, Baronet 1804. See *Mems* 108–15 ('a story of Eskgrove is still preferred to all other stories').
3 Robert Blair of Avontoun (1741–1811); adv. 1764. Dean of Faculty 1801; Lord President 1808. See *Mems*, 145–50 ('Too solid for ingenuity, and too plain for fancy, soundness of understanding was his peculiar intellectual quality.')

To James Grahame
NLS 20,437.9; *Lond. Rev. Bks*, 24 Jan 1980
Woodhall, Sunday 4 March [1810]
My dear Grahame

To proceed to business first, you will recollect that your letter concerns two things: first, whether the review of the Georgics is to be favourable or not; secondly, respecting your contributions to the Edinr Review.[1] On both of these subjects I have communed fully with Jeffrey; and tho' it is difficult to convey to another the exact import of any conversation, the following seems to be the result of that which I had with him.

First. As to the review of your poem being favourable or not, that, says Jeff., depends on what you call favourable. It must be reviewed fairly; and that fairness, according to my views and feelings, is a great and sincere love of the general tone of the whole poem, and of a great number of pleasing passages; with an unqualified condemnation of the whole agriculture as not sound – as totally unfit for poetry, even altho' it were sound. This was Jeffrey's general opinion. He objected a little, but not much, to some want of spirit and nerve in the language, and praised the uniform Scotticism of the scenery, sentiment, and manners. These are minor considerations; the above is the general scope of his considered opinion. Whether this will be favourable or not, it is your business to judge. It seemed, and seems, to me who heard what he said and saw how he said it, that either according to my opinion of the merits of your poem, or as conjecturing yours, the review will be favourable. If the other passages be well praised, you may afford to have the Agriculture respectfully abused, for I don't suppose you ever thought it the crop of your poem yourself – and you know that so far as my judgement goes, it has been abused disrespectfully already. Moreover, Jeffrey's approbation is always powerfully and feelingly conveyed when it is sincere, and even his disapprobation can make its object aimiable when he chuses. Now his love of the excellencies of the Georgics has been uniformly true, and I know, and he said, that his perfect esteem for you would make his censures, however decided, completely respectful. In these circumstances, I am satisfied that unless your poetical pulse be peculiarly feverish, this review will be thought by you Favourable. It should have been in this Number if Jeffrey had not been obliged unexpectedly to do something else; but he intends, tho' of course can by no means positively engage, to put it into the next.

1 The *British Georgics* was reviewed by Jeffrey in *ER* (April 1810), 212–23; Grahame himself did not contribute to *ER*.

Second. As to your contributions to the work, Jeff. says that he takes the unquestioned and unlimited power of alteration and rejection of all reviews into his own hands; that he never once came, and never will come, under any obligation, even to the mightiest literary giant in the Island, to insert whatever they send; that they are always told not to be surprised if their best efforts be sent back unopened, or published so changed that they cannot recognise their own offspring, or only recognise them so much as to be horrified in the change of their dress, manners, and opinions; in short that he takes and pays every contribution according to his own opinion of its merits solely; that under this unyielding, and necessary, and only respectable, condition he will be delighted to receive any contribution you may honor them with; and that if you be disposed to write you must give him some notion of your general subjects, as well as of each book you wish to review, else half a dozen will to a certainty be engaged at the same work.

These rules seem not only wise, but they were announced by Jeffrey with a plainness and honesty which ought to be pleasing to every honest man, and therefore must be pleasing to you. How they are to affect your conduct, you only can judge. It is obvious, and Jeffrey stated it, that writting for reviews, especially for the Edinr one, was not only a difficult, but a peculiar art, the possession of which could not be ascertained from almost any other exertion; as he had seen thousands of examples of men thinking they had it, who had it not, and not thinking it, when they really had it. This is a matter of judgement to yourself; only remember, that what Jeffrey particularly wished conveyed to you, viz. your contribution will give him great pleasure, but only under the above mentioned condition and that if he sends back your very first and best production as abominable, you are not to say he has either broken faith, or is unkind; no more than, if he likes it, he were to publish it with unusual pomp and exult in it publickly and privately. In short he is a Dictator. Do as you like – but remember I have told you this.

After ballancing their books merchants add 'Errors Excepted'. Perhaps I should add this to this Statement because, of course, a long conversation cannot in all its looks, tones, words, and gestures, be communicated as if these had been seen and heard by a person 400 miles off. But I am satisfied that I have stated to you, with the distinctness and unflattering plainness which can alone make the communication worth having, the result of this dialogue.

We heard of your illness here, and were much afraid of it, from the distress that both preceded it and followed it – and all these things too are much worse when they befall one in a foreign land. Your information of your recovery therefore gives us the greatest pleasure, and makes us hopeful of seeing you stout and amongst us. These diseases of rheumatism, asthma and pleurisy are bad things, but it is not improbable that they may extinguish or subdue each other, and leave you after all, for a due time, triumphant. But whether they do so or not, remember that an unconquerable spirit is the best Medicine, if it be not the only Cordial, of life. You will sigh that it is a Cordial which nature must give at the birth, and that there are some to whom she has denied it! But this is not true. She puts it to be sure into the veins of some; but there is no good man who may not put it into the veins of his own mind. When it arises from a sort of lamb-like instinctive chearfulness, it is not in the least dignified, and not nearly so independant of pain, poverty, and obscurity, as is generally supposed. When it is founded on reason, it is well founded, and can never want support; but when to this is added the purer aid of religion, it is difficult even to imagine anything that is wanting to create or insure it. This arises peculiarly from the scene of your occupation, which, to a humble mind, is altogether so pleasing that I am tempted to think that the practice of feeling the varied and sublime consolations which it is your duty to give, would almost enable anyone to convert even rhumastism [*sic*], pleurisy and asthma into objects of defiance and victory. Do so at least as far as you can, and with Poetry, Affections, perfect respectability, and a sense of usefulness there are pleasures around you which pain cannot destroy, and death will enoble.

I am sorry you find your church so damp as to oblige you to leave it. But this will not be so great a loss to you as to your parishioners, to whom, we learn here, you are much endeared both in the pulpit and out of it. Since the powers above are at such a loss for a moderate statesman, I wish they would apply to me. I should be either a Chancellor or a Bishop; and if the nation should be conquered under my management, I should not have a blot on my memory of leaving the Curate of Shipton and author of the *Sabbath* to cough away his worthy lungs in a wet church. What a belly you should have with one of my Deaneries! You would take a proud pleasure in standing alongside of Ringan Hill, like a majestic river in rolling along with a thin canal, or a 74 with her bellying sheets in towering above a one masted pinnace.

Seriously I do not rightly understand why you don't get some Christian niche in the temple. You are keen on the cause; you are a popular author on pious subjects; you have clerical friends; you have private relations with Votes in towns and counties – and every thing that should get you on. To be sure your original sin of being a Whig is dreadful; but I do believe, after all, that a Whig may be an honest man – but this is not a common belief. But the truth is, My Dear Jamie, that provided you keep your health and spirit entire, I care little about your worldly promotion. You have plenty to live upon (especially since you don't spend *so much* upon Whisky) and enough I suppose even to tocher the lass. Richardson will make one of the boys his partner when he gets the gout and can't work; and when I am Lord Advocate or President, I shall superintend the other; and what have you to fear? The Children of the Righteous shall never want bread. So live on with what gaiety becomes thee – for which purpose you must absolutely revisit us here, where all is the old way.

It wants but seven days of the vacance, and the weather is getting good natured at the very thoughts of it. From where I sit just now in a nook of the window a universal operation of the Secret Spirit of Spring is visible and pleasing. The stream and the sky are trying which can be bluest; the trees are putting out their hands, with nerves [at] the ends of their fingers, to feel the mild breeze, the blackbirds trill so shortly, that it is obvious they do not believe it has returned again; and the rustic maidens have begun to leave off the red, winter-berried cloaks, and to don the vernal white-blossomed gowns. All within doors is as well as all without them. Miss Hill, Miss Helen, Betsey, and Margaret; (of Glasgow) Janet, and Elizabeth, (Ninian's) Laurence – are all around the table, each with his or her own book, composed by the Spirit of Sabbath, and family comfort and quietness. You know where John is – and must be. They of this house have been all tolerably well this winter; but as they have told you this themselves, I need not.

As to Edinr, about which you ask me, it stands where it did. I am still in your old mansion in Charlotte Street,[1] and have still the room for you that I promised whenever you chose to come and reoccupy. Your friends, so far as I know them, are all thriving. Robert Hill is not so strong as he was, but he is, as things go, well enough; a man is not to be like a column that stands in the desert and desolation of all things, and at the end of 1000 years still says, 'This is me'. The human edifice moulders – the lines, the hieroglyphics, the very name and inscription become erased – and down it falls! And why not? Ninian is well, and fat – but not so very fat. His whole house is creeping with weans; there was one of them caught and enclosed all night in the rat trap lately. It had gone in after the cheese, and the lid closed.

Brewster[2] is getting great praise, and, they say, wealth, by his encyclopedia. Thom: Broun[3] is lecturing for Stewart with immense, and so far as I can

1 i.e. 4 North Charlotte Street.
2 David Brewster (1751–1868), kt 1832; edited the *Edinburgh Encyclopaedia* (1807–29).
3 Thomas Broun (1778–1820), Dugald Stewart's successor in the chair of moral philosophy, 1810.

judge, most just éclat; and in doing so he is not in the least affected. Geo. Thomson[1] I scarcely ever see, and never hear – sing I mean; but I do believe he is still warbling. Mrs Fletcher is still going about – doing good no doubt, tho' some people might say in the usual ostentatious way. You see I take you for one of her friends who can hear such things without believing them, else I would not say so. Archie is quite rotten in body and mind. Sir John Greenshields[2] is well; he seems flourishing rather in business, and in other respects is unchanged. George Bell[3] is encreasing the things of his name. He has a dumb-bell of one child and an expected Belle of another; and is thriving, as he eminently deserves, in his trade. Johnie[4] has a carriage with the motto '*magnus in parvo*', and is cutting away at noses, escvavating [*sic*] wens, and gouging out eyes, with great success.

Scott, Erskine, (Wm) Clerk, Murray, etc.[5] and all these Gents are just as when you left them. Gillies, J. Clerk, Mat. Ross, Cathcart,[6] etc. are still the great fee gatherers among the ancients at our bar; Jeffrey and Cranstoun are following, if not treading, on their heels among the youths. Henry Erskine[7] glimpses out a little now and then, but he is extinguishing upon the whole. Blair is giving universal and just satisfaction as President. But it is needless to tell you all these things, for in truth, except that we have got a new new town to the West, one to the North, one to the East and one to the South, there is no change on Edin, morally or materially, since you left it. Its pleasures, too, of Nocturnal parties, and a sort of half fashionable half literary slang about science and reviews, are still the same.

We had two plays by Miss Bailly acted here this winter; *The Family Legend* a new tragedy, and *De Montfort*.[8] The first did best, but neither of them, tho' excellent to read, will ever be standing plays for the theatre. Yet the first was performed about a dozen of nights with applause. Scott's *Lady of the Lake* is to be set a swimming very soon. It is, I believe, quite *Northern* and highland, and

1 George Thomson (1757–1851), Burns's friend, and collector of Scotch music.
2 unidentified
3 George Joseph Bell (1770–1843; adv. 1791), professor of Scots Law 1822, Principal Clerk of Session 1831.
4 John Bell (1763–1820), surgeon.
5 Walter Scott (1771–1832), adv. 1792, Clerk of Session 1806; William Erskine, later Lord Kinneder; William Clerk (d. 1845) adv. 1792, Clerk of the Jury Court; and John Archibald Murray.
6 Adam Gillies, (1766–1842), adv. 1787; SCJ 1811, John Clerk (1757–1832), adv. 1785; SCJ 1823–8. Matthew Ross (1750–1823), adv. 1772; James Cathcart (1768–1835) adv. 1791.
7 Henry Erskine(1746–1817; adv 1768), brother of Lord Buchan.
8 *The Family Legend* had been produced at Drury Lane in 1810; *De Montfort* dated from 1810.

is much praised by those who have seen it. He still keeps the printer's devil chasing him for sheets, like a fool. I know no poet who has committed such suicide as Watty. He writes so quick that he must either be very fond of money, or cannot live without being talked of for something new, or fancies that people take poetry, like cash, less of it paid down than a larger sum at a long credit. But he is quite wrong. It is just the reverse. If they get *good* coin, they would do so; but it enrages them when this ready payment is a pretence of slipping base money into their hands.

Lord Buchan[1] is still trotting and lisping about the streets, saying that he is God or Apollo or Dr Anderson – or any thing that he thinks he should be but is not. Your friend Pillans,[2] you would hear, has got the High School rectorship, to the great delight of the worthy. Blair's conduct was noble. He was one of a committee referred to by the Baillies – and was well plied with Jacobinisms [?] against Pillans by his antagonists; he enquired; never spoke a word; but when the day came, went, and in full council made a fulmination an hour [*rest missing*]

To James Grahame
NLS 20768. 74, 84,117 (variant transcripts)
Caroline Park, 29 March 1811
Dear Grahame

I am writing to you with a married man's hand. I was cleeket to a decent, well-behaved, thickish woman about a fortnight ago, and as yet have no reason to repent of my choice.[3] We are scarcely fairly settled, having never been at home, but we mean to be so in a day or two in your old house in Charlotte Street, to which, as usual, you will always be gratefully welcome; tho' man you must really put a curb upon some of your practices if you even enter my threshold.

I suppose that Blackwood[4] would convey to you an opinion of mine anent the Sermons. It was rather unfavourable to their public publication, tho' not to their circulation in print within the sphere of their peculiar local attraction. This opinion remains unchanged. I liked the one about educating the poor

1 David Stewart Erskine (1742–1829), 11th Earl of Buchan, antiquarian, eccentric and 'character'.
2 James Pillans (1778–1864), Rector of the High School 1810–20; Professor of Humanity (Latin), Edinburgh University 1820–63.
3 On 18 March HC had married Elizabeth (d.1857), eldest daughter of James McDowall of Castle Semple, Renfrewshire, Auditor of Excise.
4 William Blackwood (1776–1834), the publisher.

better than that about incarcerating debtors. The Miss Hills praised them both. I hope they are right – but cannot allow the partialities of friendship to mar the *immisericors mens* of criticism. But I need say nothing about the matter now, for I presume your mind is made up respecting these discourses.

I was delighted to hear from your friend Gamlin of the success of your sermon for Greathead, an appellation as worthy of the preacher as of the boat-maker. No mitre can be as noble as the crown of such charities. It is the power – or rather the temptation – to do such things that renders the life of a clergyman calculated to pass pleasingly away amidst pleasures made sacred by duty – and his eye to close amidst blessings and recollections, before which all the pains, the troubles, and the perils of his professional labours fade out of sight. A Doctor has no such soothing remembrances from pilling a dropsied alderman into proper slimness; nor does a lawyer lay up such a sinking fund of charity from blearing the eyes of a poor Judge about an ill-bought house.

Gamlin seemed an excellent fellow. I could show him no attention – being very busy, my house polluted by painters, and my horror-struck mind startling at the brink of matrimony just before me. But I scarcely ever saw a man who carried a better letter of recommendation than he did in the plain sense of his manner, the honest heartiness of his face and the cheerful wisdom of his talk. You are a good hypocrite – you never let out that you could sing. But upon all these your private virtues Gamlin was duly informed and by this time I suspect you can have been sufficiently tortured on account of your potatory and cantatory powers.

The Hills are going this very day to Woodhall. I am glad of it for their sakes; for tho' like plants they did not actually wither in the windows of the town, yet they would have languished if they had staid after the breath of Spring had begun to bless the earth. Ninian is still the old man; good natured, thoughtless, and much occupied about porter. I have taken Bonaly from him; and there I mean to rusticate as much as a rigid attention to business will allow.[1] If you come to Scotland when we are there, you shall always find carrotts and water, a bad bed, and a sincere welcome.

You have heard, no doubt, of Richardson's intention to avail himself of my divorce and to marry again.[2] Betsey is very well – an excellent girl – tapering away like the new bursting poplar.

---

1 The first mention of Cockburn's own connection with the property he was to rent, then buy, rebuild and occupy for the rest of his life as a rural retreat which formed an essenbtial counterpart to his busy Edinburgh life during the session.
2 Richardson (jocularly 'married' to HC) married Miss Elizabeth Hill on 5 August 1811.

Oh! If you had been in the Outer House to observe the amusing contrast of the Clerks, Gibson and all that crew, during the Prince's phases! Their impertinence, confidence, decided hope, and devotion to the Prince – the greatest patriot in the country, their dealing folk of offices, and altering courts and campaigns, *before* he was made regent; and their chap-fallenness, amazement, stupour, disbelief, frantic rage, loud despair, contemptuous disregard, grief for the failings of Princes, hopes that all would go well, and settled furrows of thought and pain, *after* he was appointed, were as amusing as any scene of human life.

Monipenny's [*sic*] appointment of Solr-General gave satisfaction because he is a well behaved inoffensive lad and because it kept it from Sandy Maconnochie.[1] Mackenzie's being made Sheriff also pleased – but all the other appointments are made by the ordinary principle of equalising the happiness of the world by bestowing them upon those on whom God has been pleased to bestow least. Very right. What would Boyle have done, if it had not been for this?[2] He is a good natured fellow – but looks, upon the Bench, very like as if he were surprised to find himself there. His face is flushed, and he is always kirpling on his seat, and swinging his arm over the bench – and never says anything except that the case is of great importance, and has never before been decided, and that he is for a hearing. This, he thinks, looks candid and wise, two of the qualities of which he knows he is least suspected.

Jeffrey made some admirable speeches this last session – and is fast advancing as high in the profession as a bad manner, and a wrong sided review, will let him. He and Cranstoun are decidedly at the [head] of our juniors – and are certainly in every thing, except age and impudence, very far before Clerk or Gillies. My own progress is continuing steady tho' slow, and I have no reason to fear its permanency. I made as near £800 as £500 this Session. These particulars I mention merely because I like to let you in to my exact condition, of which they give you a better notion than any description can do.

Well. What are you doing? Gamlin talked of your getting a situation about ten miles from Durham.[3] How do you like it? And what are your circum-

---

1 David Monypenny of Pitmilly (1769–1850); adv. 1791. Solicitor-General 1811; SCJ (as Lord Pitmilly) 1813–30. Alexander Maconochie (1777–1861), son of Lord Meadowbank; adv. 1799. Solicitor-General 1813; Lord Advocate 1816; SCJ (as Lord Meadowbank *secundus*) 1819.

2 David Boyle (1772–1853), of Shewalton, Ayrshire; adv. 1793. Solicitor-General 1807; MP Ayrshire 1807–11. SCJ February 1811; Lord Justice-Clerk November 1811; Lord President 1841. See *Sedition Trials*, ii, 175 for HC's comments.

3 Graham had moved to Durham, and thence to a curacy at Sedgefield nearby, where he died (of hydrocephalus) 14 September 1811.

stances and news? I met some time ago with Hume of Carolside. He talked very kindly of you, and discussed the possibility of your getting a Chapel built here for yourself. I doubted – and still doubt – the possibility of making the erection – and of its turning out lucratively. I should think it would be much better to wait till a vacancy occurrs in some of the present Chapels – when, if you start early (and with a loyal sermon) you are the surer of it from your last failure.

Talking of Loyalty – I must tell you that a bundle of papers were lately sent to London by the mail to Clathick, with a *large official* fee for merely signing them as a King's counsel; and he called the next day at the Sollicitor's for 2/6d as the carriage of the parcel.

We have changed sides so much of late that I have just been obliged to write a long criminal information, against my own former one, to show that Combination is no Crime. But what are these vain and passing things to you? Yet I don't know. For I have an unlucky tendency to think things of more importance after they are pas[t] than at the time they occur. When a process comes in, I feel nothing but dismay, vexations, and a desire to get done with it. But when it presents itself to me years afterwards, the interest of the parties stands out undiminished by any feeling of personal annoyance: and I am touched by a sense of their sufferings. And so it is I suppose with all the duties of life – the nasty little selfish obstacles which throw out their full discharge at the moment, seem when it is all over so insignificant that we are actually amazed how we ever cared for them. Yet even this is useful; for what would become of the world, if the laziness of counsel did not moderate the keenness of clients?

Poor Thos. Martin of Langholm has lately met with some new losses – from being security for a sea captain that he would manage a farm right. Your friend John Haggart[1] is almost at zero now; but his estate is improving, so his county influence rises, while his forensic falls. I don't know what W. Scott is about – tho' there can be little doubt that ten or twelve presses are groaning to feed the public maw with his crops. Willie Erskine[2] is still reciting at suppers. The Principal novelty in Edinr this winter has been Mr Morgan an English parson who sings divinely any tune to any words. He affects to be a sort of musical improvisatore, and will sing anything from a Playbill up to a Chapter in the Revelations. His music is admitted to be good, but the common and just opinion is that he is crazy.

1 John Haggart (d.1816); adv. 1784.
2 Later Lord Kinneder.

I have not heard one word of Thom. Campbell these six months.[1] It is a pity that his heart-sticking genius should be so lazy, tho' upon the whole it is much better to be so than to the intolerable and sickening defect of perpetual parturition. I have often thought, and *still think*, that the best thing you could do would be greatly to increase and polish your *Sabbath* – and give it to the world anew. After all, it is the poem on which you stand – and by which your reputation will principally live. Now there are many pleasing solemn, curious, Scottish views and sentiments which, tho' strictly applicable, it does not contain. Under a description of a peasant's life, from Saturday evening till Monday morning, there is little interesting in the feelings of Scotsmen you might not introduce. The *Cottar's Saturday Night* and *Deserted Village* interfere with you on some pleasing topics, but there is substance in the subject for a third poet – especially since you put more of religion into it than any of the other two. All this is clear; but you will think the grafting is so delicate and that the public may be surfeited with Sunday. Erroneous. You have only to eik scenes and sentiments here and there till you perhaps double the size of the poem; and if this be skilfully done, adhering strictly to the peculiar character of the groundwork, the previous publication will only have the effect of preparing the public taste to receive gratefully the new charms that are added to the old stock. Think seriously of this; but I entreat you to beware of what you add, and let the new colouring be put on with a very light and delicate hand indeed. You will be worse than an Infidel if you don't dedicate the work, thus improved, to a Bishop.

Have you such a thing as a Burn near you? Lord pity you if you have not! But to a true Scotsman the burns of his native land are ever tinkling in his ears and trickling over his heart – and the breezes which he recollects to have felt come over in his imagination, softened and endeared by the distance from which they have blown. These remembrances, if abused, may easily be converted into so many sources of wretchedness. But when thought of as the poetry of life, as pleasures long enjoyed actually, and more intensely enjoyed in memory; when connected with changes which suggest the idea of increased usefulness elsewhere; and used as evidences of the power of man to be delighted with whatever he accustoms his heart to love; they become, like past duties and future hopes, treasures of felicity which distance can only endear and time can only perfect.

---

1 Thomas Campbell (1777–1844), the poet, then in mourning for his son, who in 1810 died of scarlet fever.

But I must, at last, be done, so adieu. Did Ninian's[1] whiskey produce no verse from you? Was it not a very characteristic gift from him? Remember my wife expects some tythe pigs, petticoats, and tea chests from you as a matrimonial gift.

God bless you
H. Cockburn

To Mrs John Richardson (née Hill)
NLS 3989.12

[28 December 1812]

My Dear Betsey

Good new year to you. May they often return in equal peace to you, to your husband, to your mother, to your bairn, to your manservant, and your maidservant, to the poney, to the stranger, and to all that you have within your door. When you receive this, Elizabeth and I will be at Hermand[2] – no by the bye we will be here, for tho' we are going to be there today we return to dine with little Dumpie on the first of January 1813, which is the first time that I have written the new year. The Lord (Hermand) has his kirn[3] this evening – and I hope you are not so denaturalized, as Bonaparte calls it, by going to England as not to know what a kirn is.

I meant to have walked, but the day is very bad – chill without frost, raw, grey, soft, drizzly and dirty. Rutherfurd (who has actually made 25 guineas already at the bar)[4] and I walked out to Duddingstone yesterday and stood upon the ice – tho' it was weakish – but it will be gone today. He is going directly to pay poor Laury [Hill] a visit. I wrote him a letter of condolence lately. Margaret sent in some snatches of his bride in the form of drawings of flowers executed by her. They were very pretty but I *observed* that they had all been done before she was bride, else they would all have been *Laurestinas*. Was not that a very good remark?

Your aunts are well. Miss Helen getting round as she says – tho' upon that too I made, or rather always make, another good observation, saying that a

---

1 Ninian Hill (1775–1814), younger brother, by twenty years, of Lawrence Hill, to whom he had been apprenticed.
2 George Fergusson built Hermand, near West Calder, in 1799, the year he became a judge (as Lord Hermand).
3 At this season a general celebration rather than a harvest-home.
4 Andrew Rutherfurd, born Greenfield (1791–1854) adv. 30 June 1812. Solicitor-General 1837; Lord Advocate 1839–41, 1846–51; MP Leith 1839–51. SCJ 1851.

Lady of her length will never *get round* again. How's my young friend Johnie? Margaret knows John's picture here perfectly, and from the habit of being held up it never comes into this room without roaring and kicking and looking at it.

Rokeby is to be born in a day or two. Report speaks well of it – but Watty, I think, is a good deal lower in this intellectual city than he was. He has withdrawn himself very much from his friends, and not to be cozie in his own nest – for that he is not – but to share it with players and printers and low Torries. Talking of the word cozie, I don't know a better translation than Zachary Boyd's[1] account of Joseph's garment –

> Now Jacob gied his dautie Josie
> A Tartan coat to keep him cozie.

Nothing in English could express this.

Laury is wrong if he goes and lives at Dalbeath – for no pleasure (I think) can be greater than that which contented new married people have in sitting in their own house, and toasting their toes on their own rugg, and ringing their own bells, and handing their own forks. As I told him (another good saying), going there will make him Dull-beth. Do you know that in place of Hopkirk, he calls her Skip-Church?

This moment have I received your worthy husband's last epistle. Tell him that his autumnal schemes for next year are highly judicious. What a handsome angel his son must be – for he has legs like mine. I confess I doubt it – for such a pair never were framed before, or since.

Oh! These cursed accou[nts – !] my wicked wife is buying China every day. But the chaise has come for Hermand – and we must be off. Adieu and God bless you. I have been meditating a congratulatory epistle to your mother upon this second nuptial occasion, but dare say her thoughts are so likely like mine respecting it that I need not express them. I'll lay an egg that your laddie will have black eyes – for they change very much. Margaret's have been all the colours of the rainbow already.

Ever and Ever

Each Sea

[*Addressed:*] Mrs Richardson, 5 Fludyer Street, London

---

1 Zachary Boyd (1585–1653), author of much religious poetry 'of dubious merit' (*Oxford DNB*).

To Andrew Rutherfurd
NLS 9687.5

Bonaly Castle, 21 October 1813

Dear Rutherfurd

I have been looking anxiously for an epistle from you – but since you won't send one I know no better way of punishing you than by making you receive one from me. We are living here in the old way. A very few days before you went off, I went to Jedburgh – no faith, it was before, and I think I told you this already.

Since this I have only been twice from home; once at Perth, about the sticking boys[1], and once on a visit to Mr Tod's near Melrose.[2] Richardson and I rode there by Peebles and home again by Gala water. The stage (22 miles long) from Peebles to Melrose is one of the finest I almost know of – surrounded by pastoral hills, skirted by oak copse wood, frowned upon by a few of the savage old private castles, and humanised by the constant attendance of the Tweed, of which the very name is enough to make the country-side pleasing. The weather was horrible, but by the help of an ingenious greatcoat which it cost me four days to plan, and Elizabeth three minutes to execute, I rode it out dry.

Richardson made the most beautiful descent yesterday in Maitland Street from the back of a tall grey hack you ever beheld. It was a stupid brute, totally incapable of making one unnecessary motion, and it lay so slowly and patiently down upon its knees and its nose, while the sollicitor pitched so effectually upon his best London hat, and then rolled so thoroughly over upon his clean brushed *Town* greatcoat; danger being quite out of the question, from the pacific indifference with which the beast stood still and snorted the dust off his mouth, and the unintended neatness with which John's feet came out of the stirrups – as if for the very purpose of not impeding him in his plunge; while there were just enough of spectators to enjoy it and give it a zest, and not so many as to make it shameful; and then the half jocose ruefulness with which he led the dirty kneed steed back to the stable, with an unconscious dimple in the said hat, his discomfiture marked on his dirty back, his cane bent useless, everybody smiling (and he seeing this) at the impossibility of either getting quit of the beast, or of mounting him again; the day's ride visibly quite spoiled, tho' the hire must be paid, and the chairmen galling the wounded spirit by running from sundry quarters offering their aid,

1 strikers?
2 Archibald Tod (1759–1816) of Drygrange, near Melrose.

and publickly naming the knight by way of showing their regard. It was perfect.

He leaves this on Tuesday, but I have less regret for this, because (mirabile dictu) I shall see him soon in London. I have been asked to go up about the Roxburgh fews [*sic*],[1] and notwithstanding my abhorrence of the place, arising from want of sympathy with it, and my conviction of the inutility of any Scots counsel in an English court, yet in order to avoid explanations and expostulations, and to try the experiment at least for once, I have resolved to go. The time is not yet fixed, but I believe I will need to depart about the time the Court of Session meets. Elizabeth is going – which, with the help of the Richardsons, will make it very pleasant. I hope we shall see you before we depart.

We go to town in about eight days or so. If you have any desire to assist at an execution, you had better come and aid me at a criminal trial on the 8th, being that of two idiots for robbery. I have seen Gordon at last. He is to dine here on Saturday (the day on which I suppose you will get this) along with a shoal of children, who have claimed their annual feast. I wish you had been here to assist in decorating the room. Horner has been in Edinr a few days.[2] An excellent fellow, but too sage in his demeanor – tho' on a bench it would do admirably.

After Murray[3] got his trunks that morning, we proceeded till we came to Inverkeithing when he unlocked a whole trunk full of books and began to read, but after giving forth about half a page he forgot the plan, and the books were utterly forgot. He then saw his brother at a distance coming. Seized hold of the letters he had brought from Edinr for him, and stopped his chaise. Got out and talked about ten minutes. When we got near Perth, 'Good God,' cried he, 'I've brought on my brother's letters.' He went to Scone that night, and altho' I put my luggage into a separate room from his, he contrived to take it all with him. At twelve at night he sent it back, but forgot the best part of it – and swore the next day that that part was not with him. After rummaging the whole Inn and teizing the whole waiters, it was resolved that it *must* be at Scone – and on going to my friend's room, there it was. Did you ever hear that even in his youth he had an instinctive abhorrence of the present tense at School and always lost places at it?

1 Estate business following the determination of the Roxburghe peerages dormancy in 1812.
2 More likely Francis Horner (1778–1817), the politician and economist, than his younger brother Leonard.
3 John Archibald Murray, whose brother William, elder son of the judge Lord Henderland, was at the English bar.

Adieu. Elizabeth begs you to keep her in your holy remembrance. I hope I shall see James in London. We live at Richardson's.

Ever Yours
H. C.

[*Addressed:*] Andrew Rutherfurd Esq, Corbridge, by Newcastle on Tyne

To Andrew Rutherfurd
NLS 9687.7

Bonaly Castle, 21 July 1814

My Dear Aundra

I am truly sorry to disturb your autumnal studies, especially since by this time you will have got into the very thick of them from the literary talk of your learned and abstruse friend Tom, but your worthy mother has entreated me to send you some lighter reading than you commonly indulge in, and therefore I send you a letter, in the hope that the weight of the postage at least will bring you to your senses.

The Bivouac does *not* hold for Tuesday, partly because there was a difficulty in getting you all assuredly to meet – and chiefly because Lauder has the weakness to attend lectures on Chemistry at that very season of the year in which nature provokes her true sons to partake of the pleasures she affords, without troubling their heads about their causes.[1] So it is now fixed for Saturday se'ennight – and you will therefore be at head quarters on the evening of the Friday preceding. I envy you the pleasure of this postponement – as it will enable you to enjoy for nearly a week longer that retired and severe mental labour which, tho' it be (as your mother says) wearing your frame away, is rearing the scaffold of your notoriety. However as it may be of use to you to get near a library, let me tell you that Fullerton who is at Carstairs[2] wants us very much to go to him for a day or two. I am not disinclined – for I am sensible of the value of your judicious commentaries on all things (chiefly Muscovite), but if we are to go, we must do so before Saturday se'ennight, for Fullerton will be in Edinburgh about that time. I cannot – at least will not – positively pledge myself to go until the time comes, for as I would propose

1 Dick Lauder was interested in chemistry and from 1815 began to contribute papers on the subject to *Annals of Philosophy*.
2 John Fullerton (1775–1853); adv. 1798, SCJ 1829. He was the second son of William Fullerton of Carstairs.

walking, it may depend upon the state of the weather, shoes, small cloathes, or any of these thousand things which are great to little men. But if you can tear yourself away from the learned Tomasius Podicis-Cutis,[1] come over when you proposed at first and we shall hold what the old agents called a consult over a bottle of the purest water even *you* ever drank – or I believe 'you ever drunk' would be truer.

Richardson's household, including even my John, is now on board a Smack bound for Leith. He will follow when our Senators disperse. Talking of Senators, I am, glad to inform you that our Slave Trade Petition has been sent off at last – with above 15,000 signatures. It was more than 200 feet long. Our division of the town into districts more than doubled the produce in three days. Maclaurin get about 400 himself. It will be a black spot in Tom's history if he has lived ten days near Dundee without attempting sedition there. The review about this matter is (I think) in as bad a tone as possible. Full of party spirit, rancour, and abuse. Its great knowledge and great cleverness (for the question does not need these) weigh not a feather in comparison against this defect.

Waverly [*sic*] is admirable, in my opinion. You will no doubt have slipped over that fragment with many other enormous morsels of lore which you have been devouring. For God's sake, Andrew, take care of your eyes. Severe Students too are very apt to suffer sorely from their bowels. It is this that vexes [your] other. Do call at Alexander the druggist's shop in Dundee and ask for the Idler's pill, or the Scholar's belly salve, or the Sedentary man's doup plaster, or the Student's windy cordial, or the Philosopher's clearer, or the Lawyer's delightful pocket companion, or the Judge's rectifier, or Vacance Powder – or anything else that will keep you as well and make you walk as stately as during the idleness of last winter. Sleep's my foot, Andra, and Study's yours. I sometimes study in my sleep; do you ever sleep in your study? Na never!

Keay,[2] Home,[3] Fullerton and I went to the Launch on the deck of a hackney coach last Monday – and then dined at the New Club.[4] I see that it is a Club that is very apt, somehow or other, to knock one in the head. But I beg your pardon for intruding on your reading so long. I hope to see you soon. Would not a bivouac do Tom much good? Bring him with you if

1 Arse-skin.
2 James Keay (d.1837); adv. 1799, of Snaigow, Perthshire.
3 David Hume (1757–1838); adv. 1779, Principal Clerk of Session 1811; Baron of Exchequer 1822.
4 A social club founded 1787 and still extant. HC does not appear to have been a member.

you can. He may go to Carstairs too. I saw the sun rise, with Gordon and Jack last Sunday.

Yours Ever

H. Cockburn

You should really not rise before 5 in the morning – for the dew is still in the air then.

[*Addressed*:] Andrew Rutherfurd Esq, Student, Linlethen, Dundee

George Joseph Bell
Huntington RB131334(2)

14 Charlotte Square, 10 June 1816

My Dear Bell

Many thanks for your valuable present.[1] Estimable as it is from its contents, I confess that, coming as it does, I prize it more for the friendship that sent it. Tho' in fine long vacation days it is impossible to think without a sigh of the labour it has cost you, yet – now that the toil is over – it is still less possible not to envy the steady and unclouded fame by which you are quite certain of being rewarded, as long as Jurisprudence shall be cultivated in Europe. *The worthies* (myself included) are a set of idle wretches. But since the only test of excellence is the average of the court, why should we work? I trust the day is coming in which your spectacles shall scowl down upon us from the bench, and make us ashamed of the easy felicity of our youth. One pleasure you have already given us, which I defy even yourself to take away – the enjoyment of your own eminence, and the consciousness of its being partly reflected upon the friends with whom you associate. Long may you live to extend it.

Ever Yours

H. Cockburn

[*Addressed*:] Geo. Jos. Bell Esq., Advocate, York Place.

1 Bell's *Commentaries on the Law of Scotland in relation to Mercantile and Maritime Law* (1810) had been published in a second edition. (For an assessment, see D.M.Walker, *The Scottish Jurists* (1985), 338–51.)

To Andrew Rutherfurd
NLS 9687.11
Bonaly Castle, 9 April 1817, 9 p.m.

My Dear Rutherfurd

I am so extremely sleepy that if I did not foresee that if I did not write to you tonight, I would not get written to you at all, I would not do it. We are living here in the old way – only I have not had one screed this vacation. The ejection of David Niven,[1] and the getting his garden and house, has diverted your humble servant much in the digging, wheeling, and directing way – and the weather has been singularly excellent. I have tried to read Sismondi's republics, but have only mastered his two first volumes. You may say what you like, but he is heavy, methodical, bookmaking fellow. For the first fortnight my throat was like the rock at the Linn – nothing fell over it but pure water. The worthy doctor and the Colonel came out one day, but went back in a city coach in the Evening. Old military men and old apothecaries get very like each other.

The most interesting event however has been that we have had two of the famous State trials discussed.[2] The first was that of two most excellent men, one a white faced, steady looking weaver, and the other a red faced, sappy grocer – both from Kilmarnock – who were accused of Sedition. Their words, *per se*, were seditious; but considering them as spoken casually, at a lawful meeting, for reform, by starved people, they were innocent, and there ought to have been no conviction. But convicted they were – tho' strongly recommended to mercy – and they were only sentenced to be imprisoned six months. Clerk and Rothy were for the weaver – and did everything that obstinacy, folly, and the desire of getting up a senseless attack on the Court in the House of Commons could do, to ruin their cause. Ruined it would have been had not Jeffrey (who, with me, was for the grocer) made a most capital speech – full of an amiable and correct tone, sparkling with occasional brilliancy, and well calculated to excite a prejudice in favour of the prisoners by showing the miserable littleness of the whole affair. There were many Whig quality present – who are all in raptures with 'the argument' as Eskgrove called it – but all judicious people agree that it was at least an hour too long (it was three in all), and it was the only speech of Jeffr[ey]'s in which I ever saw

---

1 The farmer at Bonaly.
2 For McLaren and Baird (*State Trials*, XXXIII), convicted of sedition, see HC's *Jeffrey*, i, 253, ii, 170n), and HC's *An Examination of the Trials for Sedition which have hitherto occurred in Scotland* (1888), ii, 177–92.

anything injudicious. Yet he was so injudicious as to harrangue *ad longum* in favor of the free practice of England, where people were not even tried for Spafields orations and breaking frames. These words – dwelt upon long – made one curdle for Scots prejudices. Yet it was a noble Speech.

Today we had the first of an endless set of poor devils who gulped the oath which Maconochie[1] proclaimed to the House of Commons – a capital offence and charged as *treasonably* committed. We came to the field, according to agreement and as before, in due force – for I think there were for the culprit Clerk, Cranny, Jeffrey, Creefy, Murray, myself, young Stewart, Campbell, and Timotheus in a corner with his great coat and hat on. Cranny objected to the Relevancy in a speech in his best style – for learning, cunning, and precision. Maconochie, seeing he was in a devil of a scrape, set H. Drummond and the dull wasp to defend the case and remained mum. Then Clerk came forth with a shot in his usual style – pithy, confident, loud, slow, and on the whole, tho' effectual, rather absurd. The result was that the court had great doubts if any crime had been committed at all and still more if it was well laid – and therefore ordered informations.

I think it is at least an equal chance that it will be found that the oath is not criminal at all – in which case all the apparatus of the Castle, and the drawbridge and the sabres outside the door, and inside the door, and the secrecy, so great that the Lord Advocate actually refused to let the agent and counsel for the prisoner in to see the witnesses – will all turn out to be as oppressive as foolish. Creefy is to write the information. Eh man! It was a true, heartfelt, satisfaction to see the perfect contemptibility of the crown counsel. Macc's speech against the seditious men was universally admitted to be his chef d'oeuvre for poorness. It was not even pompous. Pure doited. When Clerk in reply uttered his first sentence, which was 'Ma Lord! In this case the Lord Aadvocate has exerted his *whole* abilities', there was a general smile. Drummond today was even worse than Wedderburn – and no wonder, for Cranny was openly praised by the court as superexcellent – and they rose to answer him, after having told us at the beginning that they could not conceive what we had to say, and after Macc. had been chuckling that we might *bother* as long as we pleased at the relevancy, 'but tho' their Lordships should sit forty-eight hours, *I* am determined that the trial shall go on'. Singet whelp. There has been a strong combination against Rothie, who has not got a word in. Indeed nobody has, but those I have mentioned as talkers – but then nobody else desired it.

1 At the time Maconochie was Lord Advocate and MP for Yarmouth, Isle of Wight.

Thinking you might like to hear of the outer house I have given you these details. By the bye the Sherrif tells me that in examining the bodies what they meant to do with the Regent if they had got uppermost, what do you think was the answer? There were two opinions and votes. One, to 'tak him aff the throne, an' let him gang his waes, an' tak up a shop – or just gang about his business'; the other 'To send him to St Helena!' The last always carried. How would he look, at Longwood with Boney?

Now what have you been doing? I hope you and Fullerton have found your two friends as agreeable as you expected. Humph. Napier and Elphinston! Has the Chrystalline cleaned either of you yet? Richardson tells me that you have had (what he calls) a punch club at Hampstead. A miserable poor imitation – I suppose. Mrs Cockburn is looking anxiously for your china and old silver packages. Murray is to be in London in a few days. Nobody could get wigs or gowns today, and it was found that the man was carrying some books for Mr Murray into the court – where Jack was not to be found.

We had the usual Maitland, Tod, and Cockburn party last night to see Kean.[1] A little vulgar body. I am going to Glasgow for a few jury cases next week. Carstairs would have been a good halfway house – but Fullerton is a prudent man. Has he got a literary boat from Oxford yet? Oh Lord man I'm sleepy!

Take care of your manners Andrew. You are now in Town – and avail yourself of the opportunities of improvement afforded by that mart of fashion. You know my views on these subjects. *Sat verbum.* Do you see any worthy virgins fit to be taken up? Give Fullerton a serious advice. What bandy legged dogs your young ones will be. If Fullerton falls in with one of the south country red and white women, his will be albinos. Gask[2] was here for a whole day, and Morelli[3] for dinner. He looked very natural by the hills. I have not seen your mother since your departure. I must have her out here next summer– for she is an excellent person. Morelli inflamed my desire of going abroad by telling me what I did not know, that even his pulpit legs had carried up the Swiss [Alps. I] should delight to pass a long [vacation there]. Do let us get green jackets, strong shoes [?li]ght hats and long poles, and set forth. I shall put and keep on my very best Arcadian temper if you will pay all – and sure you have the best bargain because you

1 Charles Kean (1811–68), the celebrated actor.
2 Laurence Oliphant, 9th of Gask (d.1824).
3 Unidentified.

only give what when lost can be got again. Oh! Sleep! Sleep! So Andrew,
Adieu – till I knew thee I knew nothing.

Ever yours

H. Cockburn

If Napier[1] admits, in morals, as in mathematics, that things related to the same
thing are related to each other, present my respects to him, and assure him that
I sacredly recognise the same tie.

[*Addressed*:] Andrew Rutherfurd Esq., Care of Richard Napier Esq., 2 Tanfield Court,
Temple, London

To John Richardson
NLS 3989.31

14 Charlotte Square, Sunday 8 November 1818

My Dear John

I was glad to know from yourself that all your travelling plans had turned
out well, and that you had at last got safely home. I trust that long before this
you have joined Mrs Richardson and that she is getting strong. She will be ill
used if she is not allowed to bathe, journey, be idle, or do anything she chuses,
for at least a long year. Remember me to her and Miss Hill, and Johnathan,
and Christy, and Hope. Now that the Autumn is closed, I feel great
gratification [in] reflecting on my having seen them all, so well and so happy.
This season has indeed been rich in pleasures for us – for to say nothing of our
expeditions on the Thames, Boxhill, the top of Moses's (cunctator like old
Fabius) coach,[2] Hampstead, the streets and the sights of London, and Tarbert
and Greenock and Ayr; and the Pentlands, both of our dearer parts have
recovered from long weakness and great danger. How long all this may last,
God knows; but it is our duty, and our only pleasure, to enjoy such things in
due moderation while we can.

I had a week's hard work at Bonaly, after you went away, with the Bowling
Green – which is now finished, and gives an immense look of neatness and
antiquity to the place. It is in this shape, viz: [small diagram follows]. A is
beech hedge, which I have got high enough to be a shelter already. B is a
mound of turf two feet high to keep in the bowls at that end next the house.

1 Perhaps Macvey Napier (1776–1847), Librarian of the Signet Library 1805–37; Professor of
  Conveyancing (1816–47) at Edinburgh University; editor of the *ER*, 1829. 'The Pundit'.
2 Moses the slow coachman, after the emperor Fabius Cunctator, 'the delayer'.

CC are entering places. E is at present a seat, but is to be a bower. The dotts are a border of flowers behind the bower and within the hedge. All the other thorn hedges are put in, and the border up towards the tent stuffed full of roses etc. The *built* wall, in front of the house, is to be continued westward (instead of the present Galloway dyke) till it goes round the little seat at the end of Peter's path, by which means the farm house will be nearly, and its filth altogether, excluded.

Kirkhill is, by a letter from Craig, to be set up at £2600.[1] But that vision is at an end, and the more I think of it, the more I, and everybody else, is satisfied that it would not have done – even tho' attainable, which it is not. But the little spot will be ever sacred in my memory for its beauty and associations. These rural labours did no good to my awkward disorder – but on the contrary obliged me to give up going to Stirling, and to lay on my back for three days entirely, and very much ever since. But I am now as well as I have been for eight years or ever will be.

We were for some days at Caroline Park and for some at Hermand; from both of which you were much missed. We get to town on Thursday, and I am at this moment comfortably settled in the book room with a fire and a lamp, waiting till Sir Harry begin a sermon he is to preach this evening in the adjoining church, and which Eliz. and I mean to hear. I have got two or three good books since you went away – particularly a splendid Parisian 4to moroco bound Tasso, a venerably magnificent Spelman's *Concilia*, a large three vol[ume]d 4to Montaigne, and Sully of the same kind. Oh! If you could tempt me by discovering a worthy Hackluyt, Purchas, and Fuller. If you ever fall in with them let me know.

Jeffrey has come back. I am told better. What a frightful and lamentable event this is of poor Romily.[2] I cannot get him out of my head. If you know any private circumstances, do tell me them – for every thing about such a man, and such a catastrophe, is interresting, t[hough] horrible. It is awful to think of the strange events to which, apparently, the surest of us may be subject every moment. When I think that a few months have removed Horner, Gordon, and Romily whom it required no personal acquaintance with to love, the world looks sadder than one originally believed it would; and the reflection of what may yet be done by a few months more, makes

1 Estate at Gorebridge, the house earlier than that built in 1828 (by Thomas Hamilton) for John Tod.
2 Sir Samuel Romilly (1757–1818), the law reformer, had committed suicide following the death of his wife.

me feel the necessity of seriously anticipating these things, lest one be utterly struck down when they happen. There is too a distressing and alarming sense of loneliness and responsibility, on finding oneself every year left to carry on the business of life with fewer of those early supports on which one has always relied. But the natural remedy is to cherish the connections that remain the more, and to encourage those that are opening – and to do one's duty actively and firmly – and with an anticipation of those ruptures to which our best pleasures are exposed, as constant and vivid as is consistant with their present enjoyment.

This last calamity is an awful loss to the country – chiefly by its creating a number of servile wretches whom the dread of Romily's moral worth kept in check. I trust that there are thousands who will see it in a different light, and who will perceive from his example that the meed of public glory is only to be got by zealously denouncing folly or villainy wherever and whenever it may exist – and that all the calumny, public and private, by which a patriot is assailed, dies away when its end is severed, and leaves the true character undisturbed to posterity.

God bless you

H. C.

The (too long delayed) Turnips and carrots shall be dispatched this evening.

[Addressed:] John Richardson Esq., 5 Fludyer Street, London

To Mrs John Richardson
NLS 3989.35

Bonaly, by Collington, 2 April 1819

My Dear Mrs Richardson

It is a long time since we have heard from you. Do give us a line now and then – for it is very agreeable to receive a letter from you. We are all well here. Elizabeth was called suddenly into town on Tuesday morning last to attend Mrs Fullerton[1] who, before she arrived, had become the mother of a stout girl. She and her child are doing well – both indeed wonderfully so. And, that I may complete the intelligence, I may add that she is nursing with such success that is thought that is her forte. The worthy husband, who (from want of experience) was very anxious about her, is the happiest man in Charlotte

---

1 Fullerton had married Mrs Cockburn's sister Georgina on 30 September 1817.

Square. I went to Edinr too, and wrote papers, and got my beautiful visage finished by Raeburn – which last is a great deliverance.[1]

We returned here this forenoon – one of the most lovely days I ever saw. Indeed this Spring has been more wonderful in this region than even last summer. I am at this moment sitting without coat or neckcloth. The sun never descended more sweetly than he did two hours ago. I went up to Torphin hill and saw him casting his last splendour on all the western windows over the land, amidst the songs of two or three mavises who were perched on full blown broom bushes. A number of people were prolonging their field labours by sowing long after six – the smoke, symptomatic of rural porridge, ascended from the low-laying Collington and various other villages; the first lambs were beginning to appear on the hills; it was so calm that the wheels of the solitary carts were heard on the Lanark road; and altogether it was very pleasing – tho' very sad. When I think of the number of persons whom I used to know on these glens and hills, and will now know no more – including poor Ninian and John, the Miss Hills, yourself and mother, Mrs Ninian[2] and others – the strange changes of a few years seem at first view frightful, and we wonder how we can enjoy the places when all their shades arise. But a little reflection teaches us that it is the very rising of their shades that endear them to us, that such thoughts, when idly dreamt over, are hurtful, and that, considering the precariousness of all things, there is more reason to be grateful for what is left than despairing for what seems to be taken away. I had a long letter from the Miss Hill[s] two or three days ago. Both well – but uncertain as to their motions. I wish they could be told of Redford.

My seeing you in London this Spring is now completely out of the question, for the agent went off yesterday who was to have taken me. I am to be at Dumfries on the 10th of April, Aberdeen the 22nd, Forres the 27th, and Glasgow the 5th of May. So a day or two here and there is all I shall get of this place after the end of next week. I wish you saw our hyacynths here. They are in full blow, tho' they have been out and uncovered all winter. Bid Richardson ask some of the seedsmen for a new flower that they have got in Leith Walk. It is called (by the sound, for I never saw it written) a Delhi, or Dallia.[3] It is cultivated in France and other hot countries for the root, which is eat. It is bulbous root – like a Jerusalem artichoke. It is kept out of the ground

---

1 Raeburn's portrait is now owned by the Faculty of Advocates.
2 Ninian Hill, WS, had married Isabella Lang in 1801.
3 The Dahlia, a Mexican native named after the Swedish botanist Anders Dahl, introduced into Europe in 1789.

all winter, and put in April into a *poor* light soil, in a sunny situation. It flowers in August, and keeps the flowers till October. They are of various colours – some scarlett, some blue, etc – grow from two to five feet high, and are very showy particularly on a wall. But all this account is needless, for Elizabeth says that she knows that they are common about London. I hope *my* grass is greener than the rest of your domain.

By the bye – I almost forgot what I began for. The Bonaly butter is famous all over the Earth. *Mrs* Hill, who is the farmer here, supplies all the people of taste in Edinr. So are the Bonaly eggs – that is to say ours. Our hen house is out of sight the most successful thing we have done here. The idiots lay for ever. Elizabeth and Mrs Porteous have been making a pose[1] since we came here for you – and the box left Leith today. I can't say what number breakage and stealing will leave to you, but when it left Edinr it contained 16 dozen, and four bottles of Whiskey. Don't let them stay an hour in the package, lest they taste of the bran. Tell John that two of the bottles of Whiskey, *with black seals*, are the two he got from Will Macdowall at Greenock. I think they are both very bad. The other two are from my store – and are not good, but better than their brethern. Mine are sealed *red*. The *long necked* bottle, tho' it does not please my perfect palate, is reckoned excellent. I am afraid lest the presence of these exciseable articles may get the whole box seized. Adieu. Remember me very kindly to Mrs Hill, Hope, Christy, and John.

Ever Yours
H. Cockburn

[*Addressed*:] Mrs Richardson, 5 Fludyer Street, London

To Sir Thomas Dick Lauder
NLS Dep.235(1)
14 Charlotte Square, 6 November 1820
My dear Lauder

The Convention of Royal Burghs have an agent or Sollicitor at London. Mr Langlands, who has long held this office, is dead, and my friend John Richardson is a candidate for the situation. It depends on a vote of the Convention, which meets annually at Edinr in July; but that vote of course depends on influence used with the burghs, and chiefly with their Provosts, as soon as possible. Now it has occurred to me that you may possibly have

---

1 A pile, or collection.

something to say with some of these personages at Forres, Elgin, or Nairne, or with some of those by whom they are ruled. If you have, I have to impart to you that Richardson and I have been so long and so intimately connected, that he used to be called my wife, and may more truly be styled (which you know is a very different thing) Myself – for indeed I am as much wrapped up in his interest as in my own. To you, I am sure that I need say no more. But I have not such regard for him, or for any body, as to ask you to do anything you dislike. So if you feel disinclined to interfere, I beg you to abstain. I do not know if he is to have any competitor. If he has, it will probably be a Mr Campbell.[1] He is supported by all sorts of people in this quarter, from radical Whigs up to Sir Walter Scott, and from chief magistrates under indictment up to the Lord Advocate; but still his success depends on his more private and effectual friends.

I beg to be remembered to Mrs Lauder and Mrs Cummin; in which Mrs Cockburn prays to be united. You have heard I presume of Macbean's misfortunes.[2] He was thrown from his gig three weeks ago, and got a knock on the head and on the leg. The former was well in a day or two, but the latter kept him in bed till four days ago. When he got up he had exposed himself to cold, and for the last three days has had a slight rhumatic fever. I saw John Thomson and Turner today. They say he will be well very soon –perhaps in forty-eight hours – but at present he sees nobody and can do nothing. He is rather lonely, as all batchelors in that state must be, but his maid is a good nurse, and Thomson thinks that his being quite alone is much in his favour. As I know the anxiety you must feel when even a slight affair is the matter with him, I shall write to you again soon about him. In the mean time *you may depend upon it* that as long as I *don't* write, all is going on well. If he be in the slightest degree worse, I shall let you known instantly. Rely upon this; and be easy.

Ever Yours

H. Cockburn

7 November. Macbean is better. As Thomson assures me he will be well in a day or two, I won't write again. But if he gets worse I will.

This letter, *cum multis aliis*, goes to you thro' Richardson's agent, who has opened a battery on almost all the burghs, and of course, as is usual on such occasions, pays the post. So don't take it amiss that you are not obliged to come forth with a shilling for this application.

[*Addressed*:] Thomas Lauder Dick Esq., Relugas, Forres

1 James Campbell, solicitor in London, later a member of the Bannatyne Club.
2 Aeneas Macbean (1776–1857), WS.

Note on David Haggart
NLS 135
[1821]

One of the many evangelical pieces of absurdity which honoured the execution of my client David Haggart, murderer – one of the greatest villains I ever had to do with; and a fellow who committed crimes to the very last moment, but gained the affection of saints and phrenologists by affecting piety in the eleventh hour, while at the very same moment he was preparing posthumous lies by dictating a volume of the falsest possible account of his life and adventures.[1]

H. C.

To Sir Thomas Dick Lauder[2]
NLS Dep 235(1). (*SL* 20)
14 Charlotte Square, 15 February 1822
My dear Sir Thomas

I wish, for my own sake, that I had time to write you a long letter; because in communicating with you, a fresh scene of beauty and of kindness rises at every line. But it is 12 at night, and the accurate Pitmilly comes out tomorrow morning at 9 to a moment.

Old Findhorn flows – or overflows – at Macbean's, with all his subject streams, on Saturday the 2nd of March. He wants an appropriate Cap – a crown. And after deep revolving, he has settled that it must be made of Peat. There is none of that article to be got easily here – at any rate none that has ever heard his growl. So direct a mass of Peaty Material to be cut, put into a box, and sent to me by the coach. It must be in one mass – a sort of cube, of about 18 inches by 12. The head-covering structure shall be cut out after it arrives. What I want you to do is merely to send me the raw material, in so soft a state as to admit of cutting and carving – and yet so firm as to keep together,

---

1 Haggart stuck in HCs memory, as in his Spring 1848 account in *CJ*, 339: 'He was young, good looking, gay, and *amiable to the eye*, but there never was a riper scoundrel, a most perfect and inveterate miscreant in all the darker walks of crime', etc. He also appears under several headings ('defective in Love of Approbation', Conscientiousness, large in Combativeness, Destructiveness, Self-Esteem') in George Combe's *System of Phrenology* (e.g. 5th ed., 1843), which includes at i, 147 a diagram of Haggart's head. Combe wrote an appendix on Haggart's phrenological development in an appendix to *The Life of David Haggart* (1821). Cockburn took an amused interest in the pseudo-scentific phrenological frenzy, admitting that it encouraged 'sound moral views and educational principles' (1836: *Jnl*, i, 117).
2 Dick Lauder had inherited the baronetcy on 6 December 1820.

after a skull cap is cut out of it, and after plumes of yew and holly are inserted into its corners and summit. It must be square at the corners, and not round. Do this, and Findhorn calms his torrent to receive thee! Do it not, and Findhorn rises, till he rushes up and overwhelms thee!!

There wants but one thing more to complete the feast of Aquarius. Turn the lower end of thy stream a little southward, and join us. You will see Williams's[1] exhibition – a most beautiful display of art and of taste. It is succeeding very well – and I have no doubt that he will not only pay his expences (above £200) but make some money. It is becoming a fashionable lounge and if he can only get some pore blind [*sic*], snuffy old card-playing Haridan of a Dowager to take him up, Greece may do after all. Old Niddry has got the third part of the estate of Cakemuir[2]. 'The damned body' is looking beautiful – but very dissipated. I trust that you have got a letter some time lately about the Parthenon.[3] By Minerva, let me implore you to inspire taste and patriotism in the Shire of Moray.

We are all well here. Mrs Cockburn in daily expectation of a bairn.[4] I'm done. How many are you to have? Read Malthus once every nine months.

Oh! What a glorious – what a Godlike bouze had we on the opening of Williams's exhibition, in the room. Jeffrey, Murray, Keay, Rutherfurd, Pillans, Lambton, G. Jos. Bell, Maitland, Cunninghame, Williams, Horner, and myself – twelve in all, being the nine muses and three graces – dined surrounded by Greek scenes, with two fireplaces, two lustres, nobody but ourselves in the house – and had we not a night of it? Geo. Jos. was appointed that day to succeed Hume as Professor of Scotch Law – and had you but seen the two Professors, Pillans and he, engaged, with Jeff piping as a little Pan, with a Pyrrhic dance. But the villains set me at one in the morning to a side table to make punch and then eat all the Devils. Put £10 in your pocket (not a farthing more) and come here for a week, and see these things.

Ever Yours
H. Cockburn

My Dear Lady Lauder – How are you? and the young ones? and Miss Kettle? and all your concerns? Macbean is hatching a variety of Jury Court jobs, some

1 Hugh William Williams (1792–1867), known after his travels in 1820 as 'Grecian' Williams.
2 Capt. Andrew Wauchope of Niddrie was born in 1735. Cakemuir is a tower, south of Pathhead, built by a Wauchope in the 16th century.
3 The uncompleted national memorial on the Calton Hill to those fallen in the Napoleonic wars; work began in 1826 but petered out by 1829.
4 Laurence Cockburn (his name from the Hill family) was born on 25 February 1822.

of which will certainly break the shell, and appear in the form of a visit to Relugas[1] in due time. I think I hear the sound of the water at this distance. But you keep dreadful late hours – and indulge in murderous long drinks. I mean you let your guests do so. Has the new stable succeeded to your wishes? Build no more – and above all, don't touch your house. But whether you do so or not, keep a cozie corner, with a lovely view, for me – for I verily believe that very few years, if one, will pass always without my intruding [on] you. I even intend some day to appear in the shape of a circuitous Lord – blowing away with a brace of brazen trumpets, like Esky himself. Mrs Cockburn is sound sleeping – but if she were awake she would certainly unite with me in begging you hold us both in your remembrance.

Ever Yours
H. C.

My Dear Mrs Cummin – Remember that there is a pair of capital shoes of mine at Relugas – and don't let them be worn, except in cases of necessity, as for example if you should want to kick a creditor. An Irishman, by way of kindness, would make a heavy colt walk here with them on for me.

Ever Yours
Each Sea

[Addressed:] Sir Thomas Dick Lauder Bart., Relugas, Forres

To John Richardson
NLS 3989.44

Bonaly, Sunday 24 March 1822

My Dear John

I bid hail to the lad! and trust that Mrs Richardson is doing well. You are surely glad that it is male – for tho' you say nothing on this point, it is plain that this is what you ought to have been wishing. Write soon how the infant and the mother are. Georgina produced a son last night – which ends my catalogue of anxieties of that kind for at least one year. I need not say how well Elizabeth is, for the place from which this is written attests it. We came here yesterday; and for our reward, all this day has been one interrupted hurricane – made visible by hail and snow. Yet the children have been running out to the hill every moment, and renewing their acquaintance, amidst great raptures,

---

1 The Lauders' Nairnshire estate, near Forres.

with the burn, and the bridge, and the bath, and the pig, and the cow, and all the other wonders of last season that they had forgot. How we are to do in this small and damp den, when they get a little bigger, I do not know. We have abundance of spring flowers out, but these endless and cursed winds, which have blown, like untired Devils, here for three months without one moment's interruption, have beat everything down, and seem to have exhausted and sickened the very primroses, which have pretty strong stomachs for winter too.

Murray I believe is gone to London. Fullerton will be there soon – and Jeffrey also. Creeffy talked of going, but I expect that this unlooked for calamity of his brother George's death will prevent him.[1] Poor old Sir Harry is sadly struck with it. So you have beat the Provost and his police Bill! Thank God therefore. A more infamous attempt never was made – nor for a more contemptible purpose. You have no notion of how ludicrously low and piteous they look, as they go about the Streets mourning. They are chuckling mysteriously however about the arrangement being to be broken up by the Chancellor in the House of Lords. But this I presume is nonsense.

James Stuart is going to make another blow up.[2] He has got hold of the actual papers of the Glasgow Sentinel, formerly the Clydesdale Journal – both being the Beacon of the West; and thus found out the supporters of, and the contributors to, that disgraceful paper. In order to get these back, a charge of theft or breach of trust has been made against the persons who delivered them up; the Sherrif seizes the documents, and these go, with the other papers, into the hands of the Crown counsel, as part of the precognition – after which they are never seen more. The Lord Advocate[3] is one of the supporters of the paper – and his scamps write in it. So here we have an Advocate who first sets up a libellous paper, and then employs the machinery of his office to get the evidence out of the hands of those who could detect his connection with it. Stuart leads a strange life with these fellows – but it is far more his misfortune than his fault.

1 Sir Harry's fourth son George (1782–1822) had died on 15 March.
2 James Stuart of Dunearn WS (1775–1849), a Whig friend of HC's, had been repeatedly insulted in print, first in the (Edinburgh) *Beacon* and later in the (Glasgow) *Sentinel.* Evidence was procured that Sir Alexander Boswell, the baronet son of James Boswell and an ardent Tory, was the author of the scurrilous articles. Further attacks evinced a challenge to a duel, which took place on 25 March 1822. Boswell, perhaps repentant, fired into the air, but Stuart (certainly inexperienced) discharged a bullet that wounded Boswell, who died soon afterwards. Stuart fled to France merely to avoid immediate imprisonment, but returned voluntarily to be tried on 10 June. Jeffrey defended him before a jury which returned a unanimous verdict of Not Guilty. See letters below as the story unfolds.
3 Sir William Rae (1769–1842), adv. 1791. Lord Advocate 1819–30, and later.

Have you seen an edition of John Home's works by old H. Mackenzie?[1] The works are useless – but the life is curious. It is not good – far from it; but it is about Edinburgh long ago, and contains some capital letters by David Hume. The excellent Playfair's works too have been published by his nephew;[2] with the most unsatisfactory and detestible Life that could have been planned. I see some books in Payne's last Catalogue which I think I must have you to get for me when you are at leisure. The second vol. of Scott's *Fortunes of Nigel* is printed. I never read his *Pirate* till t'other day. Very bad. Williams's exhibition is to close in a few days. It has been a most beautiful and instructive Spectacle. He has been strongly urged, but won't send it to London. Have you seen Nasmyth's view of Edinr that I wrote you about?

Remember me to Mrs Hill and the wife – and young – what is he to be called? Ours is Laurence – and new name among the Cockburns.

Ever Yours
H. Cockburn

[*Addressed:*] John Richardson esq., 5 Fludyer Street, London

To Andrew Rutherfurd
NLS 9687.16

Bonaly, Thursday 26 March 1822, 8 p.m.

My Dear Rutherfurd

I long to hear of your proceedings – past and future – but chiefly the latter. Dowager Mrs Ruthefurd told me t'other day something about your projects, but nothing satisfactorily. When are you to be married – and when am I to see your wife?[3] I have not forgotten my promise of writing to her; but tho' I am very anxious for the commencement of that acquaintance which I trust is only to terminate with the life of one of us; I really have not courage. Give her my kindest benediction; and let her know – if you can – how sincerely Elizabeth and I are disposed to love her. I feel the event that is about to happen, as a new tie to my life. I need not explain to you how much my happiness is involved in yours, and the step you have resolved upon is the only one that was wanting to make yours steady.

1 The collected works of the dramatist John Home (1722–1808), author of *Douglas,* edited by Henry Mackenzie.
2 John Playfair's works were edited by James G. Playfair in 1822.
3 Rutherfurd married Sophia Frances (d.1852), daughter of Sir James Stewart of Fort Stewart, on 10 April.

We are all well in this Hyperborean region. We came here two days ago, and have been rewarded by all the balmy verdure of a Scotch spring. It has been an absolute hurricane ever since, and this day I had to cut my way up to the bath thro' snow in many places two feet deep. I took the boys up a hill this forenoon, and diverted ourselves by rolling down little pellets of snow, and seeing them become huge masses before they reached the bottom. There was great magnificence in the expanse of dreary, dazzling whiteness; and wherever there was a projecting cliff, the wind and the drift swirled into eddies as elegant and natural as a waltz with Miss Horner.

The mention of this name puts it into my head to tell you (tho' I dare say you know it) that we have got a complete triumph in the Police contest. Professor Bell said to John Forbes[1] t'other day that he was glad it had been compromised. To which the sore Torry answered, 'Why it is an odd sort of *compromise*, where the one party gives up everything, and the other gets more than he asked.' Mrs Fullerton has got a son – which to my certain knowledge is not more than she asked. My lad is ycleped Laurence.

James Stuart has again been playing the Devil among the Taylors. One of the partners of the Sentinel, alarmed at his action, offered to give up the proofs of the authors if he was let free. This of course was agreed to, and he gave up various papers to Stuart, who has thus made curious, certain and shameful detections. How he means to use his information I don't know – for he is as yet very mysterious. He won't even reveal an author; but Affleck[2] I am told is a great writer, and our worthy Lord Advocate the great patron. Stuart got the papers perfectly lawfully and honorably. Yet, merely in order to get them back, they have instituted a charge of Theft or Breach of Trust against the *Partner* who gave them to him; and they give out that their design is to bring both him and Stuart to trial. A regular precognition has been going on – which, it is said, makes all idea of guilt out of the question, yet I should not at all wonder if the malice of attempting to degrade Stuart by forcing him to stand publickly between two officers at a criminal bar, should prove too strong a temptation for them. They have succeeded already in getting the papers. Duff[3] seized them as part of his precognition – and of course they go into the hands of the very culprits – after which, all the said Duff's affected precautions are idle. So you see we have a Lord Advocate nowadays who first sets up the trade of a libeller, and then puts the machinery of his office in operation in order to

1 John (Hay) Forbes (1776–1854); adv. 1799; SCJ (as Lord Medwyn) 1825.
2 Sir Alexander Boswell (1775–1822), 1st Baronet.
3 Robert Duff of Fetteresso (1790–1861); adv. 1812.

stiffle the evidence of his personal guilt. I wonder he does not assassinate on the same security.

Murray and Clerk are gone – Jeffrey and Fullerton going – to London. We had the promised Festival at Craigcrook, but the Marshall destroyed it. He got into one of his fractious fits with James Brougham who did not understand or like it, and the scene was very disagreeable. Between ourselves, that vice of the excellent Marshall's is not to be laughed at. Williams closes by a day for that Parthenon of his on 8th April – by which time he will have drawn about £530 or £550.

Poor old Sir Harry[1] is sadly felled by the sudden death of his son George. He has published another vol. of sensible sermons. I have been reading a life by old Mackenzie of John Home. A poor performance, but interesting from its being about old Edinburgh, and containing some admirable letters by David Hume. There is one upon fat men that is a masterpiece. I have also read (besides the *Pirate*) Playfair's life of his Uncle – the most abominable production conceivable. I saw Ellis t'other day.[2] He said he was going to send me his Memoir of Gordon to read before printing.

Is there such a thing as a *Tent* in Bath? How am I to point out the glories of the setting sun from these hills to Mrs Rutherfurd, if you don't get me one? I trust she can walk – and that she likes bad company. Instruct her in the moral beauty of jollity. Pray do you mean to get like Mr James Keay! Or Mr John Fullerton!! Or Mr Robert Hunter!!! Eschew them. Keep to the old man – and a good many of his works; under which last class I rank myself. Upon my soul if you get absurd, I shall give you up. So if you will please get less domestic – less temperate – less townish – and speak Scotch. If you renounce me, and my hills, and my ploys, and attempt to set up for a respectable married man, you will certainly fail in the latter [*sic*], and what can you get in exchange for the latter? It shall be my first business to lay this down to your spouse as soon as I see her. In the mean time, do you expound to her, that her general rule of government in this region is to addict herself to me, and to force her husband to conform to her. So shall I be sure of you both. Meanwhile, God bless you two. May we dwell in unity of affection during the time that is to come, as we have done during that which is past. Adieu. I don't expect to hear from you, except to warn us of your approach.

Yours Faithfully

H. Cockburn

1 The Revd Sir Henry Moncreiff, 8th Bt (later Wellwood)(1750–1827), Minister of the Kirk.
2 Daniel Ellis, author of a memoir of Dr John Gordon (d.1818), the Edinburgh anatomist.

I have got a scold from Elizabeth for not desiring that she may be commended to Miss Stewart. I have great pleasure in anticipating their friendship. What a queer thing it would be if they were to fight like cat and dog. What an odds this simple change would make to the whole vision. For then you and I would be obliged to pretend to take it up. Let's be very fierce, that they may think us in earnest.

[*Addressed*:] Andrew Rutherfurd Esq, 24 Marlborough Buildings, Bath

To Andrew Rutherfurd
NLS 9687.18
Bonaly, 28 March 1822
My Dear Rutherfurd
　　Lest you be kept on the rack, as I was for a day, by just hearing of Stuart's affair without knowing the particulars, I think it may be acceptable if I tell you them, so far as they are yet known. They are simply these.

　　On getting possession of the *Sentinel* papers he found that Affleck was the author of the most audacious attacks on him. After a pause of about a fortnight, during which he seemed to be preparing summonses and submitting to precognitions with great coolness, he challenged Affleck, who was living in Edinr. It was settled that they should meet in Fife, as Stuart had been bound over in Stevenson's affair to keep the peace in Midlothian. James Brougham (I understand) went over with Stuart as his second early in the morning of Wednesday last the 26th inst. Brougham only went in case Lord Rosslyn was not to be found. But Rosslyn was found, and went out. Affleck had Douglas the Commissioner of Excise. And each had a doctor – Stuart, Liston; Affleck, George Wood.

　　They met at 11 a.m. on the 26th at Auchtertool, near Balmuto. It was agreed that they should wheel round on a signal, and fire at once. They both wheeled, but Stuart's shot took effect before Boswell had fired. He was taking a steady aim (it was said) and was too slow. But the fact is that his pistol only went off as he was falling. He died next day at 3 o'clock p.m. The ball struck somewhere about his neck, and made a slant down the spine – which last was the cause of his death. He was instantly paralyzed – and never spoke again. Stuart was in Edinburgh in two hours after the affair, and in a few minutes after, Duff had his officers at his door. But he was either out or was denied; but so it is, that after seeing Gibson, he and Lord Rosslyn both went off – whether separately or alone I don't know. What has become of Douglas I do not know either. As soon as they were fairly out of reach, Gibson waited on the Crown Agent, and explained that their flight was only to avoid jail, and that whenever they were to be tried they would appear.

These, as far as I can ascertain, are the facts – tho' I dare say there are some inaccuracies. I have not been in town since, so I do not know the sough [sc. gossip] personally. But I understand that the Torries are inwardly cheering themselves by the prospect of Stuart being tried by a Sentinel Lord Advocate, and a well picked jury of country gentlemen; and they are very anxious for grounds for asserting that Stuart fired too soon. But this last they have not as yet dared to speak out. There is not the slightest foundation for such an imputation – and indeed the presence of such seconds makes the thing ridiculous. Yet there is no saying what Douglas may state; for tho' Boswell's not having fired may just as well have arisen from the deliberateness of his aim as from any other cause, it is certainly unfortunate that he did not fire. It is a strong circumstance for Stuart, that before taking their ground he distinctly asked Boswell whether he had any explanations to give? To which a decided negative was given.

Any calamity that puts so excellent a man as Stuart in jeopardy, or deprives a widow and ten children of their protector, is to be deplored; but I must say that if the thing was to happen, there are few who could have diminished the grievousness of the event, by his provoking it, and by his general insolence, so much as Affleck.

As I wrote t'other day, I have nothing more to say. Miss Stewart[1] will think us all savages here. And so we are. I wish she were here to civilize us. Renew the falling down upon her head of the dew of my blessing. Elizabeth says she is positively determined not to quarrel with her. I am glad of this; because it will the more easily enable us to leave these two domestic household fowls brooding together at home, while their jolly spouses are pursuing their own avocations. Do wean her from the foolish habit, if she has it, of expecting to be regularly attended to by solemn visitations, and of staring when her friends enter to meals without being formally invited. I expect that she is to keep an easy and soshial house. I mean to intimate to all my other friends that I don't intend to sup with them all next Session – being pre-engaged. Shall I take the East House of Bonaly for you?

Ever Yours

H. Cockburn

1 Rutherfurd's fiancée.

I am told that the last Sentinel is the most villainous that has appeared, and that poor Boswell was its author. This however is not unlike a thing that would be said without foundation.

[*Addressed*.] Andrew Rutherfurd Esq, 24 Marlborough Buildings, Bath

To T. F. Kennedy[1]
LAS 69

Edinburgh, 25 December 1822

My Dear Kennedy

As to the Fox dinner,[2] I hereby repel all your objections; which are singularly feeble. If you be a public man, we require you as such; but if you be not, we need you the more. The very use of these meetings is to indicate the opinions and spirit of private men, whose views are otherwise never heard of. Upon your notion, who would act? Are Leo. Horner, Moncreiff, Alexander Young, W.S.,[3] or Scott, the apothecary, public men in your sense of the word? or Lord Minto or Admiral Fleming? You shall therefore be advertised in all probability, and if you be so, I trust to yourself for your appearing and doing your duty on the day appointed.

As to Abercromby[4] – I wrote to him fully a few days ago, and have heard from him since. He is to be in Edinburgh about the 4th or 5th of January. He is coming by Carlisle to Glasgow, from thence to his brother's at Tullibody, and then here. I was too sorry for the annoyance our poor Scotch affairs had already given him, to urge him to go on with Borthwick's case,[5] so I only

1 Thomas Francis Kennedy (1788–1879), Whig MP for Ayr 1818–34, carried the Jury Bill 1825 reforming the selection of juries in Scottish criminal cases; prepared the (Scottish) Reform Bill; a Lord of the Treasury 1832–4. Paymaster, Irish Civil Service 1837–50; Commissioner of Woods and Forests 1850–54. Married 1820 Sophie (d.1879), daughter of Sir Samuel Romilly. A Friday Club member since 1811. His edition of *Letters on the Affairs of Scotland* (1874), largely from HC to himself, was published without the Cockburn family's approval. His printed texts contain various small omissions, duly indicated.

2 For these demonstratively Whig occasions, nominally in memory of C.J.Fox and important for declaring support up to the passing of the Reform Bill, see *Mems*, 83, 355, etc. Kennedy was invited to be a Steward.

3 Alexander Young (1759–1842); WS (1786).

4 James Abercromby (1776–1858), barrister 1801; M.P. for Midhurst 1807, Calne 1812–30, Edinburgh 1832. Judge Advocate-General 1827, Speaker of the House of Commons 1835–9; created Baron Dunfermline 1829. Prominent in Commons in discussion of Scotch business; see *Sedition Cases*, ii, 223, for his work on Jury trial reform.

5 One of the editors of the *Sentinel.*

communicated the fact that the interest of the affair, though it was less talked of, was not impaired, and that all parties remembered the last discussion and anticipated the next. I advised him, however, not to chain himself to the stake for us, but to be guided solely from the consideration (of which he alone could judge) of what was due to himself as a Member of Parliament; adding that his totally abandoning the affair would not deprive him of one particle of the gratitude which he had gained from all liberal men in this country. On this statement he seems resolved to act on his pledge of proceeding; and I have no doubt that his visit here is partly to get information. His being here is an additional reason why you should appear on the 13th, for you will of course come a week before that, and help us to entertain and instruct the worthy member for Calne.

But these matters are as nothing compared to what you say of yourself. I don't know that I ever read an intimation with greater regret than that in which you disclose your intention of ceasing to be Parliamentary. I do sincerely hope that the project is not irrecoverably fixed; for nothing can be more certain than that it ought not to be adhered to. It is melancholy for us that even one should be taken from the slender number of efficient Scots members – but particularly so that this one should be you. There will probably be no session for many years in which some effort will not be made for the improvement of this part of the kingdom. It was therefore of immense consequence for the public that there should be one person in the House acquainted by birth, habit, or education with Scots affairs. The Jury Bill[1] is a fair example. I don't know what you may profess, but I believe that that measure would not have been carried if your present scheme had beset you a year ago. Brougham disdains us, Maxwell is ——; Abercromby and Mackintosh require great instruction on our matters, which besides are not in their natural path. Hume, Fergusson, and Lord Archibald are ignorant, and, on these subjects, slight; so who have we?

But our loss, great though it be, moves me less than yours. You seem to feel the step you are planning as a temporary one. If it take place at all, I trust it will prove so; but I have not the slightest expectation that it will. A man can neither dally with Parliament, nor with his habits, nor with time. You will become a mere Ayrshire gentleman before you know what you are about. What this implies, look around you, and you will see. You have not a conception at present what two or three years of spiritless, unintellectual residence there will do for the understanding, the taste, and the temper. If you

1 For discussion of Jury Bill matters in Parliament, see, e.g., *Sedition Trials*, ii, 221–2

had been born and bred a clod of Dumbiedykes, it might have done very well. But any young man who has known higher things, and renounces them for the purpose of pacing over his own acres, and giving the law to his own people, must either degenerate into a fool, or a tyrant, or both.

As to your reasons for this fatal design, I can speak of them plainly without the presumption of knowing or of meddling with your private affairs. I dare say living with an establishment for half the year in London must be a severe addition to the calamities of the times; and you obviously assume this to be necessary. But how it is so, I cannot see. How many members are there who leave their families in the country, and only run up themselves when their presence is necessary? To be sure they don't do so much good as if they were always on the spot. But is this any reason why they should do none? I am satisfied that by little occasional visits, not exceeding a month or six weeks in all, performed by yourself, you might do a deal of public good, without any private loss, and to your own complete personal salvation? I know that you will demur to leaving Mrs Kennedy to rusticate, and in ninety-nine cases out of a hundred this is the consideration which leads to such resolutions. But if she knew, as well as your other friends do, how necessary your remaining in Parliament as long as you can is to your happiness and respectability, she would be the first to abjure this claim, and if the thing were stated to her distinctly, she would see it exactly as everybody else must. If you should say that your fortune will not even permit your absence from home, or your residence in London, occasionally and humbly, I ask you if you seriously mean to shut Parliament against all those who are not richer than you? What does Mackintosh do? The idea is absurd; and it must be owing solely to some vague notions of magnificence that you can indulge it at all.

Thomson,[1] on my telling him generally that I had had a letter from you, instantly opened on this subject, and I wish you heard what he said. He promised to remonstrate in writing, but I presume this as usual with him will be some years hence. But he perfectly and powerfully concurs in what I have said, and is particularly fierce at the idea that if you could otherwise go to London occasionally you should hinder yourself, or be hindered from doing so, by the mere silly unwillingness of parting from your family and home pursuits for a fortnight now and then. I don't believe that any friend you have

---

1 Thomas Thomson (1768–1852); adv. 1793. Deputy Clerk Register (a post created for him), 1806: 'The man to whom, more than to any other, we owe the preservation of the public records of Scotland', wrote James Fergusson (in spite of casual accounting, which led to his summary dismissal in 1841). Also a Clerk of Session 1828–52.

can approve of your scheme. I assume in saying so, that you have consulted Wishaw and other sages in the south, and that they don't absolutely say No. But they know nothing about the matter. Nobody can, who does not know you out of London, and the effect of five years' residence in Ayrshire. I would lay my life that in ten minutes I would convince Wishaw that the plan was absolutely ruinous.

So you will find ere you are aware, and after it is too late. If therefore there be any opening, even a chink, left, I implore you not to close it. You are doing a thing which is to affect your whole life, with all its plans, and views, and habits. Excuse the plainness with which I have remonstrated. If I cared less for you, I should have said less about it.

Mrs Cockburn desires to be remembered to Mrs Kennedy, in which I join. Oh, that I had half an hour's free talk with her on this cursed and nonsensical subject.

Ever yours
H. Cockburn

To John Richardson
NLS 3989.48
14 Charlotte Square, 14 January 1823
My Dear John
Peter Maclaurin[1] has not yet appeared, which gives me leisure to tie the broken thread of our acquaintance. I cannot find out where I last left you – but I think it was about the period of which Solomon sings when he talks of 'now is the time of the coming of the buns, and the crunching of the short bread is near'. I sympathised with your annual festivities, and was with you in spirit. On the same night – Hogmanay – we were at Hermand; where we had a glorious forenoon of curling and skating on Sandy Young's five acre pond[2] – and a glorious night of Plotty and Brandy posset of the old octogenarian Lord [Hermand]. Would he could live it over again. But quod voluit non *posset*. He has not been very well – and we must now begin to look for his place being void among us. A sad void it will be. He is not made much better by his coachman driving over a woman today as he was taking his master to court. She is not dead, but he is in jail – and I fear is in a scrape.

1 Apparently Cockburn's clerk.
2 Alexander Young of Harburn, near West Calder.

I went to Glasgow on the 2nd of Jan. to do honor to the new Rector[1] – and was away two days. Dined at Elderslie[2] one day with a mob. What a beast the Knight of Elderslie is! Lying is actually the best of him – which few other men can make it. Lord how we abused him at night. Next day saw the installation, and heard Sir James make a very bad extraordinary speech. Went that day to Cumbernauld[3] with Murray and Thomson – and had a long, wet, late night at Fleming's, and came home next day. I saw Abercromby for half an hour in Glasgow. Eight days ago he came here – and ever since I have been with him constantly. He dined, supped, breakfasted here; I took [him] thro' the town, round the Calton, down Leith Walk, along the Craggs – in short every where, and every day we have feasted till he declares his poor English stomach to be demolished. Kennedy too came in, and others – so that what with [them] and Sir James exhibited as a lion, we have had a busy and rather strange week of it.

Abercromby went away today – and is to be in London about Saturday or Sunday. He is an admirable person, and I shall ever treasure it as one of the fortunate circumstances of my life that I have now made a very intimate *speaking* acquaintance with him. We have not *advised* him to proceed with his parliamentary affair; but the facts he has learned leave him no choice – and convince him that he ought not to abandon it tho' he could. He was at our Fox dinner yesterday – and is utterly confounded at the scene. Ask him about it. Macintosh made some excellent and successful speeches – and Cranny croupiered him with matchless excellence. He never [made] such an appearance in his life – and never will again – as in his two pure, limpid, noble, well composed, finely conceived, and beautifully given, little orations. Jeffrey not *very* good, for him; Creefy excellent; old Rosslyn[4] admirable; Abercromby himself perfect – for thought, feeling, and propriety; the citizens most respectable; and your humble servant prodigiously cheered both in his lofty and in his jocular strains – but very inferior to all these. I am quite satisfied that no such meeting, not composed of packed, select men, could be got up in any other part of the world.

Abercromby says that Peter Brown speaks better than Joseph Hume.[5] Not saying much perhaps for speaking, but surely a good deal for Peter – who cannot be bad for a citizen of Edinburgh, since Joseph is so efficient in

1 Sir James Mackintosh (1765–1832) had succeeded Jeffrey as Rector.
2 Seat of Alexander Speirs (1758–1832), MP.
3 Sir Malcolm Fleming's.
4 2nd Earl of Rosslyn (1762–1837).
5 Joseph Hume (1777–1855), the radical politician, then MP for Aberdeen (1813–30). Brown not identified.

Parliament. I this day too heard Macculloch's first public lecture in political economy.[1] There were about 130 present – and it was excellent. But I presume his class won't consist of above twenty or thirty – if so many. But in time, he will create a taste for it, and do.

Write soon. Send all the books you have for me by sea. The Cluverius you mentioned in your last seems a good one – knabb it. Archie is never above 18 and never below 25. A good medium. Laurence has been very ill of cold, teething, earache, bowels, and bad temper.

Remember me to all at home. Go and talk with Abercromby.

Ever Yours
H. Cockburn

[*Addressed:*] John Richardson Esq, 5 Fludyer Street, London

To John Richardson
NLS 2257.156

14 Charlotte Square, Sunday evening 16 February 1823

My Dear John

The sight of your antique hand of writing was to me like the reappearance of the green grass after a long storm of snow. What a devil of a *givetar*[?] it has been. There were about thirty mails due here at once. But now, except where the drift was deep, all is soft and springlike. We have dined for a fortnight by daylight, and the children are beginning to long for Bonaly. By the bye, that project is done. I offered, in the most regular manner, to give them a feu duty of double their present nineteen years' rack rent, and they have refused – and won't specify what they want. So I am done with all permanent visions about Bonaly. And it is perhaps as well. For it would have been very expensive – and I have never entirely overcome my dread of laying out money building a house on poor soil and in a stormy sky. So I mean to fight on there as long as I can or must – and to pounce on any half made and saleable place I can ever fall upon.[2]

We are all well. The children immensely happy, and Elizabeth as stout as

1 John Ramsay McCulloch (1789–1864), professor of Political Economy at London University 1828–37. Jeffrey and others backed an abortive scheme to get him appointed to a new chair at Edinburgh (*Life Jeff.*, i, 277–8).

2 Only a temporary setback, but strongly felt at the time: 'It [will be] a sore pang to quit the wildness, the solitude, and the prospects of the hills, associated as they are with the sports and progress of the children' (To Mrs Jeffrey, 2 Feb 1823, (Dep.235.1).

ever she was in her life. This is the consequence of her not being obliged 'to pay me a visit in June'. I don't know if you ever saw an excellent person, a sister of my father, who has lived at Caroline Park since even we went there. She died two days ago – to her and our great relief. She, from the bad usage of a near relation, got broken hearted, or at least low spirited, about 1806, and never was herself again. I never saw her after that event – tho' I was her great favourite before. She died in a moment, without any previous illness, aged 79.

The Spottiswoodes dined here t'other day. They can['t] get away for snow. Thomson and our worthy Sollicitor General[1] have gone too. As the latter is for Harden, I presume you will see him – and of course when you contemplate his tall figure, will imagine you behold a bottle of sour, cold, bad hock. I have had some communications from Abercromby of late – in one of which he gives prodigious praise to Brougham's Holy Alliance speech. Tell Timotheus [Thomson] that his namesake the bookbinder had his workshop burnt to the ground this forenoon. The Bannatyne Manuscript, which he had, was saved, along with a good number of other books, but still the loss is supposed to be great.

Are you never going to send me any books? Talking of which, I have another commission to give you – to which pray attend. I have a beautiful copy of the Memoires of Phillip de Commines, with the original engraved Dedication, which is rare, but without the Portrait, which is still rarer, of Marshal Saxe. Now go to Colnaghi or some such, and get me *a* portrait of that hero which I shall insert into the book. The volume is about the size of Robertson's 4to works.

Lord Ashburton has died suddenly today or yesterday.[2] Old Hermand has not been well all winter. But he always suffers severely from cold weather. The little Hills have got something which they call Smallpox. The citizens are preparing a vigorous application to Parliament for extending the right of voting to a certain class of householders. It will keep us in a stew for a fortnight – but they are quite right. I suspect that I shall be obliged to pen another 'Letter to the Inhabitants' – or keep them right in some other form. It looks visionary – but I don't despair of seeing the Hustings erected at the Cross.

What are you doing with my friend John? Doddie and Graham go to a reading school for two hours a day, and vary in their positions from Dux to Boobie – they being the class. Remember me to Mrs Richardson – and Miss

1 James Wedderburn
2 Richard Dunning, 2nd and last Baron Ashburton (1782–1823) had died on the 15th, at Friar's Hall, Roxburghshire.

Hill, Christian, Hope, Isabella, and Roland. I wish you would tell me what I am to do with an idle £1000? Is this a good time to buy into the Funds? Remember my books, and Marshall Saxe.

Ever Yours

H. Cockburn

[*Addressed*:] John Richardson Esq, 5 Fludyer Street, London

To John Richardson
NLS 2257.158

Bonaly, 2 May 1823

My Dear John

About a fortnight ago, Eliz and I and Jane went from this to Glasgow, where at one o'clock we met Rutherfurd. We then had a beautiful sail down the Clyde to Greenock, where we dined, and staid all night, at Will. Macdowall's.[1] Very pleasant evening. Next morning, being a Sunday, we crossed in the Custom House boat to Helensburgh, and went from that place up Loch Long to Arrochar, where we dined and staid all night. We were the only Inn-mates, and the evening reminded me of our heavenly Windermere one seventeen years ago.

Never was Highland lake more glorious with calm light or dark shadows, than Loch Long as the sun went down, and after the moon rose. I could not see the clear, fantastic Cobler[2] [*sic*] without feeling again our many youthful days, when we used to wonder at him from the same spot.

The Saint shuddered as I described my inward [*illegible*] pangs when we passed and repassed the neat white manse of your departed and redfaced friend the minister. The noggin with which the scenery was preceded, and attended, and followed, was scarcely inferior to that which solaced us at Crookston last autumn. Next forenoon we went up Glen Crou, where there is a new and delightfully smooth road. But, thank Nature, they cannot, with all their improvements, level Rest and Be Thankful. Tho' some miscreants have, as the Surveyor told me, thrown down the old stone with the inscription into the valley three times this year. But he is to fix it.

At Cairndow we bated [*sic*] the horses – and ourselves on rural eggs, highland cheese, and distilled nectar. Thus refreshed, the Saint and I got Eliz.

1 William MacDowall, 17th of Garthland, Lochwinnoch.
2 The Cobbler, otherwise Ben Arthur, Cowal, Argyllshire, at the head of Loch Long.

into a boat and rowed three times across the Loch entirely – landing each time, and riffling a bank of its glorious primroses, which we took by the roots for Bonaly. We then got to Inverary by 4. And such another night! Almost worthy of the day on which you and I first and last saw Elizabeth at that place in 1807. Strange thoughts went over me.

Next day I had a trial – which was over by 4. Rutherfurd had left us in the morning to pursue his way to Ballachellish, where he was bent; and I had sent Eliz. back in the chaise in the forenoon to Cairndow, to be ready to start when I should appear. I had been sent to Inverary by the Board of Customs to defend one of their sailors accused of official murder. He got splendidly off, and the Captain of the cutter sent his boat with me to Cairndow – which we reached in an hour, *I steering*. Observe that – *I steering*. We instantly got into the chaise and that night at 8 reached Arrochar, again in its glory.

Next day we went down the Loch Lomondside to Luss, and from that to Helensburgh. Coll. Walker tipsyfies I am told. The Loch was beautiful, with bright sunshine, and soft warm rain. We crossed at Helensburgh to Greenock, where we again staid all night; and next morning splashed up the Clyde to breakfast, and got here in the evening.

In about eight days after this, Eliz and I went to Hermand last Sunday to breakfast – where she remained. I went on to Glasgow. Got some trials dispatched on Monday forenoon, and was back at Hermand that evening. Staid there all Tuesday, colded and stupid, and came on Wednesday, being the day before yesterday; where we remain till next Wednesday the 7th, when we go to town. The weather has been cold, but is now delicious again. We saw two swallows on the 13th of April on the Clyde, two here about ten days ago – and yesterday plenty.

Such is the logbook of my life. What have you been doing? Talking of books, I don't know to what you allude when in your last letter you speak of the spare copies of the Edinr Roxburgh club. It is called the Bannatyne Club – and I am not aware of its having any books.[1] If you mean the copies of the reprints which the members are to get, I should suppose there would be no difficulty in securing them for you – if they ever print anything. You of course can always have mine.

When am I to get a box from you? Take Arch's Cluverius, if you approve of it. But I forget what else we have corresponded about in this line. I remember only some De Foes, Wakefield's *Ireland*, Philopatris Varvicensis – but there were more. *But there is one thing I am seriously anxious about*: after a rummage I

1 The Club was founded in October 1822.

have found all the reports of the Commissioners on our Scotch courts which you have sent me carefully put up. They consist solely of the 1st, 10th and 11th Reports. Now these are so much in my way professionally, and will in all ages be so useful, that I must have them complete *at any cost*. So observe that I rely upon you, and shall take the liberty of regularly boring you about them every time I ever write to you till they be all here.

Anything known yet about our appeals?[1] What a remedy, to make the Appeal be virtually to a permanent Scotch judge – with all his local prejudices and factiousness – and whose unfitness is apparent everywhere except on the foreign and mysterious place to which he is raised – and where it is most mischievous. If they would give us a good judge now and then here – an active English man of law in the House of Lords, aided by the presence of a Scots judge or two sitting beside him in *rotation*, and this improved in their turn, and each correcting the follies of the other – and by the practice of giving proper and not nominal costs – the system would work perfectly, without subjecting us to the national, personal, unexposible ignorance, crotchets, and prejudices of a permanent individual. Not that anything will prevent appeals – for who will renounce another chance? – but that it would get them well and easily disposed of, without annoying anybody.

Ever Yours

H. Cockburn

[*Addressed.*] John Richardson Esq, 5 Fludyer Street, London

To John Richardson
NLS 2257.164

14 Charlotte Square, 17 November 1824

My Dear John

A petition has been sent to you today for an unfortunate young rogue – a client of mine – now under sentence of death for robbing a house in this Square. I have assured the agents that nothing of the kind ever fails in your hands. His petition, drawn by me, states the grounds for mercy. He is only nineteen; this is his very first offence; he was seduced in a moment by a hardened and already convicted blackguard who did the principal part of the job; his relations are very respectable; and the public feeling is against hanging the lad. He pleaded guilty, which prevented a public exposition of the facts. I

---

1 Lord Colchester's Appellate Jurisdiction Committee of 1822. See Walker, vi.307.

have reason to believe that, if a remit be made to the Justice Clerk by the King, his Lordship will report favourably, and I know that the Prosecutor wishes that he should. So that the great thing is to prevent the youth's suspension without the ceremony of a remit; of which it is said that there is a recent example in a case in which Pitmilly had actually made a report that would have saved him.

All business has been suspended here for two days by a series of strange and horrible fires.[1] The first broke out on Monday evening a little below the old one, on the south side of the High Street, and before morning left tenements with fifteen windows in front standing black and smoking, from the front of the Street down to the Cowgate. On Tuesday, when we were in court, an alarm was given that the Tron church, which was above 100 yards, or more, from the nearest burnt house, was on fire. I rushed out, with many others, wiged and unwiged, and saw the whole spire shrivelled to dust in one hour. Never was there, tho' it was in the forenoon, a more beautiful sight. The upper part was all wood, iron, and lead, and burned and melted like paper and wax. It was a Dutch thing two centuries old, and of course was full of edgy ornaments, all quite dry. The fire ran along them as if it had been led by art. The covering, being thinner than the beams, was eat away first, and the beams left standing, crackling and red. It was like a piece of hellish phillagree.

The highest stage of it, with a radiant and long triumphant cock on its summit, at last bent inwards and made a glorious plunge into the flaming gulph below. The handle [sic] of the clock was pointing at quarter from twelve, and of course stood horizontally. When the heat destroyed the muscular power of the machinery, the handle [sic] fell, suddenly and silently, down, so as to stand at half past eleven. There was something awful in the cessation of its powers, and its thus dropping dead. It seemed to say, It is finished. The second stage fell in a little after this. The cutting off of each of these sections left the tower better in point of architecture than before.

The watering and confusion lasted all that day, and towards night people were getting easy; when a new alarm was given about 10 o'clock of more fire in the Parliament Square – tho' this was in the very opposite direction to the wind – which was all along violent. I went over at half past ten and staid till three in the morning. The flames, the roaring, the crackling, the heat, the fallings of roofs and walls were all magnificent; the wretchedness of the poor inmates, the disorder, the want of engines, and the utter helplessness of man to stop that beautiful but terrible element, was almost sickening.

1 Cf the more formal account written up later for *Mems*, 393–7.

[81]

The great fear was for the Libraries, and the public buildings. But these were all saved. The whole Parliament Square however in so far as it consisted of houses is down – or rather standing, tottering, full of window pierced gables. And all behind it to the Cowgate is down. The Jury Court, as I heard a man say in the crowd, does not require an Act to destroy it.[1] It is gone – with all the chief's new carpets and desks; having only tried one case. I fear that poor Johny Brougham has suffered. His premises, Guthrie Wright's office, Jardine & Wilson, and many others you know are all annihilated. Old St Giles, whitened by the light, loaded on every pinnacle with people, and hovered over by startled pigeons, was very striking.

Today the courts could not meet, and I sat from nine to three at a window, gazing on the horrid scene – which was still raging with fire, and water, and military, and constables, and people, and noise, and alarm, and confusion. Sundry houses were pulled down as the best way of stopping the devil. But there were constant new alarms in new places – and what sort of a night this is to be, nobody can tell; but as it must have an end, I hope it is come. There was an alarming fire in Carrubbers Close this forenoon. But it was got under. Of course its breaking out in detached places is ascribed to design – but whirling embers and a high wind can account for it all – for I observed last night that the sparks did not always fly down the wind, but circled and tossed.

Mind my half hanged man.

Yours
H. Cockburn

[*Addressed*:] John Richardson Esq, 5 Fludyer Street, London

To Mrs John Richardson
NLS 3989.86

Bonaly, Sunday 1 May 1825

My Dear Mrs Richardson,

I have so often spoken to your husband on the duty of avoiding professional suicide by getting a confidential clerk in vain, that I am somewhat afraid to speak to any one for that office untill I know something of the terms

---

1 It had been established in 1815 to try civil cases with a jury. William Adam (1751–1838), nephew of the architect, a barrister and parliamentarian (MP for a succession of Scotch constituencies) returned to Edinburgh as Lord Chief Commissioner. It became part of the Court of Session in 1830. See *Mems* 283–6.

– which of course will be the very first question put if I should. What will the emoluments likely be? If John wishes that I should first hook a fish, and keep him on the line till I can communicate with him about hauling the creature up, I shall willingly do so; but I should think it much easier to let him know the bait he jumps at, at first. But tell me which way you wish me to proceed and I shall be astir directly. My chief reason for consulting you now is that unless John be decidedly serious in the affair, it is awkward and perhaps cruel to excite hopes in any poor youth. I cannot too strongly urge you and him to get a clerk who can relieve him of some of the clerks' labour which he at present does himself. The life he is leading is perfectly absurd, and, if persisted in, may be repented of sooner than he thinks.

I was very glad to see your hand writing in your letter to Elizabeth; for I really don't think we have been so intimate of late as we used to be. We are delighted that you are well; tho' Eliz and I are of opinion that you too err in the same way with your excellent and anxious spouse. Two hours a day overhearing even your own children practice music is a dreadful and useless piece of self immolation. There is a dilemma mentioned as to whether a certain person should be a nurse or a governess. She should be neither; but should take care of herself.

Remember me to Mrs Hill and your bairns. Tell John that I hope to have another tramp up a Scotch Mountain with him soon. Remember me too to the Bells. I am told that Charles is drawing crowds at his new lecture.[1] Mungo Brown gave me an account of Inverleithen [sic] fishing yesterday that would have made his teeth water. He, and Jack Stewart, and Peter Tytler went there for three days, and slaughtered terribly both of trout and of salmon.[2] They had plenty warm noggins too, and laughter, and no sentiment – yet to my surprise seem to have been very happy.

What are your or John's schemes for this Autumn? You don't surely intend to live at Hampstead the whole year. He absolutely requires rural activity – and where can he get this so easily and usefully as on the Pentland Hills? I never passed so delightful a spring vacation as this. For the first six weeks after we came here, which was on the 13th of March we never had a single shower – but generally bright warm weather. During this time I had my Irishmen working busily and got everything done without interruption or dirt.[3] And at last when I was just ready with my evergreens, and longing for moisture,

1 In the nascent London University, where he became Professor in 1828, returning to Edinburgh in 1836.
2 Mungo Brown (d.1832), adv. 1816; John Shaw Stewart (1793–1840), adv. 1816; and Patrick Fraser Tytler (1791–1849), adv. 1813.
3 Clearly settling in, despite earlier uncertainties about the lease or purchase of the property.

which transplanted ones require, the heavens opened, and the earth has been soaked, and is now smoking with heat and glittering with water by turns.

Except the approach and the house, I am nearly finished. The garden is totally changed; two houses of the village are gone; and the Terrace is completed. I have stuck in about 1500 feet of holly hedge, about 22,000 trees, and about 1500 evergreens. Don't start at the magnificence of 22,000 trees – for the only misfortune is that after all few people ever observe them till I point them out, and it takes about 4 or 5000 to plant an acre, if they be very small – which mine all are. Of the evergreens, I got about 1100 from James Stuart. The holly hedges are chiefly along the south side of the Terrace and in the garden.

In one week more I dismiss all my men except the gardener and his boy. These operations have not been dear – they have been a source of great pleasure to the whole family – and of many a hard day's fag of bodily labour and health. I see that the removal of the village, which will be compl[et]ed in six weeks, will be an immense improvement, beyond what I ever expected. I have been rather less abused than most improvers are – tho' there are daily criticisms made which I listen to, as if I listened not. I have always taken my own way – because all objections which come from people who don't know a place by living in it are absurd. My great object has been sheltered walks – and as these people only walk here in a good day, this is an object they cannot be made to think of. In ten years Bonaly will be the calmest place in the world; which you, who remember its zephyrs, will admit to be no small atchievement. The very cuckoo testified his approbation this day, for the first time this season. The children are all in riotous health. Eliz. growling at a rhumatic shoulder.

Ever Yours
H. Cockburn

[Addressed:] Mrs Richardson, 5 Fludyer Street, London

To Charles Anderson
NLS 3546.55

Edinr, 6 February 1826

My Dear Charlie

Kennedy says that he thinks – or rather is confident – that Charles Grant[1] will this session move for a Royal Commission to enquire into and

---

1 Charles Grant (1778–1866), then MP for Inverness-shire, Vice-President of the Board of Trade 1823–7. Later Lord Glenelg.

report on the state of education generally in Scotland – and that he will get this commission for the asking of it. The Commissioners will probably be three – of whom Pillans will be one. This will do immense good, and will amass much valuable matter, and lead to the putting [of] everything to rights before the present bill will be out.

Now what you should do is this. Send two copies of the pamphlet to Richardson, telling him to present them to Mr Grant with a letter of your own to him (Grant). In this letter just say – 'Sir, As it [is] well known that you are one of the Scotch members who feel a deep interest in the state of education in this country, I take the liberty of enclosing two copies of some remarks which I lately published on this very important subject. My reason for troubling you with them at present is that it is understood that a bill for regulating the provisions to schoolmasters is to be introduced into Parliament this Session, and I am afraid that the great and permanent importance of this measure is not so generally known as it should be. It is a very great sentiment among intelligent persons in Scotland that it is a pity any such measure should be decided upon without something moré being done to investigate and collect facts. I have the honor to be, etc. (signed Charles Anderson, Minister of the Parish of Closeburn.'

Don't allude to his Commission design, because it is still private. But such a letter, from a minister unknown to him, will probably fix him to go forward. (N.B. I rather think this is well conceived.) And if it, under Providence, should tend to make you and that very excellent man, with whom you were at the Speculative, acquainted, it will do no harm thereby to either.

Robertson's guess about the confession of faith, tho' that ancient corrector Time has disproved it, was a sound guess at the time. I don't think Patronage will ever be a serious question again in Scotland, till the dissenters shall so multiply as to make it one in England; and you may take it as a general rule that now that we have emancipated ourselves from the old, hereditary, local, jobbing tyranny that used to rule us at pleasure in Scotland, and must settle all our contests in Parliament, our course of improvement or of change will be in the same line with that of England.

Your question about the Highlanders is answered by what is stated above. It will fall under Grant's Commission.

Sir Harry is well – preaching every fortnight with all the pleasing vigour of a powerful dogmatist, mellowed by Time, and exalted by the approaching prospect of eternity.[1]

1 He died 9 August 1827.

We are sadly annoyed here by Constable's failure.[1] It is a great blow to Scottish literature – for no man here will venture to call up such spirits as he has done from the depths of genius and poverty. Several literary people have suffered – but none so much as Scott, who from being a man thought coining gold has come down to about £20,000 *below* zero, after all he can pay is made allowance for. He has behaved nobly – being cheerful and firm – delighted with his friends, and strong in unexhausted genius. Some of his friends went to him and offered him any money he chose. After a pause, he said 'No! this right hand shall work it all off!!' Few better things have been said – at least few better thought. How little men are known. How few people thought that a man of his strong sense should become a bill merchant and printer, when by an easy process he could give out brains, and draw in gold, without risk, at his pleasure.

Ever Yours

H. Cockburn

[*Addressed*] Revd Charles Anderson, Closeburn, by Thornhill

To T. F. Kennedy

LAS 136

Edinburgh, 27 February 1826

My dear Kennedy

The minister of Closeburn published a pamphlet a year ago about Parochial Schools. He wrote to me about a month ago asking if I thought he could do any good (which is his object) by sending any copies to London among Scotch members. I advised him to write a letter to Charles Grant, and to deliver it and two copies to him through Richardson's hands, who is a great friend of the said minister. All which I presume has been done. Now Horner is going to London on Friday first, and he is to get a letter of introduction to Mr Grant on some other subject. There can never be a better opportunity of fixing or of inspiring Grant to proceed with his commission, for if Horner, with his sense and method, be let out upon him, he's gone. You should write to Grant telling him Horner's intelligence on all these subjects, and it would not be amiss if *by return of post* you sent also a

---

1 See W.E.K.Anderson's helpful summary in *The Journal of Sir Walter Scott* (1972), xxiii-xxxi. For a similar report of Scott's first Court appearance after the calamity became known, when 'he said a very fine thing', see *Mems,* 402.

letter to Horner, addressed to him here, introducing him to Grant. It would be a most valuable commission, not only useful to Scotland, but the salvation of Pillans if he be on it, and if this opportunity be lost such another may not soon occur.

I have written fully to Abercromby on Scotch judges. Our reform petition has succeeded perfectly. We have got about 7,200 signatures, being 397 above those of 1823, without a public meeting, without calling at any houses, without opposition, and in a season of great mercantile depression. If Blyth, the merchant, had not failed in the midst of it, we should probably have had 500 names more.

The Provost[1] has turned out an idiot. Imagine his being the means of making Sir William Forbes, etc., plot with me against the local powers, and call public meetings, and all that he may ruin the town by building up Princes Street. He is in a devil of a scrape at present, out of which, if he does not back this week, he will cut but a sorry figure at another public meeting which these radical Tories will call. It is a great addition to the satisfaction of the whole insanity that his great mentor is Mr Solicitor General.[2]

Pray remember Mrs Cockburn and me to Mrs Kennedy.

The fashionable place here now is the College; where Dr Thomas Charles Hope lectures to ladies on Chemistry.[3] He receives 300 of them by a back window, which he has converted into a door. Each of them brings a beau, and the ladies declare that there was never anything so delightful as these chemical flirtations. The Doctor is in an absolute extacy with his audience of veils and feathers, and can't leave the Affinities. The only thing that inwardly corrodes him, is that in an evil moment, when he did not expect to draw £200, he published that he was to give the fees to found a Chemical prize, and that he can't now retract, though the said fees amount to about £700. Horrible ———. I wish some of his experiments would blow him up. Each female student would get a bit of him.

Ever Yours
H. Cockburn

1 William Trotter of Ballindean, head of the upholstery firm, Lord Provost 1825–7.
2 John Hope (1794–1858); adv. 1816. Solicitor-General from 1822; Dean of Faculty, December 1830; Lord Justice-Clerk 1841.
3 Hope (1766–1844) was Professor of Chemistry 1799–1843.

To Thomas Chalmers[1]
NCL CHA4.549.125

Edinr, 30 November 1826

My Dear Sir

I am much obliged to you for your communication about Dr Brown.[2] I was neither one of his pupils, nor one of his intimate friends; but I was often in his company, and often heard him lecture, and I have read all his works – and have the highest admiration of his genius and virtues. I shall therefore be of any use that the promoters of this scheme may think I can be of; but I assure you that this is very little; perhaps beyond the contribution of a mite it is nothing at all. If, as I suppose, you take charge of the measure, I cannot too strongly urge you to write to Mr Jeffrey, who was very intimate with Brown, and I know has the highest opinion of him. He will do more good than anybody else here.

I think that I know enough of the turn which such proposals take here to be able to predict that if you trust to mere subscription papers being sent round, and do not fix what the monument is to be, and where it is to be placed, you will get very little money. There ought to be a meeting – not public but upon pretty extensive private invitation – of his friends, and a committee appointed to collect funds, for a specific memorial, on a specific spot. The most popular measure, with reference to Edinr subscriptions, would be to erect an architectural edifice in Edinr. But this is dear. Playfair's monument on the Calton Hill has cost, simple tho' it be, about £800.[3] If it be plain that nothing like this can be got, perhaps it may be right to limit the object at once to a Bust in the College, or a small monument at his birth place; but I am pretty confident that neither of these would excite much interest here. You had better write to Jeffrey

Yours Faithfully
H. Cockburn

<hr>

1 Thomas Chalmers (1780–1847), then Professor of Moral Philosophy, St Andrews (1823–8); later Professor of Divinity, Edinburgh, 1828–43.

2 Thomas Brown (1778–1820), Professor of Moral Philosophy, Edinburgh, from 1810.

3 W.H.Playfair's monument, 1825, commemorating his uncle the scientist John Playfair (1748–1819).

To John Richardson
NLS 3989.97
Sunday 24 December 1826

My Dear John

I am infinitely indebted to you for the various kindnesses, disclosed and expressed, in your last letter. It is agreeable to receive friendship from an old friend, but doubly so to find that he has been working, like Providence, unseen, in friendship's labour.

The Writership is most consolatory to a man with six boys.[1] I cannot guess on which of them the lot will fall, for I never speak to them of their future destinies – as I think it better to let them ripen in peace; but of course the earlier one hives off the better, else the chance may be lost. I suspect it will be James, with whom Greek and Latin are up hill work, but I would rather have it Archie, who I don't think has James's abilities. But whoever it be – or even should the scheme fail – I shall ever treasure the promise as knitting me the more to you and to Loch. Elizabeth heard from her Indian brother three days ago. He has got some military appointment which seems to give him great delight. I never saw him, but he writes with singular kindness, and his sisters are all extravagantly fond of him.

As to the gown – I have scarcely recovered my surprise at anything whatever having seriously been done in my behalf in that direction.[2] I am excessively glad that you have done it, because it is an object I am more anxious about every day, and it is satisfactory to know that the King of Scotland (my worthy cousin)[3] is aware that I want it, as this deprives him at least of one pretence for not doing justice - if he thinks it justice. I have long been of opinion that personal jobbing for judicial promotion is improper, and I could not bring myself to practice what I see done by some. It is better therefore I think (a point you ask me about) not to let anybody you have spoken to know that I am aware of it – at least at present. I cannot interfere myself, and it is better that it should lie with others.

There are many others whose claims are infinitely beyond mine – particularly four, viz. Bell, Creeffy, Fullerton, and Jeffrey, to which, in my

---

1 Cockburn was beginning a long campaign of soliciting nominations to Indian and colonial administrative posts for his various sons.

2 Richardson had written telling HC of foundations that had been laid in the (London) Whig mind for HC's eventual elevation to the Bench (NLS 3989.93). HC was of course aware that he had useful Whig work to do as an advocate which would have been impossible were he 'benchified'.

3 2nd Viscount Melville (1771–1851).

opinion, ought to be added Keay. But I don't believe that Jeffrey would accept, at least he has uniformly said so. However there must soon be vacancies for the whole. Eldin, Balgray, Glenlee, Craigie, will to a certainty disappear in three or four years – the three first probably in one; and Gillies and the President in two or three more.[1] The danger that I, and all other counsel except those who, like Creeffy, have been put into stations which set them above dispute and mark them at a distance for promotion, run, is that we may begin to be passed over for a younger race of more faithful adherents, such as your McNeills and Patrick Robertsons – after which all hope is gone. And this, tho' you may laugh at it, I consider as no very great improbability.

As to Melville himself, I don't know him – and therefore may be doing him injustice. But I can have little faith in a man who would seriously prefer Sir John Connel to Bell, and I suspect that political opposition is never so offensive as when it proceeds from a relation, who was under claims of hereditary obligation and service. He and his wife have behaved very ill to me – and ten times worse to Elizabeth. But you need not let him know that I think so; and, after all, I am probably doing him injustice. So henceforth I let this flea stick i' the wa' – and take no further charge. I shall trust to you, who are on the spot, entirely – not even speaking to Robert on the subject. The old Chief [Adam] has been operated on in the Rectum – but is doing well. He won't last judicially another year – and at this moment there are just two of the whole sixteen who can try a civil cause by jury.

We had a prodigious let off at the Advocate's a few days ago in honor of the new Dean.[2] About thirty-five of all parties – and everything splendid, and well managed. Torrents of wine, and much mirth – at least in my quarter, where I was very successful in imitating our worthy host's worthy father, whose portrait was hanging over the chimney piece, with the nose as blue and the lip as enormous as in the original. Jeff. sat next the Soll. Gen. and diverted us much at their various confidances – the said Soll. being much improved of late, tho' as dogmatick and stickish as ever. It is his opinion (and of course must be true) that neither Chalmers nor Brougham are orators. And it is his further opinion that there are only three living persons to whom the character belongs – viz. George Canning, Professor Wilson, and Henry Cockburn !!!

1 Lord Eldin resigned 1828; Lord Glenlee, a judge from 1795, resigned in 1840. David William Robertson (1761–1837), adv. 1783, was on the Bench as Lord Balgray from 1811, as was Lord Craigie. Lord Gillies sat 1811–1837, and Charles Hope, Lord Granton from 1804 (Lord President, 1811–41).
2 Sir William Rae had become Lord Advocate; the new Dean was James Wellwood Moncreiff (1776–1851), adv.1799, who became SCJ in 1829.

that is, when the latter has a great occasion – for all his ordinary efforts are gross failures. He is equally positive, and equally judicious, on the subject of wines, literature, and the arts.

I have resolved nothing about Bonaly House. I am to get a little plan for an addition in a few weeks from Burn,[1] but I don't think I can stir in any thing this year. The fees are still fearfully low – fully a third lower than any of the last seven winters. But I have now ascertained that it is the same with almost everybody else. Horne[2] told me a fortnight ago that he had advised Downie to ask me to go up to his committee – and he seemed to me at the time to do it as if to forewarn me that the request was coming. There are two great cases, which I pleaded in hearings last summer – both of which are now under appeal, or are on their way. One relates to the validity of a Dr Chrichton's will,[3] the other to the legitimacy of a person claiming the estate of Cromarty.[4] But the first will be given in the House of Lords to Brougham and Fullerton, and the latter cannot I fear afford a special counsel, for the alleged bastard has not the rents in the mean time. Cranny was his other counsel here. We gained both here.

Your moving having cost £1500 astounds me. Are not Dunlop's clients liable to pay their accounts to him? What a fool – or worse – that man has proved himself. I see Belmont advertised for sale again.[5] Yes – I see you have been dumpish. Tho' calling it folly will do no good, it ought ever to be called so; for if it be not abused it will grow. You are not fifty yet – and I have no doubt whatever that if I had a good trust deed from you, I would work £20,000 out of you already. Don't think of a Tweed house for next summer. What the deuce could we make of you at the Tweed? Come into this house, and see your friends, and be seen, and let us concur in keeping some horses – a vehicle – and gad about to streams and lakes. Scott is still clear that you ought to try Newhall (was that its name?).

We are going to have a great Bannatyne festival soon – when we can boast of eighty members. We are going on actively here. Eight of them have

1 William Burn (1789–1870), the architect.
2 Perhaps William Horne of Stirkoke (d.1856); adv. 1806. Sheriff of Haddington 1813–56.
3 The £100,000 bequest of Dr James Crichton (d.1823) of Friars Carse, who 'had first thought of a university; but, owing to the failure of attempts to obtain a charter, his trustees decided [in 1823] to construct a lunatic asylum for affluent patients' (Groome, *Ordnance Gazetteer of Scotland* (1885), ii, 393).
4 i.e. relating to the Cromarty House estate rather than the earldom.
5 The Murrayfield property bought by the judge Lord Mackenzie. Playfair designed a substantial villa there in 1828.

clubbed, and are editing a Dempster – at about £20 or £25 each. You and Spotty should really – were it merely for the honor of the sollicitors –do something without delay. For observe that 'Refusing, or at least delaying' are exactly the same. Remember me kindly to John Richardson the younger. I wish I had another speel with him up Ben Lawers.

I envy your Spanish class – but does not the Orator of the Cortes disturb you? Poor fellow. I am sure that neither George Canning, Professor Wilson, nor Henry Cockburn would make so respectable a figure if they were sent to teach English in Madrid. Remember three things: 1. That if you wish your son to go into your own business, and to succeed, you must Scottify him considerably before he is a young gentleman. A young English Gentleman cannot do any good in a Writer's office. 2. That your Academy here is now perfect – absolutely perfect.[1] 3. That I have a room for him – or at least part of one – here. Why can't you at any rate send Christy down here, to teach Jane English, from next March to November? She would get health – Scotch – and cheap education of every kind, in return. Graham is very happy. Eight of her companions are to remain at Stratford during the holydays, besides her – which is exactly what could have been wished.

We have had a violent and long tulzie about our new approaches; of which I have only taken care of Princes Street which, solely by my own activity and obstinacy, I have rescued from all the wiles of that beast Trotter.[2] I don't believe that the Bill will pass after all – which I should regret, for I hold new approaches to be necessary; but I shall continue to watch and defeat the machinations of that cunning idiot. Miss H. Hill has been unwell – but only a cold – but she evidently can't last long. Hermand has rallied – and may live a year. Did I tell you of his horror at Irving's presuming to take the title of Newton – as name sacred in Hermand's eye to whist and claret? 'And I'm told that Sandy Irvine's made a judge! And they say the creature means to call himself Newton! What a wretch!!' Monteith was [illegible] on Wednesday – Murray I believe yesterday.

Ever and Ever

H. Cockburn

[*Addressed*,] John Richardson Esq, 21 Fludyer Street, London

1 The Edinburgh Academy. Scott and Cockburn were among the founders. See *Mems 388–9*; *Life of Jeffrey*, i, 304–5.
2 i.e. the Lord Povost.

To Thomas Allan[1]
Houghton bMSAm1631(78)
Bonaly, Collington, Tuesday [circa 1826]

My Dear Sir

I regret very sincerely that I cannot have the pleasure of being with you on Thursday. I am in bondage to some people here on that day.

But I do intend to invade you this summer, in order to evoke the ghost of old Mississippi to resist the horrible project of letting a modern mason demolish the scene of his early speculations. I require nothing to convince me that the plan is bad – and I am perfectly determined not to be convinced that it is good. I never yet have seen any old one monument destroyed, under any temptation, or in any circumstances, without being followed, when it was too late, by sorrow and reproach. The last you won't escape – God save you from the first. The worthy old tower! How often have I seen it nodding to old Sol, and old Sol to it, as the said Sol was sinking into his western repose. Depend upon it, the demolition is totally unnecessary, and even necessity, or what is called so – that is, the temporary convenience of a new domicil – is no justification. If you can clap two centuries of time on top of a new house the first day it is built, it may not be prophane to extinguish two centuries by pounding an old one. I trust that Murray and Clerk will have right spirits within them.

Yours Faithfully
H. Cockburn

On John Howell[2]
NLS Acc.6135
[circa 1826]

This man Howel was Janitor to the Edinburgh Academy when he wrote this book. A very able man, for his station. He had previously written the life

---

1 Probably from the mid-1820s, and addressed to Thomas Allan (1777–1833) at 19 Charlotte Square, his address 1816–29. He lived also at Lauriston Castle, where he was succeeded by Andrew Rutherfurd. His architectural adjustments at Lauriston, 'suave Jacobean extensions' (Gifford and others, *The Buildings of Scotland: Edinburgh* (1984) 550), were made there instead of a wholesale rebuilding that was averted, perhaps as a result of this heartfelt plea.

2 From the flyleaf of Cockburn's copy (a gift from the author) of Howell's *An Essay on the War-Galleys of the Ancients* (1826). Lord Murray's note in the same volume, 11 June 1853, partly defends Howell: '. . . If he had stuck to any of the best of his inventions – stereotyping, bookbinding, or limbmaking, etc, he might have been a rich man, but he does not care for money. His desire to make himself master of every kind of difficulty and to learn every sort of thing makes him open to the charge of changeableness . . . I hope he will write an autobiography.'

[93]

of John Nicol a sailor – the Journal of a Soldier – and invented a diving bell in the form of a fish – and done a number of curious things – all able. His great fault has always been his conceit, changeableness, and impracticability – the ordinary defects of ill trained clever men. One of the most skilful things in this work is the way in which he has picked up his knowledge thro' translations, and by conversation, without letting out that he knew no Greek and very little Latin.

H. C.

To Charles Anderson[1]
NLS 3546.57
22 February 1828
My Dear Charles

The Schoolmasters have agreed with that highly legal and literary man the Lord Advocate to do nothing this year; except perhaps to pass a temporary act keeping things as they are till a proper new Statute can be got. The reason of this is that their case cannot be properly considered until the report be received from the College Commissioners, who will probably glance at the situation of the parish teachers. Having no faith whatever in these Commissioners, I have done the very little that is in my power to get our parochial system made the subject of a separate commission of its own. But whether I shall succeed or not, I do not know. [In] the mean time the resolution to be patient for the present is wise.

I agree in what you say as to respublica. But I expect no good thro' public men now, or likely to be, in power; and my only hope is in the steadiness and improving character, and encreasing force, of public opinion. Everything direct seems to resolve into the will of the holder of the national purse – that is, of the King. It is evident that the people are ready for any degree of liberality in their rulers; it is plain that Parliament will support any party in power, and that in [this] situation the people's wishes can't receive effect; and therefore quoad government, the whole thing seems to be just to depend on what the King for the day may happen to chuse. The same House of Commons that carried Castlereagh and his Six Acts, cheered Canning and his liberality; and the very same individual Parliament has in the ten last months been equally unanimous in favour of four inconsistant governments. I have long had a desire to be King myself. I am quite satisfied that I would be the best monarch

1 Now Minister of Closeburn, Dumfriesshire. He died 15 June 1829.

Britain ever had; which shows how ill it has been served. But I don't see how I am to make it out. In the meantime be thinking what Church preferment you want. So Volo Episcopare [sic] and you may be Bishop of Thornhill.

Meanwhile I am very glad to hear from yourself, as I had heard from your brother, that you are well. Preach – visit – walk – read – work, incessantly work, in body and mind. Richardson, when I heard from him t'other day, was well. I duly considered, and read and reread the passage in Macbeth, and I see no reason, and feel no necessity in sound, for giving 'Frieze' two syllables; tho' perhaps it is more musical for pronouncing its one syllable long and full.

[*Addressed*:] Revd Charles Anderson, Closeburn, Thornhill

To Mrs John Richardson
NLS 3989.105
Bonaly, Saturday 30th August 1828, 9 p.m.
My Dear Mrs Richardson

I came here this forenoon, from Selkirk where I left your worthy spouse in bed. He was to go to Abbottsford, but I could not resist coming on here. I found Mrs Cockburn and all the shoal well. We have made a very curious and successful journey, and in a day sooner than we expected; of all which Richardson will have told you.[1]

I should like that Bridge Heugh were ten miles from Edinr instead of being, as it is, about forty; and I should like that the hills were more peaked and less lumpy; and that the general aspect of the district were less agricultural. But, as it is, it is really a very nice place, and easily capable of very great improvement. The land lies close along the Ettrick, and consists of a dead *flatt* haugh, a low bank of fifteen year old wood, and some farm fields. The water of the Ettrick was yesterday like liquid crystal, and its bed is rendered more beautiful to my eye from its constantly consisting of very large streaks and fields of gravel, which attest its flooded majesty. If it will only keep off the haugh, that part of the property (which is bounded by the wood on one side and by the river on the other) will continue both beautiful and valuable.

When you are at the house and looking towards the stream, the haugh is on the left hand, or up the water. The house is on the top of a bank at the lower

1 They had been viewing Bridgeheugh, along Ettrick on the road between Selkirk and Lindean. Richardson offered £5,000, unsuccessfully. Kirklands was later bought, much recommended by Scott.

end of the haugh and of the wood. It stands about a hundred feet or so above the stream, and the space between the house and the stream is a steep brae, covered with straggling wood, chiefly old firs. The proper farm fields are all behind the house, and seemed to have this year borne very good crops. So the premises stand thus [*Diagram*, marked 'N.B. My first painting'.]

Richardson raved at Hampstead about the view *up* the Ettrick, but the view *down* it is far better. In both directions it consists of the river – with its clear water and the gravelly channel, the lower fringe of its banks striped with wood; a great deal of farming in the haughs and on the hill sides; and higher up than the farming, hills with not ungraceful outlines on the tops, but all heavy, and neither sufficiently heathery for heather, nor grassy for grass – but good enough on the whole. The house stands on a slightly jutting piece of ground, which enables you to see both up the river and down. The house and offices are nearly as bad as possible, in every respect. The house has exactly six rooms, including dining and drawing room, one of which is only a light closet. The other holes that they show for cellar, garretts, etc. are utterly useless. The garret for example is a place under the slates without even a cieling. The rooms are all small – not unlike those here, or in any common Scotch farm house. Richardson thinks he could make two passable rooms out of the offices, and perhaps he might, at least as passable as those in the mansion house. But the whole offices are wretched and abominable, and their being close beside the house, and *nearer* the edge of the bank, and more in command of the views, is a great additional misfortune to the mansion house.

Richardson is confident in the powers of clearing and creeper planting to make a house out of these elements, which may save him from building for ten years. I know what wonders these powers can atchieve; but I also know that they are the dearest of all expedients. Your family won't be better put up in the present houses than you and your mother used to be in Mrs Niven's, for one summer, under £100, or probably £200; and you won't stay there ten years without throwing away any more than what would half build a new house. There is no rational way of proceeding except, after getting acquainted with the place by burrowing in it *as it is* for a few months, removing the whole present buildings, and making a very small new house nearly where the offices now stand.

Besides this the ground round the house must be remoddelled, and dressed up. The present garden is a common farm house kitchen garden, with some mossy gooseberry bushes, and a few miserable old apple trees. It should all be converted into turf, walks, and evergreens – and the vegetable part of it got out the corner of any of the farm fields. Without a new house, and its connecting ground, I can see no comfort for you. But as to the place itself, I have no doubt of its giving you all great satisfaction.

I love these south country streams; this spot is sweetly placed; with good half wild, half cultivated, scenery; it is near Scott; it is in the heart of trout-land; and you can never know, till you feel it, how strongly the attachment to one's own little place grows. I should therefore anticipate many happy days to you, and to myself, there; and since Richardson is decidedly set upon it, and with good reason, I advise you to buy it, provided in the arrangement of your own domestic affairs you see no serious objection to the distance from Edinr. Deducting altogether from your husband's very natural enthusiasm about his own scheme, I deliberately think that Bridge Heugh will permanently delight you.

Bell's Braes are absolute nonsense.

Mrs Cockburn begs to be remembered to you. As do I – who am more sensible than I shall ever say of your kindness.

Ever Yours

H. Cockburn

The only thing to be seriously thought of is the prudence of settling at such a distance from Edinr – which seems to me to be a point worthy of the most prospective deliberation. Richardson's answer, that the farer from Edinr the nearer London, would apply better to Hampstead. If you overcome this, I would close with this place, as soon as waste time in (perhaps vainly) seeking another. But never cease to take it for granted that you *must* lay out £1500 on a house and £300 on the grounds.

[*Addressed*:] Mrs Richardson, 6 High Terrace, Hampstead

To T. F. Kennedy
LAS 218

Edinburgh, 1 June 1829

My dear Kennedy,

Glad am I to see your legible hand once more. Why have you said nothing of Tailzies? I know only by rumour what state they are in. I can never but rejoice in any good happening to old Rosslyn.[1] His being Privy Seal, and Scarlett Attorney,[2] are agreeably symptomatic. But the Scotch Millennium

1 2nd Earl of Rosslyn (1762–1837), Lord Privy Seal June 1829.
2 James Scarlett (1769–1844), cr. Baron Abinger 1835, was Attorney-General 1827–8, 1829–30.

seems to me to have arrived when I see the Chairman of the Pantheon meeting made a Judge,[1] and the late editor of the *Edinburgh Review* Dean of Faculty. I call Jeffrey the late editor, for you perhaps know that he has announced his approaching retirement from the management of that great and powerful engine. It is a most graceful mode of giving it up – but, my God, what a change from the day he began it. Hope could not have carried it without showing himself in contrast with a very awkward minority; but still his conduct has been excellent – judicious, friendly, liberal, and in as good taste as was to have been expected from the man.

Your late discussion has deranged the gastric juices of fifteen supreme judges. This is perhaps not to be lamented, but I do lament what appears to me to be the total loss of the occasion. There never was so good an opportunity of stating useful truths, whatever opinion the stater may have had of the proposed increase – but it appears to have been sacrificed to a mere senseless sneer at everything Scotch. Corehouse has a scheme, which he professes his willingness to go to London to expound, about a full and final adjustment of all our courts. You and I know how this will end. I fear that since they are not to get their aliment raised until the reforms are settled, everything will be made to yield next year to the contrivance of devices to get them the appearance of more work, no matter how the work is to be done. I wish they had got their rise, and then being under less evil influence the other measures would have had a fairer chance. I must discuss this with you leisurely and fully. How deplorable to see the law of Scotland given over to Best. Gillies and his court, but particularly that court through Gillies, have made themselves so justly hated that even those who lament the late scene do not disguise their satisfaction which the ruefulness and rage of these men gives them.

I trust that Mrs Kennedy has been keeping stout. When do you mean to see Coila? It is only about an hour ago that Sir J. Fergusson passed this house in a red coat, on his way to Boyle's, whose daughter is this evening to be 'put under the fetters' (as Creefy would say) to our cool friend Charles. We are all well here. John Tait (Crawfurd's son) is Sheriff of Clackmannan, an excellent person; so that opening for Rattray is closed. Is the great Captain secure? What a fool O'Connell is.

Your roses are budding beautifully at Bonaly; but if we don't get a shower Sinclair's grass seeds will disappear. When they were burying Lord Buchan a

1 Moncreiff had presided at the Pantheon meeting (see *Mems* 353–5) and became a judge on 24 June.

few days ago, they by a blunder sunk him with his head to the East instead of to the West. This made a stir, for some foolish people wanted him lifted and turned; till Scott whispered 'Just let him lye, since he's there. Odd bless ye, I knew the worthy Earl all my life, and I never knew his head right in all my days.'!!!

Ever

H. Cockburn

Do you ever hear from Abercromby? I keep him informed of what passes here, for I never shall admit that he is indifferent about us. I heard from him t'other day.

To J. G. Barr[2]
NLS 1030.51

14 Charlotte Square, 11 June 1829

Dear Sir

I have considered the passage you referred me to about Mr Mackay,[3] in the Edinr Literary Gazzette, and have shown it to Mr Jeffrey, and some others in whose opinion I have far more confidence than in my own. The result is that we think the passage actionable – but that no action ought to be attempted.

There can be but one opinion, among fair men, of the injuriousness and malevolence of the article; and as it holds Mr Mackay up as an object of just *contempt* in the eyes of persons of *decency*, and therefore recommends the manager to get rid of him, it is beyond even the large licence of criticism to which theatrical performers are liable. So we hold it to be libellous and actionable.

But when this licence is so very wide and undefined, and there is such a mixture of fair criticism with the libellous parts of the article, that it is by no means *certain* that a jury would separate them. Besides the defendant would be allowed to establish the truth of the alleged facts on which his statement is founded; and however false these allegations may be in reality, it may always be considered as certain, in all such cases, that some individuals will be found sufficiently inaccurate, or sufficiently bold and ill natured, to swear to them; and

1 Scott's remark to his cousin Maxpopple at Buchan's funeral is reported in his *Journal*, 25 April: 'I felt something at parting with this old man though but a trumpery body', Scott added.

2 John Grandison Barr, SSC.

3 Charles Mackay (1787–1857) was appearing in *St Ronan's Well*. See Scott's *Journal* for 11 June.

hence arises a very precarious and disagreeable discussion. We cannot therefore recommend any judicial proceeding, because we feel it to be imprudent.

If Mr Mackay were to institute an action, he would be kept in court perhaps a year, and certainly half a year – all that time a subject of public discussion on a personal matter; and with a result at the last, which I do not doubt would be honorable to him, but which honor would be purchased by great vexation, and perhaps by considerable costs – and possibly, after all, be only attested by a verdict for nominal damages. In short no respectable man – and least of all one who from his profession must necessarily always be a candidate for public favour – ought ever to bring a personal action unless he be quite certain of a speedy and triumphant victory. If Mr Mackay could crush these libellers at once, and certainly, I would advise him to begin instantly – and should greatly rejoice in helping him at the operation. But I have a horror of being in court a year, at the expence of £100 or £200, and then, after all my injury has been repeated in protracted discussion, getting a farthing.

I strongly advise him therefore to leave these traducers to themselves. His true consolation is that their assertions are malicious and false, and that they can do no real harm to a gentleman who, most justly, stands so high in public, and in private, esteem. If however he should be resolved to prosecute, I trust he will allow me (and I am sure Mr Jeffrey on the same terms) to assist him – merely as a friend to him and justice.

Yours Truly
H. Cockburn

[Addressed:] J. G. Barr Esq., 7 Union Street, Edinburgh

To Mrs John Richardson
NLS 3989.112
Edinr, 23 November 1829
My Dear Mrs Richardson

The apparently impracticable tryst of two people meeting at Jedburgh – one from Edinr and the other from London – proved successfull; for we met exactly. We repaired instantly to Kirklands,[1] and walked over it all in the

---

1 Kirklands, Roxburghshire, on the Ale Water opposite Lord Lothian's seat at Ancrum, had been commended by Scott as 'an execrable house' but in a 'retired but cheerful location' (*Scott Letters* xi, 237–8). Richardson commissioned from Edward Blore a house in the Tudor style, which was later rebuilt.

company of the plausible and *honest* gentleman to whom it all belongs; and then returned to Jedburgh, and had a long talk, a long quaff, and a long sleep. Yesterday's heavy and cold sleet made seeing it again impossible; so we came here – to a longer talk, a longer quaff, and a longer sleep. Today we have been over the Calton Hill, up the High Street, down to the Cowgate, over the Castle Hill, thro' the Princes Street gardens, round the magnificent West approach, and home by the Lothian road, to a noisy family dinner with Legion.

I am rejoiced to see John so well – considering all things. *Buy Kirklands.* Excellent land, in excellent order, in an excellent situation, beside an excellent river, and with excellent wood. You will have a kind of notion of it, if you can remember the table land from Woodhall eastward, including Suttie's farm, with the sloping bank to the Water of Leith. Your farming is on the table land; the slope contains your fifteen acres of beautiful wood, and the Leith is your Ale. Only your bank is more extensive than the Juniper Green one, and it has not only a good wild path along its base, by the river's side, but a still more noble terrace walk along its top. From the grounds you have a rich distant view, with a rustic church and bridge in the foreground, within quarter of a mile of you. Buy it – and take a house for a few months in the neighbourhood, and let us have an autumn of planning next year.

I am sorry to hear of your lack [of] success in the place you went to see south of London. But you can be at no loss near house-studded London. Take care of yourself. I cannot speak to you of what is past.[1] You know how deeply you have our sympathy. No event, either of sorrow or of joy, can ever happen to you without your commanding it. But it is from time and your own mind alone that you can receive the support which enables one to survive these terrible strokes. This is the source of my hope as to you; for I know none on whose sense, principles, and feelings I have a firmer reliance. You cannot think too frequently of your absolute necessity to your husband and family; and thinking of this, you will see that you can do literally nothing too much to preserve and strengthen yourself. Would it not be prudent to send down any two of your children who can ride a poney, and who may seem to need it, to Bonaly all next summer? They should return rustic with health. Don't speak of trouble to us. The house at Bonaly you know stretches according to what is wanted. Jane is still motionless, and sleeps ill.[2] But her general health seems not bad; and she is thought to be mending. I hope Mrs Bell is aware how

1 The Richardsons' daughter Christian had died on 29 October 1829.
2 Jane Cockburn, HC's eldest daughter, was now a confirmed invalid; she died in 1878.

sensible we are of her kindness. Mrs Rutherfurd, Mrs Tod, and Mrs Maitland are all coming to supper in an hour, solely to see your enviable spouse.

Ever Faithfully

H. Cockburn

Oh Margaret Hill! – Margaret Hill! I saw her t'other day – in company that made me blush. I have not got quit of the very smell of the thumbed tracts and greasy priests yet. Hech – Hech.

[*Addressed*:] Mrs Richardson, 6 Upper Terrace, Hampstead, Middlesex

To William Sharpe[1]

WS Library

14 Charlotte Square, Monday [1829]

Dear Sir

Excuse the liberty I am going to take – which is suggested by our accidental meeting on Saturday, and your well known skill in matters equestrian.

Is there such a thing as an excellent Droskie horse in Edinr? My vehicle has a double seat, and four wheels. It scarcely ever goes except from Edinr to Bonaly, and is crammed each time with children, processes, lamb legs, women – and all sorts of domestic accommodation or incumbrance. And occasionally the steed must be degraded by bringing vegetables etc into town in a light cart.

And I don't know the head of a horse from the tail. But for these purposes I should suppose that the proper thing was a strong, broad, sensible, punchy beast – like Lord Craigie, but somewhat more active.

If you know of such a creature you will do me a great favour by letting me know where he is. I have given a commission to Laing, whose collection you need therefore not think of; but he has nothing as yet exactly the thing. I can wait this fortnight – but not longer.

Again excuse this liberty.

Yours Faithfully

H. Cockburn

[*Addressed*:] William Sharpe Esq., W.S., 5 Frederick Street, Edinburgh

1 Sharpe was of the Hoddam, Dumfriesshire, family. For the sequel to this letter, see 10 October 1845, below.

To Francis Jeffrey
NLS Dep.235 (*SL27* (–))
                    Bonaly, 21 July 1830
My Dear Dean
    Next Tuesday will in all probability be the Chief's[1] last appearance in the Jury Court, or rather at a jury trial. It occurs to me (tho' I have no other authority for it than my own fancy) that he will say something valedictory. If he shall do so – or whether he does so or not – should there not be something said from the bar? This may seem unusual; but when, except when old unpopular Sir Ilay was turned out, had we, in our day, a retiring head? It is usual in England, for I remember hearing of Pigott moving even Grant on his leaving the Rolls; and tho' it may be abused, it is, when well used, a salutary practice.[2] If *everything* were plainly spoken, much might no doubt be said in diminution of Adam's claims to praise. But much useful truth may be uttered, tho' the deductions be overlooked; and besides gratifying the old man, it seems to me that some very necessary hints may be given to his successors in addressing him.
    This is perhaps all nonsense. But if it is to be done, 'Thou art the man'. Digest this – and resolve according to propriety and expediency.
                                        Ever
                                        H. Cockburn

To Thomas Erskine of Linlathen[3]
Hanna, *Erskine*, i.53
                    19 October 1830
My dear Tom
    I was much gratified by your letter. It breathed the affection which I have ever received from you, and which I can truly say I have always been delighted to return. We have been more separated throughout life, both by distance and by pursuits, than at earlier periods I thought likely. But this has never cooled

---

1 Adam of Blair Adam was retiring as Lord Chief Commissioner of the Jury Court after serving since 1815. His office, with several others, was abolished.

2 Sir Ilay Campbell of Succoth (1734–1823), Lord President from 1789 (and created Baronet in 1808), resigned from the Bench in 1808. Sir William Grant (1752–1832), Master of the Rolls 1801–17, had been thanked by Sir Arthur Pigot (1752–1819) who had been Attorney-General in 1806.

3 Thomas Erskine of Linlathen (1788–1870), the theologian, was also an admitted advocate (1810).

my regard, nor yours. I do not think that we ever had a word of personal difference, and I am unconscious of one moment's alienation, throughout an acquaintance not far short of forty years. God bless you, my dear Tom.

To T. F. Kennedy
LAS 253

18 November 1830

My dear Kennedy

The tidings of the Captain's rout[1] reached us this forenoon, while a very long and very dull speech was under delivery by Mr Solicitor General. The fact was communicated to Thomas on a slip of paper, which he very wickedly slipped up to their Lordships, and the effect was very curious.

William Dundas's insane ——[2] has done much good; and you need not doubt the public opinion being expressed. But I see that Edinburgh must move, for McGregor and Shieldhall assure me that it would not be safe, owing to probable intemperance, in Glasgow. We shall therefore only wait till we see what the issue of the late events is. Meanwhile I wish you would advise me whether, assuming that a Reforming Government is formed, it would like meetings or would prefer being trusted with the thing in its own hand. I only ask this because my ignorance of what is felt at head quarters, and experience of its effects, makes me afraid to do harm; but I have no idea myself that any Government can be anything but the better of knowing the public sentiment.

In the new arrangements don't let Scotland be overlooked or forgotten.. She must be reformed in her representation, her Boroughs, her tone, and you know how little anyone cares for these beyond yourself and a few.

Keep the Burghs in your eye, as you next object. The subject was buried last time in details. But if I had another walk with you and Drummellan, I think I could satisfy you that it might be made a very short and easy matter.

I have arranged with the true men of the west for meetings in favour of your Bill, of the *Commissioners of Supply* of Lanarkshire and Renfrewshire, who are sound.

Ever

H. Cockburn

1 The resignation of Wellington's ministry.
2 Thus printed text. The MP for Edinburgh had declared in the House of Commons that 'the people of Scotland were neither in favour of vote by Ballot, nor of Parliamentary Reform' (*LAS* 253n.).

19th. I forgot yesterday that there was no post today. The delay has brought me your two last, the one of which is burnt. I tried after this to get hold of the Chief Baron, but could not, and I have not seen him lately. I wish he were at head quarters, permanently if the Government is to stand, and even for a week to advise.

As to the contents of the burnt note, Murray got a letter from Brougham today on the same subject, containing some absurdity, some sense, and much kindness. The chief absurdity consisted in enquiring if we were all sound politically, and whether John Hope could not be kept!!! But his principal enquiry was how the Dean, Murray, and I, felt as to the offices of Advocate and Solicitor, the last of which Hope has resigned or offered to resign.[1] We three held a wittenagemote which I wish that the slaves of office had seen, for three more disinterested fools they have no idea exist. The conference was necessary, because B. asked [for] a specific answer, and Murray wished to be able to give it.

I don't know what Murray *will* write, but if he be accurate, as no doubt he will be, all that he will convey, as from Jeffrey and me, is that we are not thirsting anyhow, but are ready to do good in any way that may be thought right, and that we can say nothing more specific till a specific proposal be made. Part of this was mere caution in reference to B.

But I must now tell you truly how the thing stands. I have – I mean Mrs Cockburn has – nine children, and somehow or other there is every appearance of a tenth,[2] and if I were rouped my saved worldly substance would probably be about £7000, including this house. That is, but for my profession, I am a beggar. The office of Lord Advocate nearly ruins the practice of any Counsel, it leads him into great expense, and obliges him to lay out at least one third of his salary yearly or so, in getting or keeping a seat. In these circumstances, nothing but *necessity* to the cause will ever make me Advocate. Especially as I would now begin the new line so late in life that I know best how little useful I would be in it, in London. But I have never hypocritically affected indifference to professional preferment, but on the contrary avow that I hunger for it, and that the honour of being John Hope's successor is what I want. Besides its other recommendations, it is the situation in which I could be of most Scotch use. These are my present feelings, but I am open to reason and to duty.

1 Hope resigned on becoming Dean, 16 December 1830. After discussions, HC became Solicitor-General in the rearrangement.
2 Johanna, the tenth and final surviving child, was born in 1831.

Jeffrey has a little of the same repugnance to the Advocateship, but not by a hundred degrees so much; he is rich; and, if asked, will accept. But he is far more anxious to push me on, in any way, than himself.

I have no right to speak for Murray, but I may tell you that he says positively that he will take no office, at least none of these. He won't on any account let himself be preferred, anyhow, either to me or to Jeffrey.

These being the facts, the result is Jeffrey Advocate and me Solicitor. For as to Brougham's crotchet about Hope, it is too absurd (though Jeffrey's facility won't let him say so) to be talked of.

You seem to indicate that Jeff is not to be. Why, I can't conceive. And this is a point not to be conceded. Murray is so clear about its being the Dean, that any doubt of it seems to make him think it a duty for everybody to decline in concert. This is nonsense. But don't yield Jeffrey, who is by far the fittest for the place; and in saying so, I am confident that I am not prejudiced by my eye being on his first lieutenant's situation.

I wish there was some communication established between us and the arranger, whoever he may be, of these matters. For if any one of us were tomorrow to get an official letter, we would either refuse, if we could only say yes or no, or answer by a written proposal, and *to whom is this to be made?*

Don't take your eye off the Burghs. Rather secure them by a notice for next session before this one be done.

Ever

H. Cockburn

Richardson has written to me on the same subject. I have not time to write to him fully, but shall refer him to you for my views, and if he wishes to know them you can communicate at your discretion.

To T. F. Kennedy
LAS 268

24 November 1830

My dear Kennedy

Murray had a letter from Brougham today, which announces that tomorrow there will be a formal notice of Jeffrey being Advocate, and Murray and I joint-Solicitors. Thank God Jeffrey is Advocate, and thank God that Hope is not! For we have had a dreadful alarm on the score of the latter very adhesive gentleman; the idea of whose being kept has given such disgust that if

[106]

a public meeting had been called to petition against it, it would have been numerously attended.

As to the joint Solicitor-Generalship,[1] I think, *first*, that it is an inexpedient measure for the public, and one which tends to get ridicule for the party. It implies a division of one cherry merely to please two Whigs – the office itself implying individual honours, duties and responsibility. What would have said if it had been shared between Pat. Robertson and Duncan McNeill?[2] *Second*, that coming as it seems to do from Brougham, who is a thousand times more the friend of Murray than of me, it is Murray's office in truth and justice, and that it is paltry in me to come, through his kindness, between him and his fair right. Though I have not positively made up my mind, therefore, my present belief is that I must decline interfering; and I perhaps come to this conclusion with the less scruple, that the half of the profits, with the whole of the deductions, is really not much of an object.

I know what I owe to your personal kindness in the matter of these appointments, and I shall not forget it.

Our public meeting is to take place on Saturday se'ennight.

Ever

H. Cockburn

To John Richardson
NLS 2257.166

3 December 1830

My Dear John

It has at last been announced to the Deacon[3] and me that our Commissions, or whatever else they are called, are to be here tomorrow; so that on Tuesday, which is the first day we can be sworn in, we are Lord Advocate and Soll Gen. Nothing could have reconciled me to the joint nomination; but the Chief was clearly of opinion, and so was Cranny, that *if* it had been so settled that it could not be unsettled without annoying government, I ought undoubtedly not to repudiate, and that it would give offence. I therefore wrote a letter in form to my proposed spouse Murray, but bearing to

1 i.e. shared between Cockburn and Murray.
2 Patrick Robertson (1794–1855), adv. 1815. Duncan McNeill (1793–1874), adv. 1816, then Sheriff of Perth. McNeill became Solicitor-General 1834–5 and 1841–2; Lord Advocate 1842–6, Dean of Faculty 1843–51, SCJ 1851, Lord President 1853–67, and was created 1st Baron Colonsay.
3 Jeffrey.

be for Brougham, which before sending off I showed to the Chief, stating that if the thing was arranged I was willing to discharge any duty [that] might be assigned to me; but that if it were open, I begged to be left out of the nomination; for which I gave reasons – all ending in the inexpediency of the proposal on public grounds.

Many other remonstrances were sent up to the same effect; so that I suppose the double appointment was soon resolved against, and the only thing was to decide on the two competitors. On this I have no doubt that I was beholden to many friends, *particularly to the Chief,* than I shall ever know. But considering Lord Brougham's and still more James Brougham's[1] most natural preference to Murray, I have no notion that he would have been postponed had it not been for his own most disinterested and friendly conduct. He did not merely withdraw, but wrote to the Chancellor, Sir J. Grahame, and Lord Lansdowne,[2] urging my claim in the strongest possible manner; in so much that from the account given me of his letters (for I did not see them), I felt myself obliged in justice to write to him saying that if I should get the promotion, I should consider myself as owing it chiefly or entirely to his friendship and magnanimity.

I am not quite satisfied with myself for having stood in his way; but it is very grateful to think that one has such a friend. I cannot refrain from further telling you that when my total exclusion (at which however I don't mean to say that I ever, inwardly or outwardly, grumbled) was probable, Jeffrey offered *and urged* that I should take his place, or that Murray should be Advocate and I Soll., leaving him to his Deanship.

All this is very pleasant – and I only trust that we may not disgrace ourselves, or prove useless, in these miraculous situations. Do you remember the days when Jeff. lived in an upper flat in the Lawn Market, and was bountiful in whiskey, and was then only considered as worthy of proscription and of Botany Bay for his 'Quarterly effusion of malevolence and falsehood'? And in which I, without a fee, and scarcely with the hope of one, sorned[3] on you up the stair in James's Square when you had nothing but the wreck of a mismanaged patrimony – Dunn *vs* The Wrights of Glasgow – the flute, verse, excellent porter, not bad rum, and a great deal of love?

Here comes a card from the said Jeff. He says that he is advised that the

1 Lord Chancellor Brougham's brother.
2 Sir James Graham, MP, First Lord of the Admiralty, and one of Grey's Reform Bill committee; and the 3rd Marquess of Lansdowne, Lord President of the Council.
3 Scrounged free lodging.

warrants or commissions may possibly be lying in some London office till some fees are paid, and 'I think you should write a line to Richardson tonight'. *Sat verbum.* Brougham's letter received today says that they will positively be in Edinr by tomorrow; but lest they should not, perhaps it would not trouble you to enquire. The delay has been, and is hourly, favourable to iniquity. One capital fellow would have walked out of jail tomorrow had not an out of the way project been fallen upon to detain him.

Mrs Cockburn says that she asked you to pay a tea account of about £20 to Dr Anthony Thomson. *Did you do it?* If not, don't do it, as we have something else to pay here.

Jane keeps well. Laurence not so well this week. I trust that Mrs Hill is not suffering. Remember me to Mrs Richardson and Hope.

Ever

H. Cockburn

I suspect you will lose your election. A day in advance, Craig's relationship, and the activity of Clan Bell are fearful odds. If defeat be certain should you, or not, persevere? The reason for holding out seems to me to be to show a respectable phalanx of friends. The reasons for giving in are to avoid open defeat, to save trouble to the Society, and to put a competitor out of pain. I told Russell today that nobody could decide this but you. *If* defeat be certain my feeling would be to give in. H.C.

Archd is a decided doctor. Clearly bit. Delights already in dissecting rooms and the hospital. A vast relief. Scotland will surely satisfy William Dundas[1] about reform now. Petitions seem bursting from every pore.

To Sir Thomas Dick Lauder
NLS Dep.235(1) (*SL* 28(–))

Edinburgh, 30 December 1830

My Dear Sir Thomas

I have not behaved well in leaving your kind letter of the 4th inst so long unanswered. But I have been very much occupied – of which it is one example that on Sunday the 19th I breakfasted here, and dined here on the next Sunday, the 26th, and yet between these two I was four entire days in London. Since that I have two days of Belladrum,[2] and a good deal of Justiciary. So

1 William Dundas (1762–1845), Keeper of the Signet and Lord Clerk Register, third son of Robert Dundas, Lord Arniston. He was MP for Edinburgh 1812–31.
2 Presumably a case involving Belladrum, an estate at Kiltarlity, Invernessshire.

that, on the whole, there is enough to let your charity ascribe my seeming neglect to other causes than insensibility of your kindness. For which kindness, from you and from the whole household of Relugas – whether expressed in good wishes, or in hurrahs, or in any other way – accept my sincerest thanks.

It remains to be seen whether the Soll. Gen'ship is to be of any use to me personally or not; but it has at least been the occasion of my receiving many congratulations, the friendship of which I deeply feel. And none more than yours. But in truth all private considerations are absorbed in those connected with the public events and prospects of these our miraculous days. Jeffrey, the proscribed reviewer, who all the powers of the bar and the bench conspired to prevent being made *Collector of Decisions*, Lord Advocate of Scotland. Brougham, long the horror of the respectable, Chancellor of England! Both by their genius and principles alone! Grey permitted to close the ends of his days by realising, in power, all the splendid visions of his youth! Torryism, with its narrowness and abuses, prostrate! Whigism, no longer the watch word of a faction, but expanded into the public creed! Government by patronage superseded by the necessity of governing by right measures! The last links of the Scotch feudal chain dropping off under the hammers that one may distinctly hear erecting the first Hustings our country ever saw! The majesty of public opinion – that true representative on earth of Omnipotence, omnipresent, just, instinctive, resistless, the assylum of all right, the exposer of all wrong – established, not in newspapers and in pamphlets, but on the very seat of government! These are the scenes that we have lived to see, and been allowed to assist in promoting.

On the other hand, black specks there are – which tho' at present no bigger than a hand may finally darken the prospect. Ireland; Poor Rates; over population; the national debt; the rise of manufactures abroad, and the consequent decline of our commercial monopoly; above all, the fearful and as yet unknown dangers which may be doomed to accompany that extraordinary rise of popular influence – each of these is well calculated to make the most sanguine ponder.

My hope is in the ultimate force of truth, reason, and common interest. By these I hope for an union of all wise and good men in the common cause; for a vigorous suppression of all undue encroachment by poverty and ignorance on property and knowledge; till by the correction of evils or abuses, even the lowest orders may be interrested in the preservation of their improved privileges and more acknowledged rights. If, as I doubt not, this country not only survives, but reappears above its present clouds in brighter splendour and greater moral force than ever, what a career is then open, under its guidance, to the rest of the world! All Holy Alliances down! Rational liberty up! America rolling its full, prodigious, tide of civilization over continents calling for inhabitants and arts! Slavery, even in our colonies, a matter of history! France, our next door neighbour and friend, so matured that it can banish a tyrant without a day's disturbance, and spare the blood even of the captured and convicted agents of his folly! The schoolmaster abroad even in the Russian armies! Poland and Italy not abased by long oppression, but smouldering, till the safe hour shall arrive, under deep felt wrongs! The church everywhere shaking in its gross temporal pillars, tho' rather strengthening in its true spiritual foundations! International rights and intercourse growing and more respected every day! The press making the world one audience, capable of receiving at once whatever instruction wisdom may have to give, or whatever feeling virtue may have to inspire! Our sons may see the fulfillment of these glorious things. Happy are we who have been permitted to 'scent the morning air'.

Sermon being done, how are you? All wellish here. Jane with ague, Laurence with astma, and Mrs Cockburn with something else.[1] She will soon be well, at least if 'coming events cast their shadows before'. Tho' it seems to be anything but a shadow. Your Elgin meeting greatly delighted me. I envy your addition of *Capitollinus* to our metropolitan Jove.

But the great good that your meeting has done is owing to the worthy *three* who formed the minority. This fact is very valuable. It forms the sum total of all spoken out opposition to reform in this country. I hope you sent a copy of the newspaper to Kennedy – who is the patron of this case. He lives 30 Albemarle Street.

Remember me to Lady Lauder and your whole household, individually and collectively.

Your supposing a vacancy in the throne of Findhorn is an atrocity only to be expiated at next assemblage of the river Gods. I agree with you as to Rae – whose case is very, very hard.

Ever

H. Cockburn

[*Addressed*:] Sir Thos Dick Lauder Bart, Relugas, Forres

---

1 An early mention of Jane Cockburn's recurrent, eventually permanent, illness. The Cockburns' youngest child, Johanna, was born a fortnight later.

To Sir Thomas Dick Lauder
NLS Dep.235(1)
                5 February 1831
My Dear Sir Thos

Sir David Baird has just been here.[1] He wants your vote on the approaching occasion, and influence with you to help you to get it. I *understand*, but I don't positively know, that all the other candidates are decidedly Antiministerial, and I know from Sir David himself that he is not. In this situation, had I a vote, Sir David should have it – and on public grounds, independantly of private friendship. I can exercise, or pretend to, no other influence with you than to state these facts.

How are you all? Frozen or thawed? Deep and universal snow here; silent streets – save when the house top avalanche comes plump upon some startled wight, waiting in delicate raiment till the bell be answered; sparrows sitting chittering round the cans, but ever and anon descending, like Torries on a sinecure, round a ball of well laid horse dung, reeking thro' the clear air; two fools from Piers Hill making people think that they have been in Russia, by driving about, each with one nankeen horse, on sledges; hackney coaches hauling their noiseless wheels, thro' accumulated masses, by means of four horses proud of their strange grandeur; occasional bickers – a stray ball nestling, till it melts, about the tangling geer of a lady's neck, or excessively discomposing the comfortable primness of a poor yellow Bengalee mincing his timid steps, 'to stop too fearful and too faint to throw'; the long white of the pavement interspersed by glorious black slides – along which, to the delight of the boys and the scandal of the decorous, a Sollicitor General is seen running and skimming; the people at the Post Office lounging at the door, and wondering when this mail, and that mail, will arrive, and certain that the cutting of today will clear the roads; the recurrence of the early and long night, undoing in one hour all that strong men and broad spades had done in ten – furious in blasts, thick in flakes – bringing back a late and dim light, to disclose window sales [*sc.* sills] inside wreathed up wherever air could blow a particle; chambermaids late – fires scarcely kindled – baker not come with his rolls – tempers short – must go forth for No. 1 at 9 o'clock – try an umbrella to save my neck – all its shoulder blades broke in a moment – proceed along the narrow track – see a fellow coming – sink my head and don't observe him – have the satisfaction of hearing his leg crunch deep thro' the snow – e'er I look up find myself deep in the arms of a decent but horrible milliner – forced

1 Sir David Baird (1757–1829), 1st Bt, of Newbyth, Haddingtonshire (E. Lothian).

to go off, after sitting five minutes; improved by the adventure; get up to court; see judge after judge shake off 'their poutherty snaw', but not one of them lost life – tenacious dogs, not a vacancy after all!

However Saturday it is! 'The long night of revelry and ease.' Jeffrey alas is gone! But here we are round Murray's cornerless table; there sits Thomson's antiquarian visage – addicted to old wine, old dates, old friends, old principles; there the judicious Keay; see the Pundit's sharp, iced steel — yet softened by heat and liquor; behold Goliah's huge form – he of morocco; hear Duloch's heavy, hearty laugh – as loud and honest as a watch dog's; observe the roseate countenance of our host, jolly in victuals, and jollier in worth; there Playfair, in miniature Ionic; here – but it is endless. Rave ye tempests – fall thou snow – blacken thou surly, dark souled night! Is it not Saturday? Have we not coals and claret, talk and time? What want we but Lauder – a heavy want – to reach whom by the pen is but a cold substitute for the present, living, laughing man.[1]

Ever

Each Sea

[*Addressed:*] Sir Thos Dick Lauder Bart., Relugas, Forres

To Andrew Rutherfurd
NLS 9687.51
8 March 1831, 7 o'clock p.m.

My Dear Rutherfurd

The roof of the bōg began to be broken in upon today, and the light was let in to that, as it is now to other, abuses.[2] Singular reform coincidence. This being Tuesday, we have no news, and are feverish. Our public meeting is arranged for tomorrow. Scene, Brown's meeting house, there being a ball in the Assembly Rooms. Chairman, Craig. Orators, Greeny, Goliah, Stuart Mackenzie, and a few others, including Union Brodie. The proposed dinner is postponed, perhaps for ever.

I saw a note from a Peer today – who shall be nameless, but who lives at Yester,[3] in which he says that if the Bill passes, he has not long to enjoy his

1 This sounds like a meeting of the Friday Club (see *Bic. Commem.*, p.181–97), 'Duloch' being John (later Lord) Cunninghame.
2 A public meeting on Reform was being held.
3 8th Marquess of Tweeddale (1787–1876).

title, nor, if it fails, his head. Disagreeable state to be in, that. The Torries threaten gallant movements, but no overt acts yet. It is quite plain however that they will be perfectly quiet if it were once fixed that the struggle was over. But under the information and directions of the Green Pear, who is their home secretary,[1] they have it all arranged entirely to their own satisfaction.

Your wife was at Cinderella last night, and was roaring here at one in the morning. We sent a little ago to see if she would return tonight, but she is out at dinner!!! Yet she is quite well. A very nice Club on Sunday, of Keay, two Murrays, Thomson, the Chief Baron, and myself. The two latter polluted that dear and dignified association by dealing in noggins of hot water and whiskey. Yet how the rest must (from duty) have assailed the claret – for the bill was near £2.

Is your case, or (as old Adam would say) are your cases, or either of them, ever to be heard – to the loss and damage of the said Trustees? Our Session is drawing to a close. Pensive event! I started today, as a tear fell on my hand, while gazing on the venerable lines of Lord Craigie's face; I sighed, 'He can never be young again!'

What progress have you made with *your* new judicature bill? If I did not make a spoon, I had at least the merit of spoiling a horn. Do uphold our laws and Lords – aye, and forms too – in the face of these conceited English bigots. I am strongly impressed with the fear that we are fast subsiding into a provincial bar and system; which can do no good to the country. Everything depends on getting the court cleared of all the bad old judges at once, and letting us see what new hands, with modern souls, can do. Hope cannot I think do much longer. His mind is yielding to a mollities ossis.[2] We must have Cranny there; or, as the Jacobite song has it, 'Geordie sits in Charlie's chair'. But even he shan't get there till Jeffrey, who has done more public good, and earned more private love, monthly all his life, than the said Geordie has since he was conceived, be completely and statelily provided for. The Pear writes that his speech was a total failure. Yet it has made a great impression here and it is very gratifying to see how much of this is owing to the universal affection for the man.

I enclose you (damn the expence) a placard – for the special comfort of Mrs Jeffrey. I must absolutely fulfil my vow of writing to that most worthy lady. The place is very dull without them. He is particularly missed by the disconsolate ladies. Don't leave London without getting their cellar key –

1 Lord Melbourne.
2 Softening of the head. (Charles Hope of Granton was Lord President 1811–1841.)

for Craigcrook in the vacance is the right of his friends. We shall make the Crown Agent preside, nose and all.

Take Notice. Go to the shop of John Wilson, bookseller, Great Mary's Buildings, and find out if he has got any De Foes for me. I sent him a list of what I wanted last year, but have not heard from him since. He is a friend of mine, and you must have known him in Tait's shop here.

Write – write – write.

Ever

H. Cockburn

To Francis Jeffrey
NLS Dep.235(1)

Edinburgh, 30 March 1831

My Dear Jeffrey

I have seen Ivory, who has explained everything. It is a mercy that you are done with it. Unless there be a popular constituency, your first adventure with Scotch Burghs should be your last.

Could you send me a few more copies of the Bill? Lord Breadalbane[1] and others have sent to me repeatedly for one; which I can't give; and it seems to be beneath the dignity of these great men to pay 1/- and read it in a newspaper.

We have had two unlucky illuminations. Here, the Reform Committee spoke to the Provost last Sunday about having one; which he on Monday about 10 a.m. begged them to give up. This they agreed to because he asked it, and promised to interfere neither for nor against it. So the meeting broke up, and every one laid out his day on the idea [that] there [were] to be no more candles than usual in the evening. I went out to Bonaly. When I was enjoying an illumination in the sky in the form of a very fine evening, one of the boys appeared about 7 and told me that the other one was going on. I went to town and found that the Provost and the Sheriff had suddenly, and without consulting the leiges, at least those he had formerly been in conference with, sent out a proclamation *about* 4 or 5 o'clock, recommending the measure.

The consequence was that nobody was prepared, and no constables were arranged; and therefore the boys very soon saw that they were masters for the night, and they exercised their power. It is said (but it can't yet be known) that £10,000 won't pay the damage. I went thro' the town, and nobody could witness what was going on without seeing that it was all done by very young

1 4th Earl of Breadalbane, created Marquess in September 1831.

lads and children going along with torches – and that a dozen of men, here and there, would have terrified them all. But there was not even the appearance of any resistance or disapprobation. The feeling is of course partly against Reformers, but far more against the local authorities. I have received officially a formal complaint against the Sherrif and the Provost signed by forty or fifty names of the highest respectability, beginning with Baron Hume's.[1] I have sent a copy of it to the Provost and Sherrif – requiring them to give any explanation they may have to give, that the truth may be laid before you or the Secretary of State.

The other is at Dundee. I was wakened this morning about seven by the Fiscal, who had escaped during the night, and after going to Perth and getting *eighty* soldiers sent off thence had come on here in search of cavalry. He says that there was a riot there at the illumination there on Monday the 28th, when some prisoners were made; and that last night the people reassembled in very great numbers, and had forced the jail and court house, rescued their friends, etc. As all this was attested by the signatures of about twelve or fifteen justices, I gave him a letter to the commander of the forces, requesting aid, if he, on conversing with the Proc. Fisc., thought it proper. I have not heard the result; but there is no cavalry here. I suppose he would go back with a general order from the Commander here, and would use it according to circumstances after reaching Dundee.

All this is unfortunate, because it creates prejudice among the foolish. But it is met by great good conduct elsewhere. Maitland saw the Glasgow illumination, and is in rapture with its propriety and good humour.

The Circuit clerks told me yesterday in the Justiciary that the Treasury has refused to give them any more money. I suspect that they must resign.

Ever

H. Cockburn

I have got your last. Don't pay a penny more for a three weeks' seat. They may do with Perth or Peebles what they like, but no member must be taken from any of the Towns which have been told they are to get them. And if you give Perth a member, observe that you leave no district. If you *are* to save a member, it ought to be by merging the Stranraer district in the counties. But this brings in Galloway again, and leaves out Port Glasgow or Renfrewshire.

[*Addressed*:] The Right Honble The Lord Advocate of Scotland, 37 Jermyn Street, London

---

1 David Hume (of Ninewells) (1757–1838), Baron of Exchequer 1822–34.

To T. F. Kennedy
LAS 385

   3 February 1832, 12 p.m., dined out, slightly elevated.
My dear Kennedy

  You are not yet in the position I should have liked;[1] because my scheme was that the Lord Advocate should be allowed to restrict himself to his proper professional or official duties, and that you should have been Secretary for Scotland. But, thank God you are in office, and double thank God that the office is not a sinecure. Occupation will do infinite good to your body and soul; and office, especially with occupation, will add immensely to your weight in Scotland. Nothing – judging without any initiation into mysteries – has ever given me more satisfaction. Go on, and work, and devise, and speak; and in all your proceedings or cogitations remember Scotland. And keep a horse – and keep up your heart, and be gay – and attend to the viscera, and become sagacious and potent. Devil take your anxieties, and your fears, and blue devils, and bad stomachs. We may be out, and they may be in; but the cause can't go wrong, and Scotland shall have ten-pound voters. This implies all the rest.

  I suppose we shall see you here in your way to your re-election. At least we should do so. Tell me how the wind sits. I see gloomy letters from foolish men; but trust that their fears are vain.

  Abercromby left this today, for London – *via* Stubbing. But how long he means to stay at the latter I don't know. Would he were fixed among you; for much as we revere and value him, he is plainly wasted here, and his sense would do much good in your House. The faithful here are disturbed by believing that Geo. Sinclair is much at Brighton, and yet voted wrong on that cursed Belgian Loan – which they connect with the King.[2] I suppose this is nonsense. I am sorry to lose Parnell; but it was plainly necessary.[3] What a head a wise man can sometimes carry.

  Fight – and on your stumps – for Cowal being joined to Bute, and Orkney to Shetland.

  Cholera and other things have made such delay already,[4] that I have

---

1 Grey had made Kennedy Clerk of the Ordnance, February 1832.
2 George Sinclair (1790–1868), MP for Caithness 1811–41; succ. as baronet 1835.
3 Sir Henry Brooke Parnell (1778–1842), MP; created 1st Baron Congleton 1841.
4 'I shudder at the Cholera in my beautiful city, and among my dear friends', Cockburn wrote to Jeffrey on 2 February about the current outbreak; 'I do not know whether the ostentatious preventatives of the Justice, or the equally ostentatious fool hardiness of Hope, be most ridiculous.' He noted that Boyle, Lord Justice-Clerk, 'did not cross the outer house till the line he was to take was sprinkled with Chloride of Lime; while Charles Hope, the President, insisted, as one of the Board of Health, on feeling the pulses of the dying.' (Adv. MS. 9.1.8, fo.128*v*.)

resolved to put off the potato rioters till the Circuit. It will only be a delay of two or three weeks, and it is perhaps better that they should feel local than metropolitan justice.

It really refreshes me to think that you are in office. Lord! Were I but thirty, and unmarried – my God, with what zeal should I plunge into public life at this inspiring crisis! One fair contunding of that whelp ——, or that military dominie ——, would be reward enough for being Newgated by the Speaker. Dogs.

Ever

H. Cockburn

To Mrs Leonard Horner
NLS 2213.71; Lyell, *Horner* (1890), i.263
Edinburgh, 8 March 1832
My Dear Mrs Horner

Your worthy husband is glorious. A blacker or dirtier man was never emptied out of a coach than he, on his first arrival, was out of the mail. But now that he is shaved and cleaned, and has bought a new vest, he looks lovely. His affair looks lovelier still. He has been treated with a degree of kindness and liberality by everybody connected with the Bank, especially by such as are politically opposed to him, that would overwhelm and soften any modest man. What may be the result cannot be known certainly, but at present I have a confident hope of success. He sometimes affects to doubt his fitness (Ha! Ha! Ha!!) and to fear the risks! Risks! Exactly those which disturbed the pensive ploughman when it occurred to him to ask what would happen 'If the Lift were to fa' and smoor the Laverocks?' That is in English, 'If the sky were to fall and crush the Larks. If he had been [*breaks off*]

14 March. A long pause. – Well, if he had been in his soda water state this delicacy would not have been wonderful. But in a man eating, as he does, four large meals of solid food every day, it is very odd. However since I began this modest fit has greatly abated and he rather begins now to think that he is the very best man they could get. He is now dubbed styled, and received as 'The Treasurer'; and we are all looking for large supplies of money from him – and so are our wives. I cannot tell the pleasure with which I anticipate the return of all here again – which experience should convince you is your city of refuge.

And then Mary – she will be married after all according to the rites of a lawful and Christian church. Leonard is going to Kinordie on Saturday to return on Wednesday, which will exactly complete his fifteenth day of quitting.[1] His stomach seems in excellent order. Completely recovered. We have not been at Bonaly yet. I go there for my vernal month next week. I was out on Saturday, the day – like all our days in this Arcadian winter – beautiful, and the grass teeming with crocuses; next day, being last Sunday, we went to Duddingstone – the minister of which has got his arm (his painting one too) eaten by a horrid dog, like the savage brute of yours that used to jump upon Frances. We came home over the hill. What a scene! Bonn! Fiddlesticks! – come here if you want views.

Jane is better; but very useless, and I do not see the upshot of it. All the rest well. Joanna (called Johny here) a very active, mimetic, pretty, clever self willed little devil. Wifie as of yore. Laurence better, tho' not strong – in spite of his gigantic largeness. Mrs Maitland is getting better. As she can't go out, and requires cheering, her house is the greatest 10 o'clock at night meeting house. Leonard casts his eye about for the spot where your household Gods are to be set up. He is bitten of late with a love of the Royal Terrace, on the Calton. Splendid and cheap, but far away, and not near accessible walks. I am just in the opposite direction, for the west end of Melville Street – near tranquil walks, hot suppers, and Bonaly.

What an annoyance it will be if he fails after all! But if he does, we shall console ourselves with the conviction that it is a low and dangerous place, and that there is no Cholera at Bonn.

We thought that we had subdued the pest here; but are wrong. It is now very bad in the village called the Water of Leith, and is appearing all over the country. But in no one instance has it yet assailed any well clad or well fed lady or gentleman. It might be very charitably employed in Ireland.

We dine today at Murray's. Mrs Rigby goes home this week. A very fine motherly body. An excellent wife for William Murray.[2] Mrs C. and I are going out in the Drosky today to visit the minister of Libberton, the most fortunate of youths.[3] If you are to settle here again, you should bring with you some

1 The Lyell seat, Kinnordy, near Kirrriemuir, Angus. The Horners' eldest daughter, Mary Elizabeth (d.1873), married on 12 July 1832 Charles Lyell (1797–1875), who was knighted 1848 and created baronet 1864.
2 William Murray of Henderland, a member of the English bar.
3 The former Cockburn family tutor William Purdie (1805–34), who had been ordained to Liberton on 26 January, but died, unmarried, on 16 November 1834.

queer Bonn chairs, cups, boxes, or other Germanic and Prussian curiosities, to make your house remarkable.[1] Remember that you won't get above a week to pack up, and very probably your spouse won't be able to go and help you. We all send out sincerest loves.

Ever

H. Cockburn

[*Addressed*:] Mrs Horner, Sandkaule, Bonn

To Mrs John A. Murray
NLS 97.1

14 Charlotte Square, 7 May 1832

My Dear Mrs Murray

Will you do me the pleasure of breakfasting here on Friday first at 9? The invitation is the greatest honor that can be done to woman. For you will meet with Justinian and a noble army of legal martyrs – men abstracted in justice, and worn by distinctions; your presence among whom will at once establish your reputation all over Quibbledom as a sage and learned lady. Be grateful and come.

Ever

H. Cockburn

[*Addressed*:] Mrs Murray, 122 George Street, Edinr

To Francis Jeffrey
NLS Dep.235(1)

14 May 1832

My Dear J.

All still perfectly quiet here. The patriots of Glasgow, it is said, wish to send a deputation of their number to assist Edinr in the King's Park tomorrow, consisting of 6,000. Of course this won't take place. I expect to see 50,000 at the least conglomerated near the residence of Charles the

---

1 The Horners were at the time based in Bonn, where Leonard (having recently resigned as Warden of London University, and also inheriting independent means from his father) had resumed his geological studies. They returned to Britain in 1833, when he took up an inspectorship of factories.

Tenth. Would that William the Fourth could have a quiet crack with him over the scene below. You deprecate meetings. But they are not only unavoidable, but are the only safety valves we have. The Town Council is narrower in its public spirit now than ever. So that R. A. Dundas[1] is quite sure. Nor do I anticipate more violence next time than last. The truth is that the people are in a calm, severe, grave, Covenanting, kind of a state. They were seriously offended last time they met in the King's Park at Lauder's frivolity in telling an Irish story. I am grieved for Rosslyn. Keay's case is nothing to his. Ireland will kill his body – and ruin his fortune.[2] The whole matter seems to me (400 miles off) to turn upon the question whether the country chuses to submit to a ministry of false and dishonest men, or whether *on account of their known principles and late sincere declarations* it chuses to oust them, *even tho' their measure be right*. For I wagered one shilling last night against Thomson, Maitland, Rutherfurd and Playfair, that the Captain will pass our very Bill; and the wise Marshall backed me that he would. Assuming this, will the Commons – even reelected – persisted in not taking the cup *because his hands present it*. I think they should. But this is too fine for a lasting practical opposition.

I tremble for Scotland. It is immaterial; unknown; and Reay etc. will get damnable things done. A strong case will be made for valued rent. Your pecuniary sacrifice is honorable, tho' lamentable, and demonstrates the absurdity of the position which the Lord Advocate is obliged to occupy. What a quantity of good wine there is in the interest of £10,000! It is horrible. We have had a public meeting today about Irish Education, which lasted from 12 to 6! – but ended, after a *debate*, rightly.

Ever H. Cockburn

Your official department here is in a very awkward state from our not knowing exactly whether you be Advocate or not. Tell me the very instant that your resignation is accepted of.

[*Addressed:*] F. Jeffrey Esq M.P., 13 Clarges Street, London

---

1 Robert Andrew Dundas (d.1877), later Christopher, later still Nisbet-Hamilton, MP for Lincolnshire.
2 The threatened Irish appointment did not materialise.

To Francis Jeffrey
NLS Dep.235(1)

15 May 1832

My Dear J.

The meeting here has this day gone off with great effect and perfect peace. There were probably from 25,000 to 30,000 present.[1] I did not attend, but saw them from a window thro' a telescope, and if I might judge from the cheers of the audience and the gestures of the speakers, the oratory was excellent. Lauder in the chair. The trades processed from the Mound; with many flags, except one Tricolor, all black – and with pithy mottoes, such as 'Cheated, not outargued', 'Defeated, not conquered', 'More in Hope than Despair', 'Right wrongs nobody'. It has been a beautiful day; and the hill, the rocks, the ridges of the houses, and all eminences, bristling with people, all turned towards the black spot where those at the meeting were, clustered like bees about to swarm, were very picturesque. I saw the Dutchess D'Angouleme walking in the Palace garden![2] There being no report today we are anxious for tomorrow, and full of lies; one of which is that the Duke has been shot.

If we were to be in power again tomorrow, we might profit by this pause and shock. The belief of our being out has unloosened some tongues, and disclosed things which we might correct. The Torries are in general ashamed of their Master the Captain, but their tone, in spite of this, is that this is another of his master strokes of policy and virtue. They are fully inclined to revenge themselves, by additional intollerance, for their late check. Very insolent. Announce your motions.

Ever

H. Cockburn

To T. F. Kennedy
LAS 407

18 May 1832

My dear Kennedy

The Edinburgh petition, with 38,000 names in two days, goes by this post to Jeffrey. I have written to him that it is essential *for himself,* as well as for Edinburgh, that justice should be done to it on its presentation. If you be

---

1 The Trades, who were counted, made up 10,000 of this total at the King's Park Meeting. See *Jnl,* i, 29.

2 Charles X, grandson of Louis XV, with his family, was in exile at Holyrood.

present, it will not only be right, but will greatly strengthen your influence here, if you help to resist the lies about a small public meeting, arts used to obtain signatures, etc., which Rae and others will no doubt assail it by. The meeting was *actually measured* – like land, by instruments, and by being paced (the pacing by Sir Edward Lees, the Tory Postmaster) – and it *certainly* contained *at the least* 25,000. Not a single exertion, literally none – beyond placarding the signing places – was made to induce anybody to sign. A few fictitious names – such as Napoleon, Hadji Baba, etc. – were detected, put down of course to the enemy, but deducting all these wretched tricks, you have 38,000 in two days.

And observe, no violence, not even any disrespect. And this from a city fretted and insulted by its degrading exclusion from the representation. Can there be a better proof of its fitness for the franchise it burns for? But all this you know.

What a scene this week has exhibited! What Providences! The noble purity of Grey and the Whigs; the spirit of the people, constitutionally and therefore safely exerted; the base and natural expiration of Toryism; the example of the worthlessness of mere military talent without public virtue.

Write – but only at your leisure.

Ever

H. Cockburn

To J. G. Lockhart
NLS 933.58

Hermiston, by Haddington, 2 August 1832

My Dear Sir

The Dean has forwarded to me here your letter to the Lord Advocate, and the Sherrif Substitute's to himself.

I have sent your letter to London, where the Advocate is; for I have no power to do anything, and the circumstances of the Court of Session not being sitting makes it, I am affraid, impossible for any arrangement to be made except thro' Government. It is impossible to doubt that whatever may be done will be dictated by every consideration for the feelings of Sir Walter's family.[1]

---

1 John Hope, as Dean of Faculty, had forwarded Lockhart's letter. HC also wrote to Kennedy, 3 August, that 'Sir Walter's incapacity to act, to resign, or to appoint a substitute, and the 15th of August approaching, makes a case I can see no light through' (*LAS*, 419). Scott died on 21 September 1832.

Since the Sheriff Substitute admits that in his opinion Sir Walter is not in a condition to enable him to receive a resignation, it seems to me that he cannot lawfully tender it. Having taken the office, he is bound to keep it, till it falls or can be effectually given up. I trust therefore that he will continue to act as long as he can. I would have written to him to this effect, had he consulted me. But as he has consulted the Dean, I do not like to interfere. You are welcome however to communicate this to him if you think it worth while. He speaks of the necessity, under the Reform Act, of his being relieved by the 15th of *August*. I am not aware that any such necessity can arise till some weeks later.

Yours Faithfully

H. Cockburn

[*Addressed*:] John Lockhart Esq, Abbotsford, Melrose

To Francis Jeffrey
NLS 235(1)

16 March 1833

My Dear J.

Consult the Pundits of the Home Office, if necessary, and advise with me as to the answer I should give the Provost, on a point which his letter to me states to be 'the only point of difficulty or doubt in the way of the successful operation of the Anatomy Bill'.

It arises out of the 7th [clause] of the Act, which permits any person 'having the lawful possession of the Body' to give it for dissection, provided that person be not 'an undertaker or any other party *intrusted with the body for the purpose only of interment*'.

The Kirk Sessions and Charity Work House[s] are obliged to take charge of corpses every day or two for the purpose of interring them at the public expence. Where the poor friends claim that the body be not dissected, of course they bury it at once. But in a *majority* of cases there are no relatives, or at least none who interfere, either by consenting or dissenting. In these cases the Kirk Sessions remove the body, which is first taken to a dead house belonging to them.

Now the doubt is whether, in the case of these unclaimed bodies, the parochial authorities can legally give them up for anatomy; and the ground of it is that, tho' they be no doubt the lawful possessors of the subject, they are intrusted with it *for the purposes only of interment*. If the relatives would consent – so that the permission to dissect might come from them – the case would be clear. But there are often none – and oftner they won't do or say anything. In either case, viz. either when there is no relation, or a dumb or sulky one, the Sessions fear that tho' they take away the body for public health or decency, they hold it solely for interment, and must only inter.

The opposite view is that they become the possessors generally, and as such may dissect.

Unless this be the right view, our lawful supply will be very limited.

What's the best, or the correct, way of getting a letter to you on the Lord's day? Perhaps you would rather not tell, so as to have one day in peace. But it is sometimes necessary.

17th March. You have heard by this time of the accident at Eldin's sale.[1] It is incredible how little so little injury has been done – one killed, and not above three or four much hurt, is the amount of it, bating several slightly injured. Moncreiff, Maclagan, and Mrs Keay, in this quarter, are in bed today, but not materially ill. It has made a terrible sensation. I fear old Geo. Thomson has got some ribbs broken. Dalmahoy, a Writer, seems to be the worst off. Ro. Jameson was so intent bidding £64 for a picture, that he declares that if it had not been for the lime dust choaking him he would never have known that he had slipped down a storey. All accounts seem to agree in the extacy of Gillies that he was not there, and in the grim joy of Willie Clerk that Ross won't get so much as he expected. It is a sad discount for Ross to be sure – both in house and pictures. Nobody seems to know how much the latter have suffered; but they must materially, as well as the china, etc., which were all in the room below. The gallant Marshall could by one step have saved himself, but went down with Mrs Keay. Sandford's wife very nearly went over the window.

I am confounded by what you say of Murray's hostile votes. He and Dalmeny had much better want such constituents than humour them so. I fear your twenty-three will make a hash of the Burgh Bill before they leave it. But it is much better to hash it at first than at last.

Meadowbank (who I have just seen) says another man is dead. But observe who the reporter is. Old George Thomson is very much crushed and smashed.

Ever

H. Cockburn

[*Addressed:*] The Right Honble The Lord Advocate of Scotland M.P., 33 Charles Street, London

1 See now Iain Gordon Brown, 'The Clerks of Penicuik and Eldin as Collectors and Connoisseurs', *Jnl. Scottish Soc. for Art History,8* (2003), 27–36. The collection was that of John Clerk of Eldin (1757–1832), adv. 1785, SCJ (as Lord Eldin) 1823–8, a clever, prosperous but violently irascible advocate who was also a cultivated connoisseur of painting, old master drawings, and the fine arts.

To Francis Jeffrey
NLS Dep.235
       20 March 1833
My Dear J.

I got such tomes from Seceders about the working of their system that I was obliged to reject them, and to beg them to answer my questions simply and shortly. This they have at last done, and Cleghorn will send you the result in a parcel. Kidston is their light in the West, Ellis and Andrew Mitchell you know. Their separations, arising from elective discord, seem to amount to nothing. Nevertheless I am for adhering to patronage; tho' not against checking its abuses. Creeffy is in horror at the Standing Committee, and I think he is right. its permanency is unnecessary, and pernicious. I hope he has written to you.

A vacancy happened in a crown living three days ago – Dryfesdale (I believe) in Dumfriesshire. Robert Hill wants it for his son in law.[1]

I went and saw Eldin's house today. It is a horrid looking hole; especially when seen from above. The whole floor is down, except a stripe of about five feet across, next the windows. It is plain that they owed their lives or limbs to the carpet, which by not giving way at once made them *slide* down and prevented their being torn by splinters. They are still raking the ruins for the wreck, and find knives, reticules, pencil cases, shoes, etc. There are about twenty hats laid out *to be claimed* in the lobby, white, dinted, torn, and smashed. James Craig, who takes charge, says that the loss exclusive of the house is not above £200. But the house is ruined in character. That room seems to have been infamously joisted, as the beams testify; and the builder seems to have been conscious of it, for they are all cobled in the most awkward and shameful manner. Old Geo. Thomson is very ill, and so are some others. Earle Monteith's head has at least a dozen skin bruises on it.[2] It was used as a stepping stone. Mrs Keay is nearly well; but all of them agree with Moncreiff, who says he feels a new bruise every hour. There is some reason for supposing that poor Smith was choaked with lime. The English auctioneer went down, but his clerk saved himself by jinking up the chimney.

Send me the various Scotch Bills as soon as you can. The Burgh one is asked for by foolish people every day.

---

1 John Henderson, Minister of Dryfesdale from 1799, who had died on 16 March, was succeeded by David Buchan Douie, Minister there until 1863, who had m. 1831 Helen, daughter of Robert Hill WS.
2 Alexander Earle Monteath of Rochsoles (1792–1861); adv. 1816. Sheriff of Fife 1816.

The Scotsman has taken up the ministerial cause, and thereby lost about ten subscribers, Hume and Sir F. McKenzie of Gairloch M.P. among others. If you fall in with a person wishing a Scotch paper, make them fill up this gap; for McLaren ought to be supported.

Of course you mean to crush Wallace's motion for leave to introduce judicial reforms.[1] He is so apt to tell an alleged saying of mine, that I should not wonder at his repeating it. A saying that never was said.

You will regret to hear that Forbes Blair, your opponent, is dangerously ill, and of a very bad [*rest missing*].

To John Richardson
NLS 3989.138
                    Edinburgh, 13 July 1833
My Dear John
        Before you leave London I think you should see Mr Lockhart, about a matter which affects Jeffrey in a way which, tho' it be remote, must be permanent. I would write to Mr Lockhart myself, were it not that I am perhaps not entitled to know that he is engaged with Sir Walter's life, and that a few words personally do more good than many pages of correspondence.[2]

Nobody knows better than you do the cordial veneration in which Jeffrey always held the genius and virtues of Scott – a feeling which neither politicks nor criticism ever abated. You also know that that the time when by Statute the Sherriff – and nobody but the Sherriff, or a substitute *specially* authorised by him – was required to set the machinery of the Reform Bill agoing, Sir Walter was utterly incapable of acting, even to the extent of authorising his substitute to act. In this situation, the absolute necessity of doing something was forced upon his own friends, and Mr Lockhart accordingly will recollect his coming to Edinr, and arranging with me and the Dean that provided his salary was saved – a condition which the rights of his creditors made necessary – a resignation in his name by Mr Lockhart should be tendered, and that if this could not be accepted from him, the knot should be cut by a Bill. It was found that it could not be accepted, and therefore a Bill was passed, and there being only one week to spare, of course it passed in a hurry. Before Mr Lockhart left this he sent me a very gratifying letter acknowledging the kindness with which the thing had been conducted.

1 Robert Wallace of Kelly, Ayrshire (1773–1855), Whig Radical MP for Greenock 1832–46.
2 See HC's letter to Lockhart, 2 August 1832, above.

Notwithstanding all this, Chambers published a life of Scott,[1] which contains these words: 'August 6th, a bill was brought into the House of Commons by the Lord Advocate Jeffrey, to enable his Majesty to authorise a person to act as Sherriff of Selkirkshire in the place of Sir Walter Scott, who was now unfitted for his office by severe illness. The bill, tho' of a most unusual kind, was immediately passed thro' all its stages. To give an idea of the duties which thus called so urgently for attention, it may be mentioned that, in five years, Sir Walter had decided forty one civil causes!' The meaning of this is that Jeffrey used him shamefully; and the result is, that so long as Scott's history is known – that is to all eternity – Jeffrey's name is connected with his by an odious, tho' most unjust, feeling.

When I first saw this, I wrote to Chambers, explaining the facts. He answered regretting his blunder, and assuring me that no new edition of his Life should be published without its being corrected. He did correct it accordingly. But I see that his first edition has been copied into many other lives; as for example in the *Annual Biography and Obituary* for 1833, where the preceding words are repeated.

I cannot doubt that on your explaining this to Lockhart, he, who must see the tendency of the error, will not grudge one sentence to do justice to our friend, and to the friend of Scott.

Ever

H. Cockburn

[*Addressed*:] John Richardson Esq, 21 Fludyer Street, London

To Francis Jeffrey
NLS Dep.235(1)
7 August 1833
My dear J.

Anxious as I am to have you among us once more, both for our pleasure and for your health, I must confess that I see our correspondence close with a pang. It has been to me a very great source of instruction and of gratification. When you are dead, or even turned out, I am thinking of turning a penny by publishing your letters.[2] What shall the title be? 'Pièces justificatifs, pour servir

---

1 The biography (1832) by Robert Chambers (1802–71).
2 They were transcribed by Cockburn's daughter Jane, and are now in NLS, Adv.MSS. Jeffrey joined the Bench in June 1834.

a l'histoire de la reformation parliamentaire en Ecosse'? – or 'London Gossip – as detected by a stranger'? – or 'Views of Scotch Lord Advocates, by one of themselves'? The only injustice some people think I have done you consists in the cautious parsimony with which I have kept you to myself. Not that the Faithful have not been duly benefited; but I always see that every thing transpires, especially if it be given as, or plainly be, confidential. It is a great deal to have had four letters a week from a man for three years, and yet to have brought him into no scrape.

I shall be very sorry if Murray explodes about the Sherrifs, because he is quite wrong. They are not scoundrels, but remarkably the reverse. And there are foolish designs about their residence, and other ignorances, which any attack will promote.

Would not ten days of Lochlomond do you more good than English visiting can? But if you can go to Malshanger[1] – give her my benediction. I fear that my long epistolary silence has put me out of favour; which would be wrong – for I have a most sincere admiration and regard for that clever, warmhearted, enthusiastic, strong minded, dutiful person.

As to your constituents, I have no doubt that all those who are sane are quite right about the Ministers and the Town. But the truth is that any of them are literally crazy on these subjects, and it is only they who make a noise. Only think of *Adam Black* going to jail before he would pay; which *I am told* is the fact.

Ever

H. Cockburn

To Sir Thomas Dick Lauder
SL 33

Friday [1833]

My Dear Sir Thomas

It will be a great delight to us to receive Mr and Miss Smith into our pastoral fraternity. Indeed a Findhorn face to me is the face of a friend.[2]

I hope that Mr Smith is aware that whatever Mr Cockburn was, His Majesty's Solicitor General is a decorous person – arrayed in solemn black, with a demure visage, an official ear, an evasive voice, suspicious palate, ascetic

---

1 The seat, near Basingstoke, of Jeffrey's friends the Penningtons (see *FJ*, ii, 227).
2 Relugas, ancestrally a Cumin seat, had become Dick Lauder's by marriage. It was sold 1846. The Smyths (mentioned later) were Dick Lauder neighbours nearby.

blood, and flinty heart. There is a fellow very like him, who traverses the Pentlands in a dirty grey jacket, white hat, with a long pole. That's not the Sol. Gen. That's Cocky – a frivolous dog; Mr Smith may use all freedom with him.

Ever

H. C.

To Jane Cockburn
NLS Dep.235 (*SL* 34 (–))

Bonaly, Sunday 11 August 1833

My Dearest Jane

Tell Dr Warren that if he has any patients who can't walk, he should send them to a Habbies How breakfast,[1] where not walking, and jumping too, is impossible. We had one yesterday in the grandest style; of which the only want, as occurred to me a thousand times, was your absence, and that of the kind friends under whose roof you are. As breakfast is not ready I shall solace your London heart by an account of it.

There were only three Lauders and three Craigs asked, but applications became thick in the course of the week, and at last we amounted to twenty-three. The day was absolutely perfect, but not altogether cloudless or breezeless. Graham, and Graham Maitland, and Frank went in the cart – the good old rural way of going, and the only respectable one. Your mother and I and Wifie went in the Droskie. Near the Hunters Tryst we fell in with Sir Thomas Lauder and a very excellent Findhorn friend of his called Smyth [*sic*] in his gig, and my Lady with Miss Smith and the three daughters in their carriage, and John and George Lauder on a poney each, and thus the two gigs, the one carriage, and the two outriders, made a very handsome procession, past Woodhouslee, and flaring up the peaceful glen, to the great disapprobation of the disturbed and stamping sheep. Near Logan House we joined the cart, with Laurence on Jessy, James on a hired beast, and his inseparable, Alex. Wright, on another of the same. At Logan House,[2] after going on a little, William Craig, and two sisters, appeared in a chaise, and Archd Davidson[3] on a poney. We had a very agreeable stroll, in detached parties, up that quiet, sunny, turfy glen, till we reached the scene of the more animal part of the

1 Habbie's Howe, about a mile NE of Carlops, was a favourite picnic spot.
2 Loganbank, near Glencorse.
3 Archibald Davidson (1805–86), adv. 1827, son of the Revd Dr Randall Davidson of Muirhouse.

proceedings. Here Professor James Pillans[1] appeared – having walked alone, from Edinr.

Then began the lighting the fire, the setting the table, the building seats, the unpacking the stores, the sighing for its being ready, the children climbing up and sliding down, etc.; till at last our hermit fare was ready, and then what clattering, what scrambling, what disappearing of elements, what helping, what roaring, what upsetting of seats, what spilling. Oh Jane, Jane – thankful was I then that you were 400 miles off. The vulgarity of their mirth was shocking. Such frivolity! Would you believe it? In that tranquil scene, they laughed! Where the Scottish Theocritus wrote, they absolutely punned! Nay, I detected flirtation! – tho' in a delicate way. For Graham and Charlotte Lauder secretly removed a small stone from Mr Smith's seat, and tumbled him back, when he sat down, nearly into the burn. And he a decent agricultural Indian aged not above sixty.

For my part, I sat, on a stone retired, and reasoned high of Patie and of Ramsay. My soul was with the Gentle Shepherd. But I trust that I kept my temper sufficiently not to let them see how I despised their low tastes. Their food (Oh! To think of food in such a place) consisted of rolls, butter, honey, marmalade, jelly, eggs, cold veal pie, tongue (no want of that), broiled salmon – *hot* (oh! oh! hot salmon, under the ray of an August morning sun, in a pastoral, classical valley!), tea, coffee, chocolate – closed on the part of the male, and a few of the female, brutes by a dram (Oh Jane, blush with me) – an absolute dram – God bless me! of whiskey!!!

Having escaped from this dreadful scene, we came home, only all the Lauders, except Charly and Corny, went away. Then we fell to bowls – then to a riottous dinner – then to bowls again, prolonging it even under candle light – then at 11 did I at last get to peace and my own meditations. Next (that is, this) morning Pillans, who had staid all night, was up and out at 5!!! Walking, like an idiot, till 9. Then appeared an Englishman – a friend of the Romily's – to breakfast, after which Pillans, the Englisher and I went up to Capelaw – and saw a glorious scene.

We dined here, and after dinner we took the bottles up to Pisgah[2] – and what a sunset! While enjoying it, Graham and the two Lauders gave a shout from the top of the hill above us, and dared us to come up. Pillans, Archd Davidson and I had the sense to sit still; but the poor little Englishman in his gallantry went up – and where do you think they took him to? Up to Capelaw

1 Formerly Rector of the High School, now Professor of Humanity.
2 Deut. iii, 27

[131]

again! After which he had to walk in to Edinr. It is now 10 at night and they are all sound – and I steal a moment (as the romantic people say) to tell all this to you.

What a mercy it is that you Town people – you, and Mrs Jeffrey, and Charly, have lost all your enjoyment of these horrid Scotch pieces of coarseness. Do cultivate fine society, weed your acquaintance, and learn to despise all happiness that can be said to be vulgar.

As for yourself, consult Dr Thomson *clearly*.[1] I have more faith in him than in most of them. But tell us without delay what is resolved about your coming home, or going to Harrowgate, or staying in London – the possibility of the last of which however I don't see. It seems to me that they have no more power over your enemy there than here. Some people are disappointed and surprised that Sir Charles does not waste five minutes in writing about you.[2] I am not; because (but don't tell him this) I know that he can't write. But I hope you won't leave London without extorting from him their views of the matter, and their remedys, in writing, so that our provincial darkness may be enlightened. Remember me to Elgin and make [her] write another letter. But she'l never do anything so good as the last.

Adieu My Dearest Jane

Ever

H. Cockburn

[Addressed:] Miss Cockburn, 35 Charles Street, Berkeley Square, London

To James Bridges
NLS 20,437.28

7 January 1834

My Dear Sir

So the Lawnmarket house is at last to come down. You know that I have long had my patriotic eye on the three carved stones which have so long looked down on the last sufferings of my poor clients below. Do tell the Commissioners to save them from the sale of the materials – which I see advertised for the 17th. They are of no value to any sane man; but very tempting to an idiot like me who has a taste for trash. Besides, I was expressly

1 Anthony Tod Thomson (1778–1849), by then Professor of Materia Medica, London University.
2 Sir Charles Bell.

promised them by Provost Trotter as a bribe. You remember the zeal with which, when they were in the dead thraw, I helped on these Improvements, and I flatter myself that your ears may yet ring with the various eloquent speeches I made in their behalf. To the public this was, and is to remain, all pure public virtue. But, among ourselves, it was all with a view to these three carved stones – which are called by botanists stone pines. If any demur be made about them, I shall plot in Faculty against the removal of the County Hall. But the Commissioners have too much justice. If any one of them talks of a price, tell him first that anything so base would destroy the chain; and secondly that, to make up for this, I mean to go and act white bonnet[1] at the sale of the other materials.

So let the bribe stand.

Yours Faithfully
H. Cockburn

To Francis Jeffrey
NLS Dep.235(1)

Edinburgh, 17 February 1834

My Dear J.

The four Sheriffs of the four disturbed counties, Lanark, Stirling, Renfrew, and Dumbarton, all concur in stating the surface of things as quiet, but by no means so below; on the contrary they all think that the bad spirit is strong, and spreading, and that as soon as the military shall be withdrawn there will be outbreakings.

All this I dare say you know. But the Sheriffs further state a fact to which your attention, and that of Government, ought to be called – the difficulty of getting justices to act. For example I understand that as yet *only* two gentlemen, Mr Macfarlane and Mr Dunlop, have interfered in the county of Stirling, and one of them (Mr Dunlop) is now exhausted, and has sent me a medical certificate of inability to act any longer. To remedy this, the Sheriff of that county proposes to create additional Sheriff Substitutes. A bad scheme. They would be raw and dangerous magistrates; there is no fund for paying them; and it would be wrong to allow the ordinary magistracy so to escape doing its duty. But it is plain that wherever there are constables or soldiers, there there ought to be a magistrate; and if they won't, or don't, act, it is idle to talk of preserving the public peace. The Sheriffs can't be everywhere, or do everything.

---

1 A pretended bidder, puffing up the price.

They want you to issue some order or recommendation. Which I dissuade you from; because it is not your business, and will do no good. But something ought clearly to be done, and without any delay, *by government.* There are no want of justices, and I suppose that the King can compel them to do their duty.

I am much struck with the total inefficiency, or rather the indifference, of all the Lord Lieutenants, and their departments.[1] I have not heard of their doing anything, or being even named, in all these scenes. If they have not all abdicated, they might be made very useful; were it only by the show of public authority.

Recollect that we have almost no civil force; and that if the new workers, instead of being protected, are to be required to act as constables, or to protect themselves, they won't remain an hour. An active Magistracy, especially if directed by a judicious Lieutenancy, might soon organise some civil force; but if everything be left, as it is, to the Sheriffs, or to soldiers unheaded by magistrates, the force of the Unions must prevail.

Ever

H. Cockburn

[Addressed:] The Lord Advocate

To Francis Jeffrey
NLS Dep 235(1) (*SL* 36–7(–))
26 May 1834

My dear J.

I have great pleasure in thinking that this will meet you with your face fairly and permanently turned towards home.[2] I am glad to learn that the people of London have been kind to you; but you may be assured that the only anchor you can ride by safely is the one that is fixed in the hearts and the habits of your old friends. Our countenances are all brightened at the prospect of seeing yours. I can think of little else than the curious and gratifying result of the career you have run, since the days when I used to walk home with [you] to Buccleugh Place, from Dugald Stewart's political class, till now. This includes the period before the Review began – when you were under proscription, and my worthy uncle Harry Dundas was the Autocrat of

---

1 The Home Secretary did admonish the Lieutenants – see Adv. MS. 9.1.10, f.70*v.*
2 Lord Craigie, a Judge since 1811, died 1 May, and Jeffrey took his place on the Bench, 6 June.

Scotland; thro' the seditious ascendancy of that work, during fifteen years of which whether you lived at Edinr or at Sydney depended entirely on the pleasure of the public accuser; till the late triumphs came thickly upon us; when, having passed thro' all attainable honors, you subside – or rise – into the secure and quiet comforts of a Scotch judge, certainly with little work – and, I hope, with encreased pay. It could not be expected of Playfair, but would that Gordon and Horner had been here to enjoy this. You have now but one honourable stage more to pass thro' – and I look forward to it as the happiest to yourself and your friends of them all.

All our calculations make the Attorney quite safe. But I need not disguise from you that, tho' I anticipate victory, defeat would not amaze me. We have not 1500 pledges. But then of the 4300 who voted for you we never could get pledges from above 2500. We do not even yet know – no not within 1000 – how many can vote, and our adversaries lie upon system, and deccive us upon their honor. If any accident should enable the radicals to fancy that Ayton may succeed, there will, during the poll, be a great accession to him, to our ruin. You don't tell me where I can write the result to you. Sir John has done admirably. He has been at no meeting without impressing them all [with] the feeling that he is a plain, able, honest man. He, and a large party, are to be here on Saturday after it is settled; for jollity if we succeed – for suspension if we fail.

Murray is nominated for tomorrow.[1] Not only he, but William, is mad if it be not a triumph. I see him daily, but never so as to talk seriously of business. He is *constantly* in Leith, or with Leith people. But hitherto all our snatches of discourse have been perfectly agreeable; except for one moment when his face got red in demonstrating the wisdom of promoting our party – by what? – dismissing poor Cullen from the Exchequer! However I hope he won't. He walked in flowered silk last Saturday. We have had various meetings to discuss the Edinr church, but have never got to it. He talks of leaving this for London on Saturday first – after his election is over, but before it is declared.

The Wild[2] predominate in this Assembly, and the Old party may be considered as done. We are confident of carrying the veto tomorrow, and would indeed be certain of it were we not split, as in the election, by our own friends. But Ma puir burghs and Alex Dunlop[3] are crazy.

1 J.A.Murray, MP for Leith 1832–8, succeeded Jeffrey as Lord Advocate.
2 The extreme Evangelical party.
3 A.C.S.M. Dunlop (1798–1870); adv. 1820. Son of Alexander Dunlop of Keppoch; church lawyer and politician; changes of party were added to changes of name. MP for Greenock 1852–67.

This is the best day for getting a good Trachea made bad that we have had this year.

Ever

H. Cockburn

Remember me to Mrs —— I don't know her new name, but I mean the married Miss Morehead.

[*Addressed:*] F.Jeffrey Esq, Post Office, Grantham

To T. F. Kennedy
LAS, 513

15 June 1834

My Dear Kennedy

We are at it again you see. The Master of the Mint[1] has been here for two days – quite well, and strong in spirit. He, and his address, appeared on the very day of Learmonth's Conservative dinner – to give it a relish. We were afraid that wine and eloquence might excite them to opposition. But it seems that they are to have sense to be quiet; so that tomorrow se'ennight the nomination and election will be on the same day, and his head will be southwards that evening probably. What a mercy his Cabinet seat is, both in itself and as a symptom. And Cambridge too! In short if the Radicals would get some patience, and the King immortality, so that the obvious growth of the public mind in knowledge and right views might be left free to operate, things would do very well.

Glorious weather. I never saw vegetable life in greater splendour. We had a riotous party at bowls yesterday at Bonaly, where the very hills seemed to be dancing in their sunshine.

Jeffrey is a Lord of Session! An actual red gowned, paper Lord. A framer and lover of acts of sederunt. An admirer of the Nobile Officium. A deviser of Interlocutors. A hater of the House of Lords. He nods over the same bench where nodded the dignified Eskgrove, and adorns the long pure cravat which typified the calm elegance of the judicial Braxfield.[2] I wish you had seen him as he took his seat. Part of the ceremony consists in his going behind their Lordships, the whole being present, from right to left, where his place is,

1 Abercromby.
2 Robert Macqueen (1722–1799); adv. 1744. SCJ (as Lord Braxfield) 1176; Lord Justice-Clerk 1788. (See *Mems,* 104–8, for a celebrated characterisation.)

shaking hands with each as he passes. Four cordial shakes there were, Mackenzie's, Moncreiff's, Cranston's, and Fullerton's. But the other nine! Had you but seen Charles Hope hailing as a brother the Editor of the *Edinburgh Review*, Balgray polluting his Perthshire palm with that of the framer of the Reform Bill; —— clenching his Beacon fingers, as the dog whom in the year 1802 he caused the Faculty to reject from being even a Collector of Decisions, approached; Glenlee grinning —— at the challenger of David Hume; and Meadowbank taking him all in his arms with ostentatious hypocrisy.

Ever

H. Cockburn

To James Abercromby
NLS 24,749.46
Edinburgh, 10 November 1834
My Dear Abercomby

Many thanks for your kindness.[1] The loss of income – especially to one who has no hope of leaving his family above destitution when he dies except by insurance – is a drawback no doubt; but a man who has 10 children must expect to be often punished for that folly; and, after all, there is no comfort, to such a person particularly, as that of having his anchor fixed in anything tolerably certain. There is not much risk of encreased Conservatism from the evil communications of the robing room, because the Whigs are now six there, and the next appointment I hope will give them a majority. I am much more affraid of getting doited. The abstraction from the ordinary share of the scenes in which one has so long been engaged, and the substitution for it of an affectation of perpetual calmness and patience – even when the Dean is roaring, as he did two days ago, for 7 hours at a breath – is very unfavourable to the preservation of the intellect. Accordingly they all suffer.

---

1 Cockburn was himself 'benchified' on 15 November. *Jnl*, i, 75 reveals his apprehensions, followed by observations on the criminal justice system. In June 1837 (*vice* Lord Gillies) he became also a criminal judge.

Soon after news of the first elevation, Jeffrey warned him to 'be rather less than you now are at Bonally, during the said time at least of your Noviciate. You are supposed to be too idle there; and if you are there it will certainly be concluded you are idle.' To which HC retorted, in a note to the transcribed letter, 'Oh! You dog! What are you at Craigcrook. I, who was never one day at Bonally during Session.' (Adv.MS. 9.1.10, f.117.)

The public is going on here in the old way. The late radical 2/6d supper of Wallace and the tradesmen was a very poor affair. Those who don't care how many hours the Councillors are imprisoned are rejoicing over the prospect of Ayton and Jameson being out-talked by Hugh Bruce, who is exactly on the Tory side what these two are on the radical. There is some chance that there might be an equality of votes in a few days for the Rector at Glasgow, which will bring it to my casting vote.[1] A very difficult card to play – in existing circumstances – Stanley and Durham being the competitors. It is provoking that the lads have had the folly to chuse any absent Rector. Peel declined being set up on this ground. They should have taken Cranstoun or Moncreiff.

Skene is able, popular, and most honorable, person, and will do his peculiar business very well.[2] His defect, for some time at least, will consist in his inexperience of public affairs, and of criminal practice. I am not quite easy as to how he is to get on with his immediate master; for there is granite in Aberdeen more hard, when he is clear that he is right.

Ever

H. Cockburn

To Sir Thomas Dick Lauder
NLS Dep.235 (*SL* 38)
1 July 1835
My Dear Sir Thomas

Ego sum vester homo.

Meanwhile my whole time, thoughts, and soul are engrossed amidst astonishment, horror, rage, disgust and indignation at a resolution of the Town Council to make the front of the Calton Jail the hanging place!!! There's a scheme for you! The Parthenon of Edinr, the Westminster Abbey of Scotland, the National Acropolis, the scene hallowed by the ashes of Hume, Burns, Playfair, and Stewart, to be voluntarily brought into connection with Jack Ketch and his subjects. And for what! To remove an established nuisance from the Old Town, from which a majority of Councillors proceed, to the New Town! If the said New Town be not degraded below the lowest dirt in spirit, it will rise into rebellion. All of

---

1 See D. Wintersgill, *Rectors of Glasgow University 1820–2000* (2001), 22.

2 George Skene of Rubislaw (1807–75); adv. 1830. After a short spell as Professor of History, University of Edinburgh, became Sheriff Substitute of Glasgow, 1841.

which I tell you in time, to warn you against rashly committing yourself in this probably coming discussion.[1] What beasts!!

Ever

H. Cockburn

[*Addressed.*] Sir T. D. Lauder Bart, The Grange House, Edinr.

To John A. Murray
NLS 97.27

Edinburgh, 24 April 1836

My Dear Murray

I take no charge of the city creditors, who have behaved like fools, and only mentioned the idea of helping to extricate matters by means of the King's Printer's patent,[2] on the suggestion of George Forbes; who, tho' he is no creditor, is a very sensible man, and with a head for these sort of things. I had little hope myself that Government would do more to lift these swine out of the Powderhall mine.

But this is no reason why the Providence of the expiration of the Patent should not be taken advantage of for better purposes. I am aware that the stationery part of it is gone, and *if* there be no profit in the Bibles and Public Papers, there is no more to be said. But this I don't believe; nor do I believe that Craig or Black know anything about the matter. But somebody must know. Was there not a Parliamentary Report about it a very few years ago? If there be profit, who is to get it? Certainly it won't now be jobbed to bribe an individual. And it would be great nonsense to let it fall into the all-receiving maw of the Consolidated, or any such, fund. Now if it goes to the Universities, as it does in England and Ireland, why not in Scotland? I see no claim so strong, and no application of the emoluments so natural, as to our beggarly Universities – that of unendowed Edinr in particular. Do immortalise yourself by securing this boon.

You may believe how deeply we have all been struck by this unexpected disaster of poor Mrs Russell. Many a one, both high and low, will miss a steady friend. A most excellent person. The funeral is tomorrow at Bathgate.

1 Schemes for the Calton had already included a Camera Obscura, which HC successfully opposed, with only a temporary success, in 1834: see *Jnl*, i, 62.

2 i.e. an appointment with special privileges in Bible printing and a responsibility for producing accurate texts.

There is nothing new in this intellectual city. It is a sad picture of poor George Combe's nocturnal labours, that he wishes to relieve their severity by lecturing on Logic in the forenoon.[1] Professor James Simpson[2] has finished his penny-a-night course 'to the youth of both sexes', with such éclat that the Hermaphrodites have given him a piece of plate. What the devil made a committee of your House let my friend bore them, as he says they did, for seven days. On that fact he claims the privilege of boring every body else. He has been vomiting his filth publickly in Glasgow, and it is said [he is] going to void upon Liverpool in a few days. We have two patriots here in jail because their consciences won't let them pay their debts. When the Quakers refused to pay the War taxes, because they could not homologate War, and their goods were seized, which was a very common case, I never heard anybody sympathise with this honest and ancient feeling. Let the Annuity be abolished by all means, but I see no justice in letting the creditor starve in the mean time, because the debtor's conscience is soothed by not paying. When I was at Liverpool lately, I endeavoured to persuade the Mayor and some of the Councillors how lovely it would be, and how becoming well, that their Corporation should pay the debts of its dear distressed brother Edinr. But they would not see it. See what your municipal reform does! Would not the Tories have done it! Clearly, since ours is a Tory debt.

I was delighted with my eight days of English civil trials – and I hope instructed. I have no idea of a better hand at that practical work than Baron Parke.[3] The gentleness, directness, and brevity of the counsel was refreshing. I could not detect one drop of sweat the whole time. I often wished I could surprise them by a blast of our high pressure Dean; who screams, and gesticulates, and perspires more, on a motion, than the English Bar does, to could do, in a century. You remember Peter Peebles's praise of a counsel – 'He's the lad for spinning a lang thread out o' a sma' tait o' woo'!' Their records, under the new rules, are excellent, and at least forty or fifty times shorter than ours. But the truth is that theirs are too short. What they could teach us chiefly is practical handiness. For which I think we could give them a good deal of matter which they want.

Remember me kindly to Mrs Murray, and to Willie, who I presume is with you. Vicious weather. Cold, rainy, and never knowing its own mind two

1 The phrenologist George Combe (1788–1858), WS 1812.
2 For Simpson, see *Jnl*, i, 118.
3 Cockburn had been visiting Liverpool, where his son Harry was then, briefly, in a mercantile house. (See also *Jnl*, i, 113–15). Sir James Parke (1782–1868), an Exchequer judge from 1834, eventually Lord Wensleydale, was presiding.

hours together. I see in the English papers a thing called 'The Pneumatic Joint Stock Company'. Should the improvement of the atmosphere not be part of their duty? We can't hear for a day or two yet what these Lords are to do with the Irish Corporations, *Take whatever they will give.* Always under protest that it is only a first installment. I got a letter t'other day which began 'Dear Captain – Sir', and ended 'Your loving Corporal'. It was a sensible letter, about civic affairs, by one of my actual old Corporals.

Ever

H. Cockburn

[*Addressed:*] The Right Honble The Lord Advocate of Scotland, M.P., Whitehall, London

To T. F. Kennedy
LAS 523

Edinburgh, 18 May 1836

My dear Kennedy,

Thanks for your enquiries. The boy, on the whole, is doing as well as possible.[1] No fever – or at least almost none – *he says* no pain – and very merry. The true nature of the loss of a right hand, and of half the arm between the wrist and the elbow, he is not at an age (11) to feel; and as he is of that temperament that denies there is any uneasiness in amputation, the present suffering is infinitely less than I could have imagined. It was a great shock to Mrs Cockburn, but she is well. We were at Bonaly and were told nothing about it till it was over.

Fullerton and I were in Liverpool eight days. I regretted excessively that I did not see Romilly.[2] He was there one forenoon and called on me; but (as a cobler always smells of wax) I was in Court, and saw James Parke try civil causes the whole nearly of every day. The youth there is doing very well, and I think has got into a most excellent house, and under very kind masters. What the result is to be God knows. But the lad knows that if he does not pay for his own porridge very soon, I won't.

Not being a merchant, and thinking that all letters and all strangers come a great deal too soon, I groan over these railways. They will destroy all privacy,

1 On the loss of HC'ss son Frank's hand following a gunpowder explosion, see Claud Cockburn, *I Claud* (1967); Cockburn family tradition had it that eleven writing boxes were given to the boy to encourage him to use his remaining hand.
2 John Romilly (1802–74), son of Sir Samuel (d.1818), later first Baron.

all provincial nature. The whole island will be a workshop; and all the peaceable independence and picturesque peculiarities, and salutary self-importance of little places will be melted in the general fusion of society.

Thomas, as was predicted, has *not* come yet – but hints about appearing when he is tired of London.[1] We are told here that he has got his job done. A very convenient thing for him.

Who can wonder that such purists as Lyndhurst and Wellington should be shocked at what is imputed to Melbourne?[2] But if there be no rash letters, the thing, as a ground of political attack, is ridiculous.

The Solicitor,[3] who has been in London, came yesterday, and reports well of most things. It is delightful to see the unanimity with which everybody attests the Speaker's [Abercromby's] health and official success. The 'foolish Lords', as they are called in Shakespeare's dramatis personae, are very distressing; especially to those who are attached to the aristocracy. No republicans ever did so much, in so short a time, so unnecessarily, to lower their order, even in the eyes of their best friends.

Our dearly beloved Venerable [the Assembly] proceeds to its annual slaughter of Mother Church tomorrow. The Commissioners say that the coarse, illiberal, vindictive brutality of the Dissenters of Glasgow was absolutely shocking. They are well met. But of the two it has always appeared to me that the Seceders were the worst. Meanwhile no eclipse of common sense seems likely to abate the fire of either.

What a beautiful spectacle that was on Sunday! The best eclipse-ometer that I have heard of is the fact (for it is a *fact*) that at Kinnordy, in Forfarshire, a row of gentians, about a foot broad and a hundred yards long, *shut its cups* during the obscuration – and opened them when the light returned.

Rutherfurd went to London for Lord Chandos[4] last Friday, but is to be back on Monday next. I wish Cuninghame were in harbour. But the old Tory Judges stick to their chairs like the Heathen God, because the chairs stick to them.

I wonder if I'm to see Dalquharran this year. I hope your meadow, and your cloaca maxima, and your tile drains, are all behaving properly.

1 See *LAS,* 532.
2 Melbourne was about be sued, notoriously, by Caroline Norton's husband.
3 John Cunninghame (1782–1854); adv. 1807, Solicitor-General, 1835; SCJ as Lord Cunninghame 1837–53. I have followed the Faculty of Advocates' draft *Biographical Directory 1800–1986* (1987) for this spelling.
4 The inquiry by George Beltz, Lancaster Herald, into the peerage claim of Sir Egerton Brydges (1762–1837), styled 13th Lord Chandos, which it was concluded was not well founded.

Remember me to Mrs Kennedy, and to your mother if she be with you. Why don't you come here and see us? We shall be very kind to you all June.

Ever

H. Cockburn

To Macvey Napier
BL 34,617.485

Bonaly, 11 July 1836

My Dear P.

Thomson and Fullerton and Rutherfurd and Pluffy came here yesterday to dinner, when Thomson read me your account to him of Brodie's having succeeded in finding the North West passage into your Mediterranean sea. Most sincerely do I rejoice in the prospect of speedy restoration. But don't come away till you be sound in *both* hemispheres. It will be great folly if you do.

The said persons made a very pleasant Sunday party – with two bottles of celestial punch, one of excellent hock, two of India sherry, one of port, and three of claret; with a rich juicy ham, a pidgeon pye cold, roast beeff, a creamy salmon, to say nothing of reeking hotch potch, and mountains of salad and all your farinaceous stomatics. I mention these things just to make your fallow teeth water, and to show the anchorite lives of the Scottish Jurists. (For God's sake don't say a word of it to John Archibald, who fancies that all the world would have enough if they have wherewith to imitate his ascetic abstinence.) The day was glorious – and we sauntered in the twilight of a mild, milky evening, amidst a glorious profusion of breathing roses of every description.

Jeff, I am told, goes to Loch Lomond tomorrow. Mr Taylor, the enthusiast, is honouring our streets. The Provost has left town unwell. I am not at ease about the election. The Comission of the church has had a field day about the University Bills, and made the usual exhibition. I am very sorry that we have lost Horner.[1] I have always taken both to him and to his family strongly; and he was very useful as a link between the lawyers and the citizens. My anxiety for Stuart's happiness makes me hope, and earnestly, that he is not to be his successor. Tytler won't be Proff. of History, and so it will go either to the son of James Skene, or to the son of John Ferrier, both at the bar.[2] They are both said to be studious and able. But it is rumoured that the Historiographer

1 He had left for England, to become a Factory Inspector.
2 It went to George Skene (1807–75); adv. 1830.

means to do the public the honor of taking it from them both. But in this kindness he won't succeed.

I am fierce at the utter desertion of Scotland and of its Judicial Institutions in the House, by both Government and individual Scotchmen. If I were not set aside from secular work, nothing could prevent me putting out something or other against the ignorant brutality which threatens to trample our whole law in the dirt. Meanwhile I have been reading Byron – with a raised admiration for his best passages, but with a lowered admiration of him on the whole.

He is always one thing; and I never observed till now by what long gaps of bad stuff his great parts are separated.

Last week was our race week – which passed off as quietly as an old county election; and tomorrow Old Forth is honoured by the keels of our first Regatta. I shall try to spy them thro' a glass from a knowe; for nothing but necessity (or one of its daughters) shall make me unmoor from this place, in the full flush of its floral glory, for some time. If you can come within a month I shall bid some good natured roses wait for you.

I hope you have not held my remembrances to McCulloch and the Stuarts (*she* particularly) to be a ceremony. I renew them gratefully. Would these two be offended now a days if we were to call them the Stot and the Broad? And remember me to all else worthy of that distinction. And remember me to yourself – and take care of yourself – in *both* hemispheres – and believe me Yours Faithfully

H. Cockburn

[*Addressed:*] Macvey Napier Esq, Union Hotel, Cockspur Street, London

To James Rutherfurd
NLS 9688.207

Bonaly, 15 March 1837

My Dear Kornel

As I was sitting next your excellent wife last Sunday at dinner at Andrew's, I vowed I would write to you; so here goes. She is perfectly well; and so I understand is Corbie. Dante is called well; but he is plainly ringing in. I was obliged to decide a cause about £100 against him lately; for which I don't expect to [be] ever again invited to see golden fish taken from the mudless waters of Cobinshaw. I rejoice to hear of your steady health. We all often talk of you. It would make you vain were I to repeat our sentiments and wishes.

You will find us nearly as you left us. Thomson has gone the way of all flesh and I fear has ruined himself by the folly.[1] She won't do. His once ever open door is closed. The light that shone from his social bower, almost thro'out the night – the Pharos of the profligate – is extinguished. A petticoat is among his tomes. With which said petticoat interferes. She won't let Voltaire into the drawing room. She compels him to go to Church. In short Thomas is done. There has not been one lemon squeezed in his house this winter. His example won't seduce William Murray or Willie Clerk. A third William – the Mason – is well.[2] But building very little. A shame to our taste. But he is about 1000 feet in the air with a tower at this once lowly abode. Donaldson's Hospital is to be decided soon. His design would make the most beautiful edifice in Scotland – Herriot's Work not excepted. Yet I fear that partiality and jobbing will leave genius very little chance. John Gordon is now promising well; to the great delight of all who remember his father.

And Andrew is Sol. Genl.[3] An event which has given all the faithful great joy and hope. It is most important for Scotland; as every step is which advances him to the head of our local affairs. The Lord Advocate's is the most difficult of all positions; so that few have survived it. I anticipate confidently for him great reputation, great usefulness, and a final retreat into the most honoured judicial position. The new line has its risks – chiefly professional. But the Gods having shown the way, a brave man must enter it. He can never fail to add to his credit. I think he must be tried soon; for Glenlee is feeble and 83, and John Archibald is longing to escape. But parties are trembling in the scale. The reforming spirit of the people however is so strong, and the Torries are such fools, that my anchor finds solid ground in the general success of the party which espouses the former. The Conservatives have, within these few days, made resistance of the Government plan for superseding Church rates, the object for which they are to stand or fall. A fatal resolution for the old infatuated Church; for it sets it directly up against the civil interests of the people and this from mere faction. In Scotland the Priests are mad, Tam Chawmers at the head of them. Jeffrey is delightfully well. No owl more wise; no lark more aerial. Charlotte still Charlotte.

Worthy Duloch's being got into port is very gratifying. His pendent lip looks very judicial. Creeffy's nose is yearly waxing redder, and rougher. Tam o' the tubs huger daily. His wife, like everybody else here, has been sorely smitten of

1 Thomson had married Ann Reed, of a Dublin family, on 25 October 1836.
2 The Williams are W.Murray (1774–1854), of Henderland, John Archibald's elder brother; W.Clerk (1771–1847), adv. 1792; and W.H.Playfair (1789–1857), the architect.
3 He had been appointed on 9 February.

late, but is better. Fullerton is not so well. Dressed as of yore, but his spirits and intellect bright as ever. Your foreign friends Emiliani, Bucher, and Push-prin, are all flourishing in their vocations. My proper household is well. Jane often and long an invalid still, but never clouded. James is in Alleppo, in a mercantile house. Harry ditto in Liverpool, George in Calcutta. Archd is keen at medicine, and will graduate this Spring. Laurence is planning being an accountant. And Frank is at the Academy, writing better, and doing more mischief, with his left hand than he formerly did with his right. I want openings for James, Henry and Laurence; so if anything comes your way, let me know.

Poor Pillans has for some months been eclipsed again. This, and perhaps some more attacks, will pass away; but it is fearful to anticipate that one will probably darken that joyous spirit permanently. The Pundit too has been a year and more ill, and is still uncured. The human hydraulics are surely ill planned. We have got Charles Bell back among us again; a great acquisition, both himself and his spouse. The Grand Marshall has just been sent by Government to search after Celtic truth, in the Western Isles, where the people are said to be starving. The last season was enough to starve both Celt and Saxon. And this one threatens not to be behind its father.

This is the second vernal month, and the snow is a foot deep, and the frost keen and obstinate. Can you not send us some of your blue sky? Think of the 'parritch-faced brutes'! They want to bring a Glasgow rail way thro' the Princes Street gardens – under the Mound – and to make the whole Eastern part of the valley a depot, with offices, steam engines, etc.[1] And, so dead are the people of Edinr to the glory of their city that this is not publicly opposed!!! The Ordnance only stipulates that the locomotive engines shan't be put on till after they pass the Castle, lest they set fire to the powder magazine!! He! He! He! Oh that we had our own Kornel to report that even the friction of the carriage wheel was dangerous to the garrison.

Are we ever to have you here again? You retain our undiminished attachment. Mrs Cockburn sends you her warmest regards. Why did you not take my advice and become a Scribe? When the Solicitor was Advocate he would have made you Crown Agent. £1800 a year's not to be sneezed at

Ever and Ever Yours
H. Cockburn.

[Addressed:] Captain Rutherfurd, Royal Engineers, Care of Messrs Cowan & Co, Barbados and Grenada

1 On this proposal see *Jnl*, i, 129–30; the scheme was temporarily halted – *ibid.* i, 135.

To Mrs Andrew Rutherfurd
NLS 9687.95
Bonaly, 29 April 1837
My Dear Mrs Rutherfurd
I don't know whether this will catch you in London or not; but I give it a chance, partly to show you that your friends in the provinces don't forget you, and partly because it is a pleasure to confer with you, especially when one has nothing to say. I got the Sol Gen's letter the day after mine to him was committed to His Majesty's post. I hope you have been well, and as happy as you ought to be out of Edinr. Don't waste too much of the 'goods in communion' on vain acquisitions, which thief can steal, and moth corrupt. Think of the destitution of the Highlands, and of your numerous friends. You no doubt have seen everybody – even Adam Black.

I hope, and cannot doubt, that your worthy helpmate has been diligently establishing himself in all places and minds of which it is proper that a Lord Advocate should have a hold. I cannot describe to you the elation, the *peck* of pleasure, which this prospect of his next step gives me; dashed tho' it be, in other views, with the anticipation of long absences, unthanked virtue, much anxiety, and very great professional risk. But the public! A good Lord Advocate! And the unquestioned command of any fixed legal honor that this poor devil of a country can present! To say nothing of great reputation. It must be queer to be the wife of a Lord Advocate. Did I ever betray to you (I certainly did to many others) Mrs Cockburn's remark on my last advance. 'Odd – Preserve me this! I never slept wi' a Lord o' Session i' my life!'

Playfair seems to be the only person of our faction now living in Edinr. You, Jeffrey, Murray, Thomson, all the judges, me, Maitland, and George Dundas – all out of town. Dundas is vexing the salmon and Worriecon [?] has hooked Goliah, who is at Cumpston.[1] I dined twice at Craigcrook last week. All well. The encreasing happiness, health, and gaiety of Jeffrey is very curious, and very delightful. It is the best possible proof of the soundness both of his heart and head. The Clermiston exchange seems to be completely and finally off. We have had one week of totally spring weather; in so much that I believe I saw a swallow today, and heard the cuckoo yesterday; but I did neither. The Tower has been rising very slowly, but is to touch the clouds soon now as they say.[2] It has certainly a very antique look. Really old towers must think it very impudent. I enclose a Bonaly violet. Playfair and I are irreconcileably opposed

1 The Maitland (Dundrennan) house, near Twynholm, Kirkcudbrightshire.
2 Bonaly now had a turret, added in 1836–7, construction much delayed by bad weather.

as to the mode of laying out a small, but important, portion of the ground, and each thinks the other very absurd. However I mean to yield – chiefly for the malicious pleasure of hearing him abused. I have been delving much, and reading little. There is a new, dull, review.

Scott's Life is a silly book.[1] And it must get worse, as he becomes more of a mere literary man, and as the interest of his youth and of the first plumings of his wings abates. I am deep in John Knox, and the reformation, and Queen Mary – the subjects of Tytler's late volume.[2] A book which I have always liked; because it is the only readable connected history of Scotland. But then, it has always been an opinion of mine that there are very few points of our history in which truth – I mean exact truth – is a bit more valuable than plausible blunders. The intollerable dogs are the nice, accurate, searching, restless wretches who won't let old beliefs alone. It is said that Glenlee has been sent out; but I don't believe it.

I hope you have seen Hope Richardson – a most excellent person. Jane has an inclination to go, in a few weeks, to see some of her friends in London; and if the wish continues, of which I have no doubt, she will go. She is as usual; powerless in the limbs, but always merry. I think I can see Ratho from the Tower. So we may establish a telegraph. Rutherfurd should fix one day in the week (besides the Lords) to be irreversibly spent there. People would very soon get into the way of not expecting him in town that day, and his affairs would go on the better of the truce. By the bye – I had nearly forgot it – I heard a person observe in company t'other day how beautifully three foreign ladies – Mrs Jeffrey, Mrs Murray, and Mrs Rutherfurd – had transplanted into the Edinr soil; which he said was owing to their sense, agreeableness, and virtues. 'Then,' said another person, 'if these things make a good transplant, there is a fourth who ought to do *better* than either – Mrs Thomson.' There's for you, with your virtues and sneering. I think I had better leave you with this morsel to ruminate upon.

Ever

H. Cockburn

[*Addressed:*] Mrs Rutherfurd, Royal Hotel, St James Street, London

1 Cf HC's comments in *Jnl.* i, 134, remarking on its 'two extraordinary revelations: that John Irving had once a particle of literary taste, and that there was a time when Lady Scott was pretty and agreeable'.
2 The latest volume (1837) in Tytler's *History of Scotland* (1828–43).

To John Richardson
NLS 3989.169

Justiciary, 22 January 1838

My Dear John

Altho' my Maitland Club letter was too late for you, I am glad to see that Young Monteith, or, as he is called at Carstairs, Maister Robert, got in by half a neck.[1] I presume you are now domesticated in Fludyer Street – despite snow, frost, and pent up coach seats. Our frost here has been *very* intense for ten days, but is plainly going to break up. Duddingstone was unskatable; very strong, but as rough as the street. I went twice out, skateless, for a walk, and returned both times over Arthur Seat – mine being the first time the only foot that had imprinted itself on its pure snow.

The bellum studentium is over; tho' the intellectual culprits are not yet disposed of, and probably will be quietly let off.[2] Roland kept out of the scrape of capture, but I am happy to say that he was by no means a mere spectator. Jane and Graham say they never saw him so excited, nor did I. I did all I could to inflame his college ardour – only always advising the evitation of con-spicuous violence or detection. He was one of several – I believe 300 – who laid out ninepence on a stout *cud*, which he exhibited here with great defiance of what he called 'the blackguards' – which I found comprehended all those who dared to oppose the students – the Provost, the police, the 79th Regt, all included. He also walked part of the way along the street in procession. All this is most natural and most proper. Would you have had him be a *nob* – as the cotton spinners call the base dogs who don't join the Association? It was a foolish affair. Nobody can tell how it began; the police are said to have behaved very ill; any man of respectability, who was known, and had a good voice, energy, and good sense, could have ended it in five minutes; and the introducing soldiers was absurd, and gave an insignificant squabble a four days' air of importance. The Academic youth has ever since been venting itself in daily squibbs – chiefly in verse – against their various or supposed foes, particularly the Provost and the 79th. I suppose Roly was engaged yesterday and the day before, for we did not see him.

My very humble, but very clear, opinion is that delving, and fully planting,

1 Robert Joseph Ignatius Monteith (1812–84) younger of Cranley, Carstairs.
2 On 'the great "Snowball Riot" of 1838 . . . in part a symptom of the bitter struggle between Town and Gown', see A.G.Fraser, *The Building of Old College* (1989), 267–8. The students accused of 'mobbing' were all found not guilty. Matters had got out of hand, the Lord Provost over-reacted, police and troops were involved, arrests were made, and a Sheriff Court trial followed. Richardson's son Roland was apparently not among the accused.

the space between your house and garden, would be *very* injurious. Probably earth would be cheaper than grass; but my objection is that grass, with a very few evergreens, is the most beautiful. The tendency of new place makers is always to encroach on the turfy verdure; of old ones to enlarge it. And in spite of the richness of masses of evergreens, you will always see that taste ultimately thins and reduces them to a few gorgeous unelbowed monarchs. You have earth round the house, and earth in the garden; and if you were to earth this stripe, you would be all earth together. In a few years you would not even see the turf of your field.

Joe is in the middle of a strong, healthy, beautiful hoping cough, and Elizabeth is beginning to take it; whereat I rejoice. The Faculty are in arms against Murray's Sheriff Bill;[1] which certainly on their point is as absurd, impracticable, and insidious, as its true author Wallace could wish. I fear that the court will not be able to be quiet under his proposed Session Bill, which, quoad Ordinaries nursing records at Chambers, is, tho' recommended by the Law Commission, very crazy.

Ever

H. Cockburn

[*Addressed:*] John Richardson Esq, 21 Fludyer Street, London

To J. T. Gibson-Craig
NLS 588.1339

Aberdeen, 18 April 1838

My Dear James

Tho' I don't like to scald my mouth with other folks' kail, it would be wrong not to let you know that the people of Elgin (which I was in yesterday, and again saw that noble Cathedral) are dismayed, and sorry, and angry, at the intended sale of the Bishop's house – which intention they ascribe to his Grace of Richmond or his managers.[2] If there really be any such intention, is it not great nonsense? The House is probably as old as the Cathedral; it is a very fine old mass; it is close beside the Cathedral; it is worth very little in the market;

---

1 The Sheriff Courts (Scotland) Act 1838 (c.119). See now David M. Walker, *A Legal History of Scotland,* vi (2001), ch. 13.

2 Elgin appears in the newly-commenced *Circuit Journeys* [*CJ*], 15–16, 22 (and also in *Jnl,* i, 170–1) as a place of much concern to HC. He was anxious not only about the Bishop's House, but also about honouring John Shanks, the long-serving custodian of the town's ecclesiastical antiquities.

and, if sold, will only be bought to make a quarry of, for the erection of some horrid spruce new villa, built by some Elgin baillie, who will be pointing out the Cathedral as a part of his garden. When I heard all this, I inwardly resolved to write to you, as probably ignorant of the design, and as an Antiquarian. It is said that the Duke does not know that it belongs to him, or any thing about it. Excuse this; from one who wishes well to the Duke, better to the Cathedral, and best of all to you.

I trust that Sir James is now safe, and taking care of himself.

Horrid weather. Hard hard work getting thro' the new fallen snow, today, in three places on this side of Huntly.

Ever

H. Cockburn

[*Addressed*:] James T. G. Craig, Esq W.S., St Andrew St, Edinr

To Mrs Andrew Rutherfurd
NLS 9687.105

Edinr, 29 April 1839

My Dearest Lady Advocate

I congratulate you, with my whole soul, on your late, and I trust upon many coming, honours.[1] Whether the Lord Advocateship be calculated to increase any man's comfort or wealth, may well be doubted; and in Rutherfurd's case, he being at the head of his profession, and with palms hourly well fee'd, his acceptance is a very heroic sacrifice for the public and his party. But if our world holds together for two years, and perhaps even for one, he may be rewarded, and made comfortable and respectable *in his old age*, by sitting down in one of our Chief's chairs. A turn-out of the present government before a vacancy happens is one evil to be dreaded; and his being left for some time in parliament after being out of office, is a still greater one.

He was this morning elected quietly for Leith, and he is now sitting below me at the trial of the pretended Earl of Stirling.[2] It is irresistible, and most agreeable, to retrace the course of talent, industry, and character, by which the

1 Rutherfurd's Advocateship dates from 19 April 1839. He was succeeded by Sir William Rae on 4 September 1841, and then by Duncan McNeill (1842–6), before holding the post again from 1846 until promoted to the Bench on 7 April 1851. For his 1839 appointment, see also *Jnl*, i, 224–5.

2 See next letter.

black-glaring-eyed boy who I remember seeing for the first time, by accident, one summer evening, at a debating society, about thirty-two years ago, has raised himself to this station. I always tremble for the fate of Scotchmen in the House of Commons; especially when they enter it after their youth is past, and with established provincial reputations; but in his case there are more grounds for hope than usual – and I do hope confidently.

Don't let him get too magnificent in his expences. He dined at Bonaly yesterday, and astounded me by saying he was going to live at the Clarendon. Pray do remember that the cessation of fees, joined to the unavoidable expences, will make your purses feel very light in autumn. What I always think of with sorrow is that his mother is not here. What disrespectful jokes she and I would have had at my Lord. I met John t'other day, and said, 'Well, John, you're getting on. You were Mr when I first knew you; and now you're My Lord! I fancy you mean to be King soon?' To which stutters John, 'Eh! Eh! God, I wud na' wonder.' And, above all, remember this, that when you cease to be an Advocate, don't reappear among us as a knight. What an incomprehensible folly this is! A most natural conclusion of the career. Sir John and Lady Murray!!! Hech! Hech![1]

We are all well. Henry is in the hungry stage, and fast recovering. But he has added a cubit to his stature. Arch'd has come home, and foolishly brought his whole whiskers with him. Graham's nonsense is to proceed. – Stuff. Jane and Eliza Maitland and I had a very pleasant circuit to Inverness, Aberdeen, and Perth. Not a drop of rain; mild clear weather; Creeffy and Mrs James Moncrieff; and much mirth. We had an evening party at the Provost of Aberdeen's; in an excellent, queer, old house, down a close; quadrilles, and a solid, leg of mutton, supper; he an octogenerian, she an undisguised Aberdonian – nice, kind, natural happy bodies. Her head was so enveloped in ribbons and carfufles, that nothing under them was visible to the world. Fancying that his Lordship's wig was awry, and anxious for the honor of the house, she dared to put it right, by an actual imposition of hands. On which he says, solemnly, 'Madam! I'll thank you to let my wig alone. *I never meddle with yours.*' I don't believe that his wig will be touched by her again.[2]

What are you doing? Do you mean to continue your early rising at Bath, and to abandon her Majesty's Advocate to his own courses in London? If he

1 Murray was knighted on 24 April, and became a Judge on 17 May.
2 For this Circuit, see *CJ* 36–47. The Provost's brown wig is recorded there too, with additional details. Asked how she he had got so many officers of the 74th to attend the Provost's party at short notice, his wife said, 'Troth . . . I just sent the lass up to the barracks and bade them a' come doon.' 'Much kindness and much laughter' they had.

and ministers will keep their places, we can't have you among us again till late August! What's to become of our profligacy! Of our social, pious Sundays! Of our Craigcrook Saturdays! I hope there is no chance of your heart taking root in any foreign soil; or of your nose turning up at your poor vulgar Scotch friends.

Jeffrey seems to be very happy and to be making a successful flirting tour. The bairn will be smothered by kindness among them.[1] I wish there were half a dozen more of them; for nothing will keep Mrs Jeffrey quiet here except having some of them with her. A hen with one chicken is always in a flutter. Our new Solicitor was sworn in today. Never saw his leg in a silk stocking before. A stately good leg. The Maitlands were in the highest huff at the silk not being on his still statelier leg. But they are softening down. The mason was with me at Bonaly yesterday. Shilpet.[2] We supped with Thomas a few nights ago – a shocking exhibition. James Campbell is polling away in Ayrshire at this moment. Will probably be ruined by the radicals. At which his visage will not be the less red.

Farewell. Don't let your worthy host, who, being a churchman is of course a Tory, corrupt you from the true faith.

Ever
H. Cockburn

Andrew Rutherfurd
NLS 9687.107

Court, Friday 3 May 1839, 10 a.m.

My Dear R.

We resumed yesterday morning at nine.[3] Ivory began at quarter past nine, and spoke exactly six hours. For a *court* it was an excellent speech: acute, sensible, full; and in good tone thro'out, in reference to the prisoner and his character, as attested. But for a Jury, or the public, it had the great defects of over-minuteness, want of strong points and general views, and, even for him, unusually stuttering articulation. It was a good speech, made bad – or at least

1 Jeffrey's daughter Charlotte had married William Empson (1791–1852), Professor of Law at Haileybury, on 27 June 1838.
2 Thin, starved.
3 The Stirling peerage case was continuing. On the litigation, see W.B.D.D.Turnbull, *The Stirling Peerage* (1839), and R.S.Lea's appendix in G.E.C., *The Complete Peerage*, xii (1953), 161–7. The claim was of Alexander Humphreys-Alexander (1783–1859), who was indicted for forgery, March 1839, a charge that was (too leniently) found not proven.

made much less good – by being somewhat misplaced. It was what Pillans would call long by position.

Robertson began at a quarter past three and spoke about three hours. A disgraceful exhibition for the bar. Absolutely degrading to his profession. Loud vulgar roaring, interspersed by constant buffoonery, even to the imitation of the tones of the French witnesses' voices, and by many efforts of tearful pathos, which however were so obviously the insincere strainings of a beast, that they generally renewed the audiences' laugh. The want of talent, and of tact, was a deeper defect. I never saw a case so plainly abandoned – I mean one of which so little was made. It is funny to know now that he convinced many *against* his own client. I certainly did not know that so little could be said for the worthy earl, till I heard his counsel.

Meadow began last night, but stopped at nine, and is now going on charging, as he calls it. It is all in his usual style. A considerable gathering together of detached circumstances, and some incidental, and apparently accidental, hits of ingenuity; but no general luminousness, or judicial weight; one sided views, and a constant strain of petulant feebleness.

Till Patrick the Beast helped you, I considered your losing the verdict, as quite certain. It is a little more doubtful now; but still you will lose it, especially as the pretty vehemence of the Charging Lord in your favour will probably correct the aid that the prisoner's counsel gave you. No intelligent mortal can be doubtful of the guilt.

I hope you got up safely, and that you will vote rightly tonight. Do put some sense into your masters. They must never court, or even coquet with, Chartists, or do, or profess to do, anything merely because the radicals wish it. But they must be a little bolder in trying to do what is right – such as to cure the since discovered defects which defeat the Reform Bill; and their being always frustrated by the Peers is in their favour. But above all, take care of yourself. A Lord Advocate generally walks over hot cinders, and sits on gun powder. But this has of late been because he has not been duly supported by Government, and Government has failed to support him, and chiefly because he had not the command of the Scotch members. And you know how much these members have been averted from acting in concert, in public matters not depending on mere party principles, by the *manner* of the Advocate not being calculated to bind them together. Excuse me for earnestly warning you steadily to avoid that fatal rock; and for telling you that your own manner has sometimes been said to be too *lofty* – a quality which people not unwilling to have a pretence for offence, never fail to take advantage of, and generally with the sympathy of those to whom they complain. I mention this because it is the only point on which I have the shadow of a doubt of your splendid success. I know it to be nonsense, but you must consider what fools and enemies think, or pretend. So, go in the name of the Lord, and prosper. I am entirely wrapped up in your success. Your wife or brother not more so. I cannot help lamenting that the excellent person who died some years ago in Forres Street is not here to see it. And pray do look after your purse. I am not easy about the funds. You should have a squeeze of Willie Clerk put into you.

I hope Charlotte is well. We hear that she is dwable (from *debolis*).[1] But I fancy it is only the novelty of the situation. Tell me occasionally all your Gossip.

11 o'clock. He's bringing it up for the Earl very well. For a Judge d——d offensive.

4 o'clock. After four hours' enclosure the Jury have come in with a long detailed verdict, the result of which is an acquital, with a finding that the charter and some other documents are forged. Upon this acquital, the poor man has fallen into a deep faint, and has been carried out – and has not been able to be brought back yet.

It has been a very painful scene. But this faint will do much good to his reputation. Tho' I am not quite clear whether his agitation be for the acquittal or for the evidence of his peerage being found forged.

Ever

H. Cockburn

[*Addressed:*] The Right Honble The Lord Advocate of Scotland M.P., London

To Andrew Rutherfurd
NLS 9687.118

Bonaly, 23 May 1839

My Dear R.

Having got your letter here, I have not seen Jeffrey – to whom 'Confidential' does not apply; but I shall confer tomorrow or next day. Meanwhile the offer to the Dean[2] seems to me wise and fair – tho' I suppose Maitland's door would never be open to me again if he, or rather his wife,

---

1 Something of a favourite coinage of HC's. Debílis (feeble, frail) gives 'debile', whence 'dwable'.
2 Now Duncan McNeill.

should discover that I said so. I greatly doubt the Deacon's accepting – which is the best reason for the offering. If he does – he is done; which is another. Either way, it is handsome for the Whig government, and is a proud answer to many accusations, and a relief in the event of many other appointments. And if Goliah is again to be postponed, his being so to so very great a man as the Dean is the minimum of mortification. So it seems to me hoc statu. Besides all which, the Deacon, professionally speaking, has really the best claim. The English and Irish prejudice I would disregard, and set them a good example; especially as it may operate in our favour in Conservative times, and is but in good taste considering that Peel made Corehouse, Fully, and Creeffy.

I really hope that Government will discharge a few of its Invalids, and get some young recruits. And if it will, or can, do nothing else, its resolutely, and as a Government, setting itself to reform the Reform Bill, so as to make it the Reform Bill but not a jot more, will give it a lift with the people fully as effectual as the discussion on Ballot.

We have ordered the respondents in Lethindy[1] to appear at the bar in three weeks; Moncreiff and Jeffrey alone holding the complaint not established. Moncreiff again gave an admirable opinion as to feeling, diction and manner, and Jeffrey a beautiful one; but I thought their reasoning a clear blunder. Duloch was the fiercest against the Church, but with some good matter. Fullerton (gout in hand and foot) and I concurred with all the rest in being quite clear that Auchterarder decided the Court's jurisdiction; after which all was clear. In the robing room, Cuninghame, Moncreiff, Jeffrey and I tried to get them from calling the Revd Gents to the bar – chiefly because it *provoked* them to be offensive, and so make bad worse. For which reason (I suppose) Gillies and Meadowbank and all the rest were clear that this was the true course.

Chalmers last night carried a vote in the Venerable for the Independance of the Church. You will see it in all the Scotch papers. What they *mean* to do in the new vacancies does not *appear*. But I understand that it is that they are to enforce the veto. So that the faster the Prison Bill passes the better for them. The important fact is that the whole three motions – Cook's *as explained* by him included – are *firm* as to *the principle of non-intrusion*, let the machinery for enforcing it be what it may; which is precisely the principle which the opinions in Auchterarder put down. As to the result of this, as you official Solomons say, 'We shall see', 'Time will show', 'It will be affected by the course that circumstances may happen to take.'

1 For the Lethindy case, and other ecclesiastical litigation of the period, see Iain F.Maciver, 'Cockburn and the Church', *Bic. Comm.* 68–103, especially 97–101.

My prediction is this. The church means to ask Government to help it to establish some sort of Veto. To which the Whigs will say, You are fierce against us, and we can't knock our heads against an English post to please you. They turn to the Torries, who say, You are against patronage and the law – go be d——d. So with the lairds, the courts, and all governments against them, their evangelical demagogues will appeal to the people; patronage will be made sterner than ever; and in a few years the majority of the population are Dissenters; and then Good Bye to the Church.

I came out here to celebrate Her Majesty's nativity – with about twenty young people, who, in special reference to Her Majesty's late proceeding, are to have the largest bonfire of whins that ever shone for any Queen from the Pentlands. Tell her this.

Glenlee can never again appear in court, it is said; yet they don't mean to let him resign till Novr. Medwyn, it is reported, says that he will only let the apple fall on the right side of the wall. Being fully ripe, I would pluck it.

Sir Jack was the only one who came unwritten to Lethinday, and spoke as might be expected. Poor Hope deplorable. Gillies is like a sulky child about the two overworked Barons being made to do Bill work besides. The truth is that the Exchequer should be given to the whole mere ordinaries in addition to the Bills – and no £600. At least this is what he should be threatened with.

Remember me to Mrs Rutherfurd.

Ever

H. Cockburn

[*Addressed:*] The Right Honble The Lord Advocate of Scotland M.P., London

To Andrew Rutherfurd
NLS.9687.126

31 May 1839

My Dear R.

I was angry with Lauder yesterday for not having told me sooner, nor ever having told you at all, that Skene had resigned his secretaryship of the Board of Trustees, and that he himself was proposed to succeed him. It is only £180 or so, now, but on the demise of Geo. Thomson will be £500 – salvation to the Baronet. Meadow and Sir Adam Hay are his steady friends, so he may be safe. But a word from on High may do good; so you ought to consider whether you should not write to the said Meadow expressive of your opinion as a Trustee – which, tho' not expressed, I hope they will take as a hint from the Treasury.

Macaulay has made a great impression by his first, Assembly Room, speech – which is unanimously allowed, and by good and not friendly judges, to have been excellent. I dined with him yesterday at Criagcrook. A vulgar looking fellow – and a cumbrous talker; but pleasant, and natural – for him. He's like a heavy strong Flanders draught horse, beside the light fiery Arabianism of Jeffrey.

The modest Duncan McLaren says, with a resigned indignation, 'this bolus will be swallowed – but don't try it again'. He will be your next candidate.

Macaulay has had two deputations of his constituents. One consisted of King Robert Thomson; who, after telling him that Mahomet did not write the Koran, and explaining all about the genealogy of Julian, asked him if he would support Presbitery? Certainly. Why? Because it's right. 'Then you agree with me that it is your duty to promote a bill for making it the religion of England and of Ireland.'

The other consisted of the little Menie, the Provost and Drysdale, about Edinr stinks – and they are to regale him over the Figgit whins tomorrow; that he may learn whence the breeze steals its odour. My excellent joke, of calling him M.P. for the Shity of Edinr, had great success.

Ever

H. C.

To Mrs Andrew Rutherfurd
NLS 9687.152

Bonaly, Sunday 4 August 1839

My Dear Mrs Rutherfurd

Since a little Scotch gossip gives you pleasure, [it] would be a shame to your friends here if you had it not to enjoy. I got your last letter – for which thanks. We heard of your illness with sincere alarm. I am confident that all the London Apothecaries could have given you nothing so soothing as what we all said, could you have but heard it. I never liked measles. Less than ever hooping cough. They are so weakening, and leave the victim so long with a tendency to all other evils. So do cherish *yourself.* A painful operation to disinterested modesty; but necessary for your friends. All the world is well here. I meant nothing about the Crow, except that she is voted dangerous from adhesion and thin skinedness, and therefore very seldom caws from the old roost. There has been no blow up; but it is not, and will never be, the old thing again. They are living very steadily and very happily at Craigcrook.

Empson reading and riding, and as pleasant as that horrid mumble will let him.

Cork Bell, Sherriff of Ayrshire, has been writing sad nonsense about the tournament to Lord Eglinton, neither forbidding, nor permitting it. His Lordship's response is very good – except that his explanation how none of the *gallant* knights *can* even be *hurt*, makes it but a poor affair. The only sense in it is that some of the fools may be finally disposed of.

How well the Kornel is looking! Just the old man. He and his spouse, and Pluffy, are to dine here today. Dante is very weak upon his pins, and is plainly ringing in. We had a grand bowling match at Craigcrook last week – Lauder, Cosmo, Ivory, Fletcher, Mr John, Sir Charles Terrott, etc., and a due sprinkling of wives. The green is so rough that nobody can play well on it but Jeffrey himself, whose feats were absolutely miraculous. His bowl seemed to know exactly what it wanted, and turned to the Jack as steadily and surely as a Torry to a sinecure. We had another day of it last Friday at Grange. A queer party. Only eight – of which Proff. Wilson, his son, two brothers, and son in law were five. The Proff. not unpleasant; and not too much shaven. But he never seems to me to be at his ease. Jane has a grand Habbie's How breakfast in preparation for this week. I hope your husband has not forgotten the days of virtue and the skep. Poor Wiliams!

Our weather is perfect. I wish you saw us at this moment. It is the Saacrament Saabbath of the parish; and therefore, tho' the Kirk has this week got a new bell which is heard up here, not one of us – not even Grahame, the betrothed of the Church – have stirred a step, but we just daundered up and down snuffing the roses and eating peas and lying on the grass, and looking at the view. And then we had a cram of excellent strawberries and cream, then I gave them a screed of Jeremy Taylor, and then made four bottles of punch and put them into the well. Then another daunder, and we went into the field and patted the Guernsy cow, and found out still better blush roses, and ate more peas, besides some soft infant beans, still cosy in their soft beany blankets. Then Joe bathed – and I keeked, and she splashed me. And, all this while, the sky and the sea are good enough to try which can be bluest – and the trees and the turf which can be greenest – and the hill lambs and the few birds that are still in love, which can be softest in the voice. And yesterday was the end of my last Bill week forever!

And only think of the addition to my delight that was made by our friend Gillies! Just as I was stepping behind Geordie to come out here, his clerk came with me with a note from his Lordship, saying that he *would* be obliged to take a sister to Jephson, and that he intended to do this about the 26th – which was his

Bill week – and begging I would take three or four days of it (!!) for him. Oh what a pain it gave me to say I was sorry I was engaged, and to put the whup across Geordie's hide. It would have been better bestowed across his Lordship's. And here I am for a month of self-possessedness, before I go forth on the Circuit. I fear August will disappear before you be free. A severe infliction.

I doubt if it will do for you to cleave unto your husband during the Londonising of 1840. If you follow his fortunes there, it should not be one day beyond the first of June; by which you would lose our cold Spring, and gain our rural summer. Many worthy ladies will supply your place – viz. Misses Crow and Laing. The Lauders are better without Sir J. Nasmyth. He is a Baronet and rather grand, but penniless. The Body is more in their way – or any such humble, well doing, independant, man of sense. It is delightful to see Sir Thomas's happiness. He sits at the Board of Trustees – i.e. in a comfortable room on the Mound – and fancies he has an enormous deal to do, and predominates over all Scottish art. He is now called *The Buird*. I have a great love for that man and of his whole family. His weaknesses are all amiable, and, as Jeffrey says, his daughters 'are always so well washed'.

10 at night. Mrs James did not come – being headachy. The Kornel and Pluffy and I sat on a hill and reasoned high. The punch excellent.

So farewell. Take care of yourself. Your Richmond is beautiful, and I hope it will recreate you. As you have had measles, an infantine disease, the infantine virtues, and other ailments, are expected – diffidence and vaccination, teething and spelling. Playfair told me that Thomasina was bathing Thomas at Rothsay. I knew that they were out of Edinr. *Can't she drown?* Pillans is with them. The cloud is settling more deeply and steadily every day over that once sunny mind. But it is time I should reli[e]ve you.

Ever

H. Cockburn

[*Addressed:*] Mrs Rutherfurd, Clarendon Hotel, London

To Andrew Rutherfurd
NLS 9687.182

Justiciary, 16 March 1840

My Dear R.

Thomas leaves this tomorrow – in obedience to the Committee's summons. And *she*, grudging him a little of his old friends, goes with him. Dined there on Saturday. Oh! Oh! Feegh! Feegh! Has Government hatched the

Kirk egg yet? Above all, avoid misleading your masters into the delusion that *any* thing will *ever* reconcile *any* church to give any steady or honest support to any *just* government. A friction bar ought to be imposed on patronage because it is right for the people; but it won't hinder our Reverend beasts from railing against any education or toleration greater than they like; and, to an absolute certainty, they will all vote against every liberal act, even by their benefactors, the very day after a vote is legalised. It is very likely that the same Toryism which supports *its* church by crushing the people and setting up patrons, will reject even your minimum; but this is rather a recommendation to granting it.

If you want a Judge to examine, Creefy's your man. An impressive witness, right views, a laborious vacation-less judge, and *with a register of his hours of work.* He says his vacation last year was *one day.*

We have had a delightful witness here in a murder case – a little, old, wrinkled, sharp, honest, Irish woman. Napier was putting a question – Ivory, before she answered, tried to put it better – and Meadowbank to help Ivory – his Lordship concluding: 'Well now, tell us how it was'. She said 'I hav'not a voice for ye all three. You'll speak to me one at once.'

The prisoner killed his wife by a blow with a stool. *Meadow:* 'Take the stool in your hand. Now, show us how he struck her.' *Witness:* 'O fie! 'O fie!' *Meadow:* 'Show us.' *Witness:*

'An' would you have me do it *exact?*' – obviously meaning to give the man next her a d—d blow.

'But my good woman' (said Meadow, after a confused pother), 'I want you to make this a little clearer.' *Witness:* 'Aye, Me Lord, but I canna' make it ony clearer; for, Me Lord, I'm no schollard, but just an ould wife like yoursell.'

Beautiful weather. The Mavises at Bonaly roaring and rioting as if they were the Strathbogie Presbitery.

Ever

H. C.

To Andrew Rutherfurd
NLS 9687.196

Stirling Court House, 30 April 1840

My Dear R.

We have just seen justice beautifully defeated by that d——d modern piece of Judge-made legal nonsense, called the option. *Six* prisoners are on their trial for theft and reset. A witness is called *in truth* against four of them; but his father and mother are the other two; and in law what he says against the four may be supposed to affect the two. So I was obliged to humiliate myself, and scandalise the administration of Justice, by explaining to the witness the nature of the Option. On which he gave the proper rebuke to the law but a most grottesque and villianous leer, saying 'Odd! I like the Hoption, Ma Lord' – and walked off, amidst the laughter of the prisoners, and the amazement of the Jury. And so it must be while our absurd objection of relationship stands.

All our families have received a great shock in the death of William Macdowall of Barr – the best of brothers, and no better man. He was only a few days ill. It happened since I left home.

Ever

H. Cockburn

To Mrs Andrew Rutherfurd
NLS 9687.198
Court of Justiciary, 14 May 1840
My Dear Mrs Rutherfurd

I rejoice to hear – and I hope on good authority – that strength is beginning to revisit your frame. Pray don't be out when it calls. I was proposing to our new Sol. Gen. that he should part with some of his for a feeble friend. But the selfish monster grunted. We are all well in these parts; tho' the three sisters have got a severe shock; which reflection, by showing the amount of the loss, makes worse. I cannot get the end of August and Mrs Cunningham, the fourth sister, out of my head. She used to live with William till she was married, and was wrapt up in him; and I cannot help following the ship which carries the intelligence, and will reach Mauritius in four months, and seeing the effect of the black seal, and its black tidings.

Mrs Cockburn is resolved to yield at last to her desire and duty, and to go and renew the acquaintance of her youth with her now only surviving brother, the India Lieut.Col.; who is at Bath, a very merry fellow we are told, very affectionate, and deprived by rhumatism of the use of his limbs. His agent is obliged to go up to him (Alex. Smith) and Elizabeth is going with him – with Wifie, I believe, next Thursday, by mails and rails. If, as I expect, Whispering Davie joins them at Bath, they will do very well. Mrs C won't be away a month; which Wifie thinks a great deal too short.

George Dundas is going to be married!!!¹ To a daughter of the late Colin Mackenzie; described as a tall, lady like, virgin of 29. I gave him my

---

1 George Dundas (1802–69), adv.1826.SCJ (Lord Manor) 1868.

benediction last night – very cordially, for I greatly esteem him. She has a great character for sense and worth, and is said to be eminently lady like. But woefully long. Some people say she has £3000, but George says not a penny. I fancy the half of it is about the truth – for she has something. Like a true Lawyer, whose love of law is greater than his love of love, he lets the Session rise before he lets her sit down.

I delight to see the settling, in the midst of us, of young friends. There has been no such addition to our Society of late; none since the fair union of Thomas and Anne. I want to be like the Banian tree; which sees itself surrounded gradually by an enlarging circle of plants, rooting themselves off from the parent stem. But take special notice that I apply this only to friends; and that I have not the least desire to have a forest of children and grand-children sticking to my ribs all my days. An offensive friend can be cut off.

Agriculturally our weather has been wett, and therefore good, for ten days; epidermically (there's a word for you) very bad. If any conceited Englisher sneers at the climate of Scotland, you may tell him that in this climate, this year, in *April, in the open air,* Lilac was out, strawberries in bloom, asparagus and *cherries ripe*. The cherries were from a remarkably early tree at Lord Blantyre's at Erskine, and were *in profusion* – and some in a Glasgow shop.

Lord Ivory dines at Bonaly on Saturday.[1] I do rejoice in the safe mooring of that disinterested and true man. Poor Mrs Crawfurd was in great spirits about their small step, and won't fear that the Whigs can ever be out. Our escape from his rival D.Ass. – a horrid beast – is most comfortable. Won't Goliah, in a single breasted coat, and *small cloathes*, be beautiful?

It is plain that the valet murdered Lord W. Russell, or knew, murderously, about it. Yet there is something very incomprehensible in its execution. What a hully-ba-loo the Conserv[ati]ves would have made, if it had pleased the foreigner to cut a Tory throat in Dublin!

Ask your learned Lord, and tell me, why Robert Stewart leaves our Treasury. I have not seen our President since 12th March; but I am told that his feebleness has considerably encreased since then. Duff, our sherrif, is *very* ill. Getting wine to support him – a fatal sign.

I long for the second coming of the Jeffries; for really this emigration of all one's friends is great nonsense. Had I kept a nick-stick, I am certain that it would appear that it was at least sixty days since I tasted Champagne. I am as dry as it. The worst of Teetotalism is its cold. One freezes at night, even between eider down. An icicle in flannel is a type of me. Were it not for the

1 James Ivory (1792–1862); adv. 1816. Sol.-Gen. May 1839; SCJ 23 May 1840.

glow at the heart, the blood would be solid. Old Lady Dundas is dead at last; and so Duloch will get into his new house.

Remember me to the Kornel and his spouse, if they be about you still.

Ever

H. Cockburn

I have some difficulty in convincing Mrs Maitland that part of a Sol. Gen's costume consists of a pig-tail. But would it not be proper in his case? A cow's tail would do.

To Elizabeth Cockburn
NLS Dep.235(1)

14 Charlotte Square, Friday evening, 9 o'clock, 29 May 1840

My very dearest Wifie

A thousand thanks for your nice, long, *sensible* letter. I am glad you like Bath; for Miss Ivory writes that there are to be four vacancies in her School soon, and that she is so glad in the prospect of having you among them. I hope you listen to the pretty English you now hear around you. They don't say *Bawth*. No news here. Except – which will please your wickedness – that Adam Maitland got such an awful thrashing yesterday at the Academy from the man hired in place of the real English master, who is ill, that I have no doubt that the Directors will dismiss the fellow tomorrow. I dine, with Jane, tomorrow at Mr Macbean's, with Ilay and his wife and a grand party.

We had a bowling party at Grange yesterday, where I was beat. On Sunday Jane, Mrs Crawford, her bairn, Joe, Mina, and I go to breakfast at Bonaly; and Mr Balfour and Crawford come out to dinner. Railways! Slow things to Geordie! – no wonder Mamma is terrified when he is pawing the wind before her. I expect you to bring Bonaly several roots of the pretty plants you see. Archd left this this morning, and will be with you a day, if not two, before you get this. I hope you take great care of mamma, and all you can of uncle Laurence. Joe is in considerable spirits. But Jane keeps us so low in food, the poor child was nearly famished today at dinner. *Lord* Ivory went to look at Spylaw yesterday, but does not like it. Sir Thomas must have got a severe fall at Bonaly last Sunday, for his arm yesterday was like a large carrot. So your hotch potch is ready. I envy you that. But our turnips are as ready as well as those at Bawth. And for strawberries! – talk not of them in England. Poor idiots – have they them rolling in the streets, amidst oceans of cream. The bodies count them one by one, and sell them in tumblers! [*Rest missing*]

To Andrew Rutherfurd
NLS 9687.214

Court of Justiciary, 8 June 1840

My Dear R.

I wrote you from Stirling about six weeks ago mentioning how justice had been defeated, and the law disgraced, by what is called 'The Option' – which you will observe is considered here as one of the necessary consequences of allowing relationship as an objection to the admissibility of witnesses still to blot our system of evidence. I have now to mention that another example, tho' with somewhat a different result, has just occurred. A man is under trial for stabbing his mother; and the mother being called for the prosecution, the doubt occurred to one of the Judges whether this woman had not 'the option' – that is, the power of giving, or of withholding, evidence as she chose. But she was admitted, on the ground that she was the party *said to have been injured.*

Now this seems to me to be adding one absurdity to another.

There is no part of all this nonsense that ever pretends to be founded on the necessities of justice. It all rests on respect for *the feelings of the witness,* who it is said to be barbarous to compel to speak truth against a parent or child; so barbarous that it is better to let a criminal escape, or an innocent accused be convicted.

Now if this be the principle, it seems to me to be *far more* cruel to compel the witness to disclose an injury to himself, than to another; because it brings him more painfully into personal contact with the case, and forces him to speak out in the very case in which generosity would lead him to be silent.

These anomalies and absurdities, at which I am pleased to see that the audiences always stare, can only be removed by quashing relationship altogether as an objection to competency; an objection which legal bigots alone uphold.

Ever

H. Cockburn

To Sir Thomas Dick Lauder
NLS Dep.235(1)

Bonaly, 3 August 1840

'That's a guid ane!' – 'Eh bod! That's a guid ane!!' And from my innermost heart, My Dear Lauder, do I rejoice thereat. You are not more anxious about your own happiness, or that of your family, than I am; and I can see nothing but good in this event. Had not Lumbago – that rigid old

[165]

gentleman, like the Laird of Niddrie, in one's back – said No, I should have rolled on the ground, and gesticulated my joy, like as a gig horse let loose on Grange clover. I sympathise with you – deeply, undoubtingly, reasonably. But you'll lose all your daughters. When it once begins, it goes on electrically. Each becomes a conducting body. Whenever it gets into a house, they all go, like snow off a dyke. See now – Watson goes off only ten days ago; and here already goes off Charlotte. There won't be one of them in your house by Christmas. All that I beg and implore is that you would insist on them settling near us; so that our friends and howffs may be multiplied, not diminished. God bless you – and yours – and all your concerns; your Trustees, and your monuments, and your herrings, your sons in law, and your works, and your inward man, and your outward man, and all that is thine.

Ever and Ever
H. Cockburn

To Sir Thomas Dick Lauder
NLS Dep.235 (*SL* 42)
Bonaly, 26 March 1841
My Dear Sir Thos

Is it true that Rae's Bill not only sanctions a Monument for Scott, but a *dwelling house* for a Keeper, and a *Theatre*!!! If the supposed tombs of dead men must have living keepers, surely this one must get a flatt in Princes Street. But as for a Theatre – necessarily and universally an odious place outside – I anticipate objections to it which will probably wreck the whole act. There are hundreds who have, as I have, the strongest aversion to the example of building anything on the southern edge of Princes Street, and whose jealousy has only been overcome in favour of Scott and a beautiful architectural design, for an inoffensive purpose.

We have been dumb, *relying on the Monumental object alone*. And now, it is said, we are to be *slyly* saddled with a theatre. If it be so, there are no words can express what will be, and ought to be, felt, on such an abuse of their confidence. But I hope that we are misinformed, and that the newspaper *quotation* of the clause is incorrect. To propose a jail, or a Chapel of Ease, or a blubber work – these would not be worse. D——m.

Ever
H. Cockburn

To Sir John A. Murray
NLS 97.47

Bonaly, Colinton, 22 April 1841

My Dear Murray

I return Mr Dean's letter. I hope I have not done wrong in taking a copy of it for Cuninghame, in order that he may see exactly how he stands. I am sorry for him. His whole life and plans have been cast, for the last ten years, on the idea that foreign employment was the most certain path to home perferrment, and now it turns out that it is something like Check Mate to it. However the sooner this is known the better; and I have to thank you again – as we all do – for your kindness on this, as on former occasions in relation to this matter.

I have not read Forbes's pamphlet. Indeed the perusal of these things, which are now above a hundred in number, is neither easy nor profitable. But I dare say Forbes's may be above the average; for I have long known him, and know him to be a very able man. An intense Tory, intollerant in all things, and fully as conceited as the Dean; but still able, and a very worthy man.

There is *no* view of this accursed Church war in which I find any comfort; and therefore I have nearly subsided into a position of a spectator of a game. The difference in opinion from old political friends would be very painful, were it not that on all the other subjects and principles which they formerly promoted, they are as united as ever.

Mrs Cockburn, and one of the Miss Maitlands, and James Crawford, and I passed half a day and a whole night at Lochmaben on the 11th, and found the Hostelrie very good. Clearly the best dinner on the whole circuit. I walked to the old Castle. It has surely been skinned of all its Ashlar stones, for it never could have been built of its present clatch of lime and round, undressed bullets.

I don't recollect particularly what Jeffrey's opinion about the Veto was when that Act passed; but I have no doubt that he thought then, as now, that the Church can't be maintained without some mitigation of patronage; and that, tho' Society may certainly do very well without a church, as an abstract principle, the maintainance of the one that happens to be incorporated with all the habits and institutions of the people of Scotland, is desirable, or at least that its suppression by force would be awkward.

But why the Devil have I come back to this? For it is a subject on the discussion of which, even with those who agree with me, I have almost put a Veto on my lips; for there is nothing in the contest, and no result, which I can feel any pleasure in contemplating. D—m them all.

What cares Loch Fine for these matters? I hope your Spring flowers are behaving themselves. Ours are beautiful, and in great profusion.

I have not heard from Jeffrey; but I saw an excellent letter from him t'other day. His trachea had been ill; but was better – and he seemed to be dissipating all day and every day.

Remember me to Lady Murray, and to Mrs Rigby, who I suppose is still with you.

Ever

H. Cockburn

To Andrew Rutherfurd
NLS 9688.11

Edinburgh, 5 June 1841

My dear Rutherfurd

Lest exaggerated accounts of Jeffrey's illness should reach you, I think it right to tell you that it has been a mere stomatic attack, and has passed off.[1] I am very thankful I did not see it; but the facts are that when Russell and Neaves[2] were discoursing before him, he fainted, and was carried into the robing room, chiefly in the strong arms of Maitland. You can easily understand the sensation this would make, and the variety of groundless fears and stories it gave rise to. One kind friend came to Mrs Jeffrey to assure her that in the *fit* he had fallen, and grievously cut his face and head. Dr Pitcairn was in court, and Charles Bell saw him the instant he came home. Bell tells me that all his fears were dissipated at once by the liveliness of the patient's description of all the sensations he had – and of many which he certainly had not. His stomach had been disordered (as Patrick Newbigging tells me – his father is out of town) for some days; he had been medicating himself; had slept none the night before; did not taste breakfast today; thought himself that he should not go to court; but went, with a bottle of Laudanum and chalk; of which he partook; and so fainted from some illness, made worse by bad treatment – and inanition. He assured them, all the while they were assisting him in Court, that his mind was quite collected, and that it was only a faint; and when he came to himself was diverted seeing a man holding his wig. It is now four, and

2 'He gave this friends a dreadful fright by fainting in Court': *Jeff*, i, 375–81. The attack marked the beginning of a long period of illness; during Jeffrey's convalescence in England HC wrote him a number of cheering letters. Jeffrey's cases were passed on to Cockburn.
3 Charles Neaves (1800–76); adv. 1822; SCJ 1853. Francis Russell (1814–94); adv. 1836

he is sleeping. I have seen Mrs Jeffrey, who is sensible and cheerful, and has no doubt that they will be at Craigcrook tomorrow. This has stopped our party there for today; and, tho' all seems right for the present, a blank summer session's Saturday, from Jeffrey's illness, fills me with the most painful anticipations. What shall we be without Jeffrey?

Ever

H. Cockburn

To Mrs Francis Jeffrey
NLS Dep.235(1) (*SL* 45)

Bonaly, 25 September 1841

My Dear Mrs Jeffrey

I came home from the Circuit today, after exactly four weeks' absence – during all which time I could learn no certain tidings whatever of Jeffrey. On enquiring at your house, the old lady who keeps it grieved and alarmed me by hints, rather than by any certainty, of his having been much worse. Rutherfurd was at Craigie Hall, and John Jeffrey was not accessible; and so, Edinr being at present a desert, I have been obliged to come out here still ignorant of the real truth; and tho' I shall learn something tomorrow or next day, I am most anxious to know from you how matters stand. [A] line from himself, I fear I cannot expect. I was surprised to hear that Fully was in London. He is probably in Lanarkshire now; but thirty miles always seem to stop intercourse as much as half the globe does; and so I need not wait till I can see him. So pray tell me how you *all* are. For tho' my anxiety be about Jeffrey, it will greatly delight me to know that the two Charlottes, and my yet unseen friend Margaret, as well as Empson, are all well. Do write to me immediately.

I can tell you nothing about Edinr or its people; for I have not been among them since things were turned upside down. When I last saw the man called Andrew Rutherfurd, he was a Lord.

We had a most delightful expedition.[1] My comrades were Mrs Cockburn, Jane, Graham Maitland, and Frank, and we had a carriage like yours that could either open or shut, and a dickie before and behind. And it seems that the rain does *not* fall on the just; for rainy tho' the season is said to be, in thirty days the carriage was only closed twice. All the rest were not merely not wet, but beautiful. We have not had one hour's rain at a time, during the day, since the 2nd of this month.

1 On this North Circuit see the unusually full entry in *CJ* 104–46.

We went to Dunira – which means Strathearn – Lochearn, Tynedrum, Glenco, and Lochness, all which I had seen before; then up Glemoriston, into Skye – where I visited Loch Corruisk and the Cullin Hills, which Jeffrey would have enjoyed, because it required only sixteen miles there, and sixteen back, in an open boat – Loch Carron, Loch Maree – unquest[ionab]ly superior to every other Scotch lake except Loch Lomond – Southern and Western Ross, and so on to Inverness – all of which was new to me. From Inverness to this was all old to me, if gone in the usual way, so we went off the direct road and paid some visits upon, and about, the Spey; and came from Aberdeen to Perth by Braemar, a beautiful strath of about seventy miles where I had never been.

Creefy, with my Lady, a daughter and a son, joined us at Inverness, and rejoined us at Aberdeen and Perth. Our intervening visits led us different ways. They spent two days at Snaigo; where they found Mrs Keay well.[1] We were all very merry. Creeffy diverting, respectable, and affectionate, as usual; and my lady really did all she could to be happy and easy. But she is sadly oppressed by the terror of impropriety, and is a visible check on any tendency towards indecorum, or even levity, on the part of her learned Lord. But, if it be often enough repeated, I would not wonder if our vulgar mirth, and hand shaking baillies, and dunches from waiters, and travellers looking into her bed room when it won't lock, and retiring with an apology, and the upsetting of tea kettles ill balanced on the fender, etc., should soften her into some practicable pliancy.

We had little criminal business, except at Perth; but Moncreiff had two days at Inverness, with Adam Anderson and Cosmo Innes, and Whigham and somebody else, in a civil cause. Our Advocate Depute was Adam Urquhart,[2] the first blossom of the new Scotch Torryism. He conducted himself very properly. But I am one of the few who have always rather had a liking for this honest bigot. Jane has kept quite well. Always ready for food, sleep, and laughter – to say nothing of liquor.

We shall be here steadily now, till October shall close our holy days. Our flowers have gratefully adhered to their stems and twigs till our return, and we are now sparkling with Carnations, Holyoaks, Dalhias, Fushias, Chinese roses, etc.

1 James Keay (who had in 1816 married Elizabeth, *née* Graham, of Fintry) had died in 1837. For an earlier visit to Snaigow, see *CJ*, 36.
2 Adam Urquhart (1794–1860), adv. 1815. Sheriff of Wigton 1843–60.

And so, God bless you all. Remember me to every body. And write about Jeffrey immediately.

Ever

H. Cockburn

To Francis Jeffrey
NLS Dep.235(1)

12 November 1841

My Dear J.

I see from your last, for which many thanks, that the best chance I have of entertaining you is by telling you the events of this one day.

We judges all *breakfasted* – really breakfasted – with Boyle. Three things remarkable: 1. A bad breakfast. 2. The late Dean[1] stalked in, late, with a Boucquet in his hand as large as his own ostentation, and presented it with vast formality to My Lady President. 3. Old Charles – the late – came in, unasked (as I understand) and was most natural, kind, and joyous.[2] I may add that tho' the clerks were not asked, there being no sworn in President, Jamie Fergusson tumbled in – conscious of no change – in a glorious frill.[3]

So we processed to Court.

Before going in to the court room, we waited nearly an hour till the Faculty could elect a Dean, etc.

During this pause Boyle read your letter to him, etc., and the kindness – the genuine and hearty kindness – of them all to you, moved me strongly. But it was only of a piece with the deep and undivided opinion of all Edinr. I love even the worst of them for it. The result was that the President is, in the name of the Court, to propose to you and the Home Office, to have your *potential* leave extended to the 20th of March, i.e. of May. They also sent you all your existing cases to me; following two precedents – one when Newton was ill, and one when Medwyn – on both of which occasions, their causes were sent to the next senior Ordinary. I begin on Tuesday next to sit, as you, on my blank day.

The first thing that struck me on our all going in was the face of Thomas, seated at the table, and looking well.

1 John Hope, Dean 1832–41, was now Lord Justice-Clerk.
2 Charles Hope, Lord Granton, Lord President 1811–41.
3 James Fergusson of Monkwood (1769–1842), adv. 1791. PCS 1826.

Boyle took his place at the table, too; and old Gillies, as senior judge,[1] was good enough to inform us that Hope had resigned, and that he understood that somebody was to come forward as his successor; after which he added some poor sentences, in a very senile voice, in praise of the departed. Boyle stepped up, presented Her Majesty's letter, was sworn in and mounted his chair; and then made a very respectable address – the address of a vulgar, but honest, good hearted man. The only folly he persists in committing is in sinking the old, known, title of President, and calling him[self] Justice General. We are to have The Lord President no more. Then came the new Justice, the Lord Advocate and the Sol.,[2] each with his tin box; after all which the Faculty had the honor of hearing *Rae* rise and announce to the Court that Mr Alexander Wood stood before their Lordships as Dean. Wood nodded. We then dispersed; and the Justice Clerk having selected me as the Ordinary who was to hatch him, I went forth and sat within the Outer House till 4 o'clock.

In the Faculty, Pat. Robertson proposed, and Marshall seconded Wood.[3] Short and inoffensive both – and no allusion to Rutherfurd. John Jardine,[4] tho' he had no other candidate, objected on the score of its being kept from Rutherfurd from politicks, and recalled the elections of forty years nearly, to show how this feeling had been abjured. Robertson disclaimed politicks. On this Maitland[5] made a good, judicious, effective speech, reading and commenting on the said Patrick's own written intimation, authorised by his party, that they were determined to have a Dean of their own politicks. The Solicitor said this only meant that having an unquestionably fit person, his agreeing with them politically was an advantage in their sight. Wood was then chosen; and on taking his seat had the folly to say that if he believed that there was *any* politics in his election, he would not have accepted!!! If there had been a vote, Geo. Dundas would *certainly* have voted for Rutherfurd. Rutherfurd was not present at this stage.

Rae then moved an address to Charles Hope, his chief point being Charles's eminence as a Statesman (poz.) and as an Orator (poz.) in the House of Commons. It wanted only little practice, he said, to have made him the greatest and most eloquent Statesman of his age. His Lordship (Rae) is looking

1 Lord Gillies, on the Bench since 1811.
2 John Hope had succeeded as Justice-Clerk. Rae was again Lord Advocate. Alexander Wood (d.1864); adv. 1811. Dean of Faculty, November 1841, SCJ November 1842 (resigned 1862).
3 Patrick Robertson (1794–1855); adv. 1815. Dean of Facullty 1842–3. SCJ November 1843.
4 John Jardine (1777–1850); adv. 1799.
5 Thomas Maitland, later Lord Dundrennan 1850–51.

red and very vulgar, and had on a queer tight wig; and Burton says he looked like a coachman proposing his master's health. Maitland seconded.

Rutherfurd, who had now come in, moved (according to custom) an address to the ex-Justice, in a speech described by all who heard it as *most admirable*. It was the justest evidence of the impropriety of his recent rejection. Ad. Anderson[1] seconded this.

D. McNeill then rose to move an address to the late Dean, and in one minute the rush outward left the mover and the new Dean almost solitary.

On the whole, the exposure of the factious promotion of Wood, Rutherfurd's excellent appearance and the strong support he could have had, joined to the guilty consciousness of his rejectors, set Rutherfurd completely up. He is taking Provinciality very well, gaily and happily; tho' this Deanship is plainly a mortification to him, and still more to her; and will sever him from Wood, Anderson, Robertson, and McNeill. I mean, not that they will quarrel, or that there will be any outward severance, but that they won't be cordial. With this exception, he is well up with everybody, and everybody with him; and the clear general opinion is that the Faculty has disgraced itself. I wish to God he could abate some of that lofty scorn, which alone tends to render him unpopular.

After all this, he and I summoned courage to go and call on Thomas, who has taken lodgings in Darnaway Street. We found Maitland and Napier there, but they soon went away. He received us very kindly, and with perfect ease. Maitland told me that he had been talking kindly of Rutherfurd before we came in, and when we got out R. said he felt his reception to have been friendly. He seems *quite* well; and neither from his look, air, or talk could I have guessed that he was not sitting in his old library. *She* also, who we had seen in [an]other room, was gracious even to R. But whether Paul is to persecute, remains to be seen.

James Craig's marriage is to be on the 23rd.[2] I predict a child. She is skittishly happy. Creeffy is well, and his nose moderate. His son rising steadily. No more girl Lauders talked of – but I suspect Sir Thomas is bringing home his Indian son with a view to the sole Miss Innes. It was discovered yesterday, or the day before, that, when abroad, one of Sir F.

1 Adam Anderson (1797–1853); adv. 1818. Dean of Faculty 1851–2; Lord Advocate 1852; SCJ 1852.
2 J.T. Gibson-Craig (1799–1886), WS, Clerk of the Signet, 2nd son of Sir James (1st Bt), married 23 November 1841 Jane (*nee* Grant), widow of Colonel Pennington.

Walker's daughters had been married to a low German *postmaster*, who has appeared here, and for whom she was selling her trinkets. They are to be married again here, after which she goes to the Post House. The Justice, it is said, really means to produce his spouse; which, as to ladies, won't do beyond a dozen. He has left Granton for economy, and *Graham Speirs*[1] has taken it.

I fancy you have had enough of this gossip. So pray do get well, and be among us again in May. You will find us sadly fallen off in virtue. Except at Rutherfurd's, there is scarcely a well principled dinner to be got in Edinr. 'Silent now the race course stands'.

God bless you
H. Cockburn

Mrs Rutherfurd is remarkably well. Mrs H. Mackenzie to be in the Isle of Wight all winter. Mrs Gillies now hopeless, tho' her bodily health good. Mrs Maitland came to town today – her ankle still immoveable. Fully has had a trial in a case which the court held it impossible to try, it was so buried in documents. But the House of Lords agreed with Fullerton that it was fit for a jury – and he has done it very well. Music at Murray's last night, and every Thursday night. He absolutely enormous. The Church mess thickening hourly. Two new actions, one by the Seven Deposed, for quashing all the decrees of the Assembly; the other by the Three Undeposed, for quashing all the Strathbogie judgements in absence of the Session. Hope Richardson's marriage on the 27th of December.

Francis Jeffrey (and his wife)
NLS Dep.235(1)

Edinburgh, 26 December 1841

My Dear J.

Lest you should hear that Duloch has wrenched his spine, and broken his thigh bone, and dislocated his hip joint – all of which we were positively assured had taken place – don't believe a word of it, for no part of it is true. But as he was walking across a field, last Thursday, near Morton Hall, alone, he slipped on some ice, and came down, with a severe blow, on the hip, and being incapable of rising lay about twenty minutes roaring for help; which came in the shape of two farm servants, who got him carted to Morton Hall;

---

1 Graham Speirs (1793–1877), of Culcreuch, Stirlingshire.

where he lies. Sir Charles, who attends him, told me yesterday that everything was quite correct, except that the *nerve* of the hip is injured, and that this was always a matter for anxiety – and that no more can be said about it at present, but that he rather thought he would get well in some days.

We ate our Xmas goose yesterday. The usual party, except four; whose healths were done due honour to – you, Mrs Jeffrey, Playfair, and Mrs Maitland. Playfair is well again, but has had something very like another touch. Mrs Maitland is not off the sofa yet, but except that she is a fixture and not yet moveable, I never saw her so well. Murray has recovered entirely, and is rapidly replenishing.

There is a Speculative rebellion here now. The Town Council have ordered the Orators to be out of the College by 12 at night – which is virtual suppression – and they question our right to our room. I have got them to suspend their order till we can hold a conference. Meanwhile we are all in a flame; and I should not wonder that they were obstinate; in which case the Speculators, having no funds to build a new hall, and injured, even tho' they had, by having no Academic dignity, will probably, in the end, evaporate. The Civic interference is chiefly instigated by a *porter*, who naturally dislikes late hours, unless his extra demands can be complied with – which they can't be *ad libitum*; and then this has roused the pious, who I can't persuade that there is less temptation for young philosophers abroad at 2 in the morning than at 12 at night. I wish you would write a note to Adam Black, who is rather disposed to be foolish, and is influential. All you have to say is to advise him not to hurt the College by driving away from it a society which has done more good to Scotland than any one private institution it contains. Why the devil can't he go on as his godly forefathers have been for eighty years.

A funny *quoad sacra* case.[1] A Presbitery, two or three years ago, ordered a Kirk and Manse to be built; which was done; and at last decreed for, and allocated the price, among the heritors. When one heritor says – No, you had a *quoad sacra* man among you. And this is now one of *thirty* actions. The Veto itself may be got quit of in the same way.[2] It was never passed. The Non intrusionists have *announced* that they have reason to fear that Government means to force some offensive measure upon them. I can discover no

1 'As regards sacred matters', i.e. regarding a parish created and functioning only for religious purposes and not for matters of civil administration.
2 The Veto [Act], passed by the Assembly in 1834, providing that no Minister should be presented to a parish against the wishes of a congregation (i.e. the issue that was to precipitate the Disruption).

symptom of any approach towards any direct mitigation of patronage by giving power to the people; and all attempts to avoid this by giving more power to the Church is only making bad worse.

My Lord Justice Clerk has been holding his virgin circuit at Glasgow, with Mackenzie – and has made it a grand affair. He got into a new Railway Hotel, because it had a room about eighty feet long. And there he made Alison[1] conglomerate nearly eighty people, to whom he gave turtle and good wine, all in silks and single breasts – who had such articles; *his own former clients and Intrusion ministers* being by far the most conspicuous portion of the Company; and so he was glorified. *All* his brethern there concur in cursing his tediousness *in every case*, and his offensiveness whenever thwarted. The agents say – and truly – that he rises at 4 a.m. merely to find out what more may possibly be got printed. We are all – or nearly all – against him in Fogo, for which treason he has made himself as impracticable in the robing room as possible. I had a Justiciary dinner at Granton last week. He neither gives Champagne nor silver covers, because they are both common and *vulgar*. Hermitage and Tin. Rae has become yellow, and his nose as thin as a pen. He won't be addressed *scripto*, except as Privy Councillor; which title is *set forth* in all his indictments.

I have been reading a 12mo vol. by Chalmers against Alison and poor rates. It refers too much to his *Economy*, but is a powerful defence of the Scotch system, *when properly worked*. He has brought me back to my (shaken) faith in the sufficiency of this system – always however if worked. He makes a gallant offer to begin now and do St John's over again, in any parish in any part of Scotland, town or country, that may be assigned to him. His respectful contempt of Archie Alison is very diverting.

The said Archie has lately decided 'That a verbal contract does not require to be stamped'. And that, there being a dispute whether a house, where articles had been left that were sought to be paid for, belonged to a mother, her daughter, or her son – who all lived in it – it must, in the absence of all other evidence, be held by the sons, 'In respect that as he admits that he is of the male sex, the presumption of law is in favour of the *dignior persona*'. Also, that when furnishings are ordered by an unmarried and minor daughter, who is living in family with her widowed father, for his house, the daughter is bound to pay '*in respect*' that she dealt, and was dealt with, as *praeposita rebus domesticis* in his family. A very curious head.

1 Archibald Alison (1792–1867); adv. 1814. Sheriff of Lanark 1834–67; created Bt 1852.

I go tomorrow to Kirklands, to see Hope taken away next day.[1] We tell Richardson that he is to be Be-Reeved.

Ever

H. Cockburn

My Dear Mrs Jeffrey

Your lady friends here are going to send you to Coventry for non-writingness. If you've nothing else to say, can't you describe your emotions?

Keilor the confectioner disposed last week of all his stock by raffle, at 1/- a ticket. A beggar boy begged till he made up a shilling, with which he bought a ticket; and the ragged little wretch got the chief prize – a grand bride's cake – valued at £6. 6. 0. He squeezed thro' the crowd to get it; but struck with its size, and purity, and magnificence, was afraid to touch it with his muddy paws. So he ran out calling, 'Eh! Keep it till I get my mother!' I have not ascertained whether they ate or sold.

Ever

H. C.

To James Ballantine
BL Add. 45,918.70

Bonaly, by Colinton, 12 October 1842

Dear Sir

In order to assist me in attempting to perform the task you have made me, very rashly and unworthily, undertake, I would wish you would tell me something of Mr Roberts's history,[2] and of what are held to be his *particular* merits as an artist. I know that Architectural representation is his principal line, and that in that he is unrivalled; but what are his peculiar excellencies in this walk? And what is his peculiar position is an artist now? What is his main triumph? Has he any object, in the prosecution of which he needs, or from Edinr can get, encouragement? In short tell me what I am to say. Because you are aware that I am one of the many who, with a strong disposition to add Art to Scotland's other eminences, and therefore occasionally presuming to appear

1 Henry Reeve married Hope Richardson (1815–42) on 28 December 1841. She died 27 November 1842, following the birth of a daughter. A *Times* journalist from 1840, Reeve became editor of the *Edinburgh Review* from 1855 till his death in 1895.

2 David Roberts (1796–1864) had by 1840 made a name for himself after working as a scenery-painter and then travelling in France, on the Rhine and in Spain. His architectural interests (they included a design for a Scott memorial) embraced an interest in John Knox House.

among artists, am *totally* ignorant of Art, and utterly unworthy to speak a word on the subject – and this I say from no affectation of humility, but because it is so true that it would be absolutely ludicrous to say anything else. So tell me a few good, and useful topicks connected with Mr Roberts, as an artist, and as a man.

And remember that this is all *private*.

Yours Faithfully
H. Cockburn

To Mrs Leonard Horner (née Lloyd)
NLS 2213.205

Edinburgh, 28 December 1842

My Dear Mrs Horner

Pray complete the address of the enclosed letter to Miss Winthrop, and put it into a post office, if she be not with you.

We have got yours, containing our first tidings of her fate, today. No doubt it would have happened long ago, had it not been for sensible men's horror of the knife – and her own remorse at violating the pledge to me which that implement attests. I could forbid the banns; but have magnanimously resolved not to do so. I do trust that she will be happy, as I am sure she deserves to be.

As to the leg – no doubt, generally speaking, two are better than one; chiefly because after one is gone, there is only one more to go. But I never can forget the case of a nice, merry, warm hearted, Hebe looking, English girl, who thirty years ago was the greatest friend of Mrs Cockburn and her sisters and associates, and is still an attached Scotch-living intimate. She came to me in great agitation, to consult about an offer she had just got, of marriage. She had hardly any relations, and not a penny; nothing but her beauty, her sunny gaiety, and her excellent virtues. The offerer was one of the best living men, very rich, universally popular, a gentleman, good looking, and very agreeable – but minus a leg. It was an offer worthy of the first girl in the land, and seemed to me like a special Providence to her. But, like an ass, she would not swallow the leg – in spite of all my demonstrations that the want of it, by making him more domestic [than] otherwise, was a positive advantage. It stuck in her throat. Some years after, she captivated a biped – a laird and a soldier; and another lady, a friend of her own, gave her heart to the surviving leg. What was the result? They are both now widows, each having lost her only child. But the spouse of the uniped lived respected and happy, and beloved by her husband, and is now mistress of a large jointure and a gorgeous house. She of the biped

[178]

got two legs, and a drunkard – who muddled away his character and substance, and after making her married life a course of wretchedness left her to poverty and bitter recollections.

From all which I conclude that there are better things [than] a leg.

We are all well – at least Wellish – for Mrs C. has for nearly two months been confined to the house by an insignificant swelled vein, for which abstinence from walking is enjoined. But in general health, and spirits, she is quite well. Jane is quite well; tho' also nursing herself as a house plant.

Archd is going to settle in Ross, *the* man whereof I hope he may prove.[1] But to help him to this, his friends must do what they can. And therefore if you be not restrained by that most contemptible piece of illiberality and nonsense which would have tended to exclude Esculapius and Sir Matthew Bailley[2] from genteel society because, tho' doctors of the first eminence, they were not doctors in London, do, I beg of you, give him an introduction or two, if you can. Not a recommendation, but a bare introduction. And tell Miss Winthrop to do the same – and to compel her spouse to do it. And Lyell – and everybody.

I am sorry to observe what you say as to Leonard's requiring Cabs. Time, care, and above all the habit of such steady exercise as is good for him, must gradually make him the same John Taaffe. My ambulatory powers are encreasing daily. Ten miles at a stretch is nothing to me. See what virtue, and chiefly temperance and exercise, do. Jeffrey, with whom I dine today, is *quite* well. In intellect, tongue, and bodily activity – as well as ever.

I hope the Memoirs are proceeding.[3] I am one of those who have a confident expectation that it must prove entertaining and useful.

Poor Hope Richardson! An irrecoverable loss.

I meditate giving myself to the Pentlands for ten days – and the more cordially should snow cover them.

Remember me to your household – including the Lyells.

Ever

H. Cockburn

1 i.e. recalling John Kyrle (1637–1724), the local benefactor lauded by Alexander Pope.
2 Matthew Baillie (1761–1823), physician and anatomist, brother of Joanna Baillie.
3 They were published in March 1843; see *Jnl,* ii, 10–12.

To William Gibson-Craig
HWUA; 2/C/4
                    Bonaly, 29 March 1843
My Dear Craig

I have just got the Aerial Transit Bill, about which I have sundry jokes and puns – all excellent – but I refrain from letting them out, because I really can't satisfy myself whether the printing of the Bill be, or be not, a House of Commons hoax. But I know one member of the Scotch bar – a very sensible young man, in a good deal of business – who *for two years* has assured me that he believes in this Atmospheric Mail coach. If they be really serious, tell our heathery headed Lord Advocate to look after section 20, which interferes with his accusative privileges.

I trust that Mrs Craig and the bairns are well. Remember me to the former.

I was glad to see your vote about the Kirk.[1] No one cares less for churches than I do; or can have less faith in parsons. And if they had only got fair play, I dare say I might have seen even the Kirk of Scotland – tho' the only good one, in the way of cheapness, working, residence, and absence of political power, in the world – extinguished, with some indifference. But I can see little in the struggle but a factious desire, operating even on the bench, by the Moderate party, to suppress their rivals. Dr Gordon's new '*Free*' church, I am told, is begun. If Government could be made to understand the subject, and to care about it, the whole case could be settled in half an hour.

Of course you have your civic eye on the Water Company.[2] They no doubt make us pay dear, for a small quantity of bad water, and are very offensive. But on the other hand, that modest man Duncan Maclaren thinks he secures his return next election, by telling the people that they may all drink liquid crystal, till they have dropsies, for nothing, if they will only believe him to be infallible. But all this is of course of no consequence, either way. The important thing is the Bonaly Burn. I hear hints of designs against it. If such a damnable project transpire, or be detectible, I rely on your sounding the Toc-fin,[3] instantly, and loudly.

1 On ecclesiastical business in the House, see *Jnl*, ii, 6–10, 12–18. 'Then for the crash!', HC remarked of the imminent Assembly, as prologue to a long and generally concerned disquisition in the Journal.
2 The growing civic demand for water had led to major changes in organisation. A Water Company had been formed in 1810, and was given enhanced powers in 1826 and again in 1843. As the new installations were fed from hills to the south, local landowners (including HC at Bonaly) had to be increasingly vigilant.
3 HC's spelling, 'toc-fin', is explained in *Sedition Trials*, ii, 5. It echoes Lord Eskgrove's habitual mispronunciation. In 1794 a time of gross national sensitivity to borrowings from the French, the word had excited much judicial disapproval.

Cold, easterly, weather. Ice half an inch thick this morning. But neither mavises nor primroses seem to feel it. Rutherfurd will be with you before this will. He likes to enjoy the pleasures of London; which he tells the Leithers is attending to their business in Parliament. By a letter from Jeffrey today, he seems to be in the heart of it. Too much for a shabby trachea. Or for an author of about 70, who is selecting his Reviews for publication. I have been greatly delighted with Horner's Memoirs.[1] Many of your derisive and fastidious people will turn up their noses at them. But as an example of what may be done at 38, without rank, fortune, office, genius, or eloquence, but by mere sense, industry, good principles, and a good heart, Horner's is an invaluable history.

How are things looking publickly? Any second coming for the Whigs? Is it not funny to see Joseph and Brougham joined in thanking Government? The noble Lord is clearly crazy.

It is comfortable to see what a degree of lunacy is consistant with high place. I know other two plainly deranged men who sit on lofty stools.

I saw Sir James t'other day – apparently quite well.

Ever

H. Cockburn

To David Roberts
NLS 14,386.101

Edinr, 27 October 1843

My Dear Sir

I regret sincerely not having seen you. You must come earlier next year, and let me know of your arrival before you be just on the wing home again.

I was at Roslyn last week; and thoroughly agree with you about that state and prospects of the Chapel.[2] I have sent your letter, as I did your former one, to Lord Roslyn's agent. He had told me, before I last heard from you, that his Lordship intended to glaze the windows, chiefly in consequence of your opinion, but he was not sanguine as to the result.

In this situation of matters, it will be prudent to abstain, for the present, from any appeal to the public thro' the press. Lord Roslyn and his father have, as I am told, laid out about £2000 on the preservation of this relic; being the largest sum, I suppose, ever laid out by any Scotchman on such

1 Francis Horner's *Memoirs* are commented on in *Jnl*, ii, 10–12.
2 On the chapel at Roslin, see McWilliam, *Buildings of Scotland: Lothian* (1978), 409–17.

an object; and therefore they are entitled to great consideration and tenderness.

But Alas! Alas! What are we talking about! Green Mould? Groined Arches? Tracery? Why, it is *said* that the Chapel is in danger of being given up for a Meeting House for living Episcopalians!!! So it is *said*. But I can't believe it. I have great faith in the triumph of rent over taste – but this is surely impossible.

Yours Faithfully
H. Cockburn

To Mrs Leonard Horner
NLS 2213.248

Bonaly, 18 February 1844

Well, My Dear Mrs Horner, since Sir George Young is such a blockhead as not to be relating to my own knife's husband, and since Something Lyall is such another blockhead as not be related to Mary Horner's Lyell, you or Leonard must do the job yourself. And a very simple one it is, if you would but set about it.

Frank's Writership is for Madrass. All I want is to get it changed for an appointment to Bengal.[1] That is, I give a Madrass appointment for a Bengal one. For health or money, the Madrass is the best. But I prefer Bengal, partly because I have some needy kin in Madrass who I wish Frank to avoid, and partly because George is rising high in Bengal, and he could help Frank.

So do, pray, catch a good natured Director, and make him be reasonable. Now don't shake your head and regret, etc. All stuff. You, Leonard, and Mary – nothing can perswade me that you three could not get this done, in a week, if you set about it. Tell Frances and Susan that I look to them too. What shawls I'll make him send them if they succeed! *Seriously*, I have seldom been as anxious about anything, and if you can aid me, you will very greatly oblige me.

We are all well. Mrs C. and I came here yesterday – our second visit since the 1st of November. We go to Edinburgh on Tuesday morning – till the 12th of March – when we settle amid our hills for a long while. The weather is that of a mild April. The mavises are in great spirits. Singing today, Sunday tho' it be, as if, like me, they belonged to the *Free* church. It is a fact that our last

1 HC achieved this improved posting; after leaving Haileybury in 1845 Frank joined the Bengal Civil Service, retiring from a judgeship there in 1873.

December was, on the whole, warmer than our last June! I have been powdering my round-the-house grass with soot; from which I expect a glorious flush of verdure.

Do you know much about carpets? You once sent us a capital one, which covers our Edinr drawing room still. I want one – or will want it soon – for the dining room here – about 22 feet by 18. I should like a Turkey, if they were not so dear as of old. What are they now in your all-producing city? *I will thank you to write and tell me this.* (Why should you not give me a present of one, as your Tower contribution?)

Archd is to be married, at last, to his long betrothed Miss Balfour, in about three weeks.[1] She is an excellent person – sensible, well principled, amiable, rather clever, a considerable musician, and not at all either elegant or good looking. He is doing very well at Ross. I suspect that I will not be able to refuse a visit there either this Autumn, or some other. If I should – in August – can we make any combined movement out of it?

Jeffrey's leg is unsound, being discoloured; and the cure – water and vegetable, seclusion and no walking – is adverse to his nature. But, except that he has what is called a disease, he is quite well; and his intellect was never more bright, nor his spirits more gay. Jeffrey's mind still sparkling, in spite of the total absence of wine, roast mutton, exercise, and society, is truly the triumph of soul over matter. He will be in London in March.

No. 11 is in his wonted youth and beauty.[2] But some silver covers have seduced the body into eighteen-seated dinners, regularly closed by balls. He never thinks of seeing us in the old natural way. But he is nailed for the 2nd of March. For Lauder and I take possession of his house that day, *with our own party;* so Goodbye to his eighteens, and silver dishes, and balls for once. Come down, my dear Leonard, and let us have one other old evening. The poor devil does not yet know his fate. But he is hooked.

Edinr is gayer with balls this winter than it has been for some winters past. And even that town is yearly encreasing in beauty. The new spire at the head of the Lawn market is perfect – and perfectly planned.[3] And Scott's monument, tho' ill, that is oddly, placed, and subject to all sorts of criticism, is fast rising into the finest modern Gothic Cross in the island. But these tyrannical beasts who own rail ways are going to be allowed by the House of Commons

1 'The Man of Ross' married Mary (d.1903), daughter of James Balfour of Pilrig.
2 Æneas Macbean.
3 The Tolbooth church, Castle Hill, at the head of the Lawnmarket, by Gillespie Graham and A.W.N. Pugin, 1839–44. Now given over to secular use.

Committee of rail way men, to bring the Glasgow one thro' the Princes Street Gardens!!! Oh! Oh!

Remember me to all your people – Lyells included. And write me a line soon about Carpets and Writerships. Tell Frances and Susan that they will find Graham Maitland in Hughes Lodgings, Dover Street, with her brother Stewart and his wife.

Ever

H. Cockburn

And kiss Miss Young's bairn for me when you next see it. And give my love to her.

To William Gibson-Craig
HWUA: 2/C/29
Edinburgh, 5 March 1844
My Dear Craig

I hope you are taking charge of Edinr, by protecting it against these railway barbarians.

The people here, even those who curse their projects, are so fond of their own purses, that, as you know, no opposition will be made, on the score of taste, to the beasts getting thro' the gardens. In this situation the only practical object is to avoid as much mischief as we can. The Promoters, as they call themselves, have professed their willingness, I am told, to do every thing practicable for the protection of the gardens; even to the *covering up* of their way thro' the ground west of the Mound. Of course all these professions will be disregarded the moment the Bill is past, if they be left free. I am aware that, to a certain extent, you must defer to the views of the worst portion of your constituents, but *if* anything can be done to lessen the abomination, do do it.

What ought to be done, I can't say. The general object is to give them as little ground as possible, to let them disfigure as little as possible by broad ugly banks, and to prevent the smoke and grunting of the engines, by making them *haul*, not steam, past Princes Street. Their proposal to heighten the Little Mound, and to remove it 100 feet further west, is horrible: because it makes the valley east of the Mound a hole. Touching this valley at all, and repealing the act which protects it, is a scandalous violation of the understanding on which the Improvement tax was submitted to.

The apathy of the public to these matters is most disgraceful. If it was proposed to erect a distillery and a slaughter house on the top of the Calton, there are not fifty gentlemen in Edinr who would give 5/- a year to prevent it. The duty of a right minded committee is the clearer.

Have you any balm to pour into my wounded taste? D—m.

Ever

H. Cockburn

To Sir Thomas Dick Lauder
NLS Acc.3733(8)

Bonaly, 23 March 1844

My Dear Sir Thos

I cannot be at the meeting on Monday.

If I were, I cannot conceive the Logic or Eloquence that could convince me that money subscribed for the honor of a man called Scott, should be applied to the honor of another man called Kemp.[1]

You are surely aware that, however wrong you or I may deem the opinion, there are dozens of Subscribers who, contributing for Scott, think the monument, architecturally, bad – yea, abominable. Does it not strike you as funny that these men should be made to pay – and out of their Scott subscriptions – for the glory of the very fabricator of what they think this abomination?

What can I say more?

Ever

H. Cockburn

To William Gibson-Craig
HWUA: 2/3/32

Bonaly, 28 March 1844

My Dear Craig

Any hope for us? I mean for Taste against the Railway? I am horrified at what I understand to be the d——ble project about the Little Mound. That Mound to be carried westward, to be raised; a Street to be driven, across the valley, direct from Princes Street, to a Station House to be erected on the *top* of the raised Mound!!! Which Station House is to stick up, in conspicuous and insulting deformity, sneering at both new town and old. God damn them all. Most cordially and

---

1 George Meikle Kemp had been drowned, falling into the Union Canal at Fountainbridge ('drunk as usual', HC commented in a letter to Jeffrey on 10 April: see *Bic. Comm.* 61) on 6 March.

devoutly do I utter this prayer. Yes – seriously – may God damn them all, conjunctly and severally. I should snicker with joy over their bankruptcy.

And there that poor, shitten, beast Rutherfurd goes to London on Saturday, no doubt to do what he, as M.P. for the Lothian Cinque Ports (Stink Ports) can do, to aid our worthy Chief Magistrate in destroying the city that he has sworn to protect. God damn them both – particularly. I wrote to Loch about it yesterday. But he ! – the iron has entered into his soul! The beauty of it all is, that if the Committee had sense and honesty to say, 'Gentlemen, Railway, you be d——d. Settle with Lord Cockburn *how* it is to be done', it would be done in three days, and the rail get thro' – *but on conditions.* But knowing that nothing of this tendency will be said, the savages go on doing it all with every aggravation of useless brutality. What do you think that some of the Town Council are said to be saying? Why – that the more destructively to Gardens that the rail way proceeds, *the better*, because it hastens the day when the Eastern valley will all be built upon, and the Western made into a *Cattle Market* – and that in this way the Grass Market might be *saved.* Oh! God, smite! – hip and thigh. *Train* them up in the way they should go!!

I rejoice in the ten hours clause.[1] Because, of course, it will prevent John Hope from speaking above ten hours. Oh! if Ashley knew the misery undergone by the factory old boys of the Second Division. But for this, what a piece of stuff that fanaticism of humanity is. I can't conceive such tyranny as to tell a strong, willing, and starving *man*, that he *shall* not sell above a certain number of hours of his own labour per day. But so [far] as the John Hope clause be carried, or understood, I wish it all success.

D——m them.

Ever

Each Sea

To Francis Jeffrey
NLS Dep 235(1)
Bonaly, 10 May 1844
My Dear J.

Thanks for your letter, which I got today. It is not so good as I would like, but is better than I expected. For we have been greatly alarmed by

---

1 The Ten Hours clause (limiting child employment in factories) had been steered through Parliament by Lord Ashley, MP. John Hope, Justice-Clerk, was known to be a noisy and tenacious speaker.

rumours, which we have had no means of appretiating. I don't think your friends here were ever more disturbed – not even on the day you were taken ill in court, 2 or 2½ years ago. I was dining at Dunfermline's last Tuesday, with Ivory, Alex Monteith, and Coventry,[1] and the first tidings we had of your being ill was by a note from somebody saying everything was bad, but nothing certain – and we had a very silent feast. I am glad now to know the truth.

I trust that you progress. Your being here by the 20th is not to be expected, nor perhaps desired. But pray do not stick to the feeling of neither dying nor resigning. Either would be very foolish. I have sent your letter to Mrs James Craig. I met her yesterday at dinner at Dreghorn, and, on comparing surmises, we could make out no probability.

Remember me to all the Charlottes, and Empson.

Jane came here yesterday; the first time she has crossed the door since October, and she has not been the worse of it. We are thinking of German baths for her. All the rest are well.

If you have seen, I hope you are not displeased with James Moncreiff's article on your Essays, in the North British.[2] I think it not only the best thing in the work, but excellent, and far beyond what I could have expected. The feeling of personal kindness and reverence is very creditable to his sense and heart.

The Pundit affects to despise his rival, but is really alarmed; they have sold about 3000, and are now printing a fourth thousand. Napier has (I understand) had a remonstrance with Brewster[3] for grinding beyond the old Edinr thirle. It seems that he considers all his men who go to the enemy as deserters. I can't say that there is much *in the No.* to disturb him. But there is a great deal *in the circumstances* which have produced a new review.[4] He has brought it on himself partly by the paltriness of never even alluding in the Edinr to the late national struggle. His Review could not sympathise with the fanaticism of the Wild; but as little could it justify the extravagances of the courts, and the suppression of the people; and a wise middle man was just what was wanted.

1 Probably Andrew Coventry (1801–77); adv. 1823.
2 See *Jnl,* ii, 71–2. Macvey Napier was anxious about the new journal as a threat to his *Edinburgh.*
3 Sir David Brewster (1791–1868), then Principal of St Andrews.
4 For a brief history and authenticated list of attributions of articles in this wholly anonymous quarterly (which continued publication till 1871), see W.E.Houghton, *Wellesley Index of Victorian Periodicals,* I (1968), 633–95. Bracketed attributions in the list below have been added from Houghton.

The authors of the ten Art[icle]s in this No. are all Free Churchmen – besides We[l]sh the Editor. They are:

1. Brewster
2. [A. Coventry Dick]
3. Chalmers
4. John Gordon
5. [R. Winter Hamilton]
6. Ed. Maitland
7. Norwegian Laing
8. Candlish
9. A. Dunlop
10. Moncreiff

By the way – Alex Dunlop! I rejoice to say it – he has become rich.[1] He is to marry a Miss Murray, who lives in Moray Place, the only child of a West India Merchant, worth, some say, £300,000 – but nobody makes it less than £150,000. The father and daughter are as Free as he is, and it is a harmonious call – on the voluntary principle. I predict that our friend will soon be in Parliament, representing the Free. Meanwhile I rejoice in his well deserved independance. He is to play bowls here tomorrow.

That is, if the rain permits. Because after five weeks' utter drought, we have had, and are still enjoying, a delicious warm, calm shower of about fourteen hours. I had not one drop of rain during the three weeks of my circuit.[2] I contrived, even still, to see something new – such as Kilravock, Cawder, and Pluscarden, one of the best, and best preserved, little old ruined Abbeys. Preserved I mean from Time; but woefully has it suffered from the improvements of Lord Fife; who, when God justly smote him bankrupt, was making it into a shooting box. Having two days over, and finding Thom Erskine, to whom I meant to give them, engaged, I retired to St Andrews – which I never knew before. A most singular and interresting spot. The most *peculiar* place in Scotland. Creeffy was very agreeable and very temperate – but, except in court, very torpid. He was shocked with Mary Fullerton,[3] who is as ardent for

---

1 Alexander Dunlop (of Corsock)(1798–1870); adv. 1820, married on 18 July Eliza Esther (d.1902), only daughter of John Murray, of Edinburgh. He was MP for Greenock 1852–68, and Procurator for the Free Church, 1843.

2 For this Circuit, see *CJ* 211–37. Kilravock (pp.218–19) includes the 'craavats' incident, and there is a particularly full account of St Andrews (see also *Jnl* ii, 61–66).

3 The *CJ* (221–2) reports a theological duel between Moncreiff and HC's niece by marriage, Miss Fullerton: 'I roared with laughter, which the combatants were too keenly occupied to notice.' She later became a Roman Catholic.

Puseyism as he is for Presbytery. They had one or two diverting onsets; in which the calm and gentle brevity of the young lady had immensely the advantage of the vehement bigotry of the Learned Lord. He says, since he came home, 'I am very sorry for her poor father'– [*Rest missing*]

To Macvey Napier
BL Add.34,624.621; Napier, *Corr.*, 1879, 473)
              Bonaly, 9 October 1844
My Dear Napier
      For this autumn, we seem to be doomed. On Saturday and Sunday, this domicil is full. And two of the fillers are Londoners, on whom I am pledged to attend, and to execute arranged ploys with them, in and about Edinr, on Monday and Tuesday, and indeed almost the whole of next week.
      At all which I do, most sincerely, assure you that I am grieved and vexed. But it really has been, and is, unavoidable.
      I regret particularly not seeing your sons; to whom I beg to be remembered.
      Mrs Cockburn saw Jeffrey yesterday; looking thin, but well; and not the worse that he is still most eloquent in his demonstrations of his dreadful maladies. I am to breakfast with him, with my Londoners (both female) on Friday.
      I rejoice in the Anticipation of another birth from the Macaulay Muse.[1] But, tho' I incur your contempt by the sentiment, I think the brilliancy of his style, especially on historical subjects, the worst thing about him. Delighting, as I always do, in his thoughts, views and knowledge, I feel too often compelled to curse, and roar at, his words, and the structure of his composition. As a corruptor of stile, he is more dangerous to the young than Gibbon. His seductive powers greater; his defects worse. But still I rejoice in all his deliveries.
                                        Ever
                                        H. Cockburn

To Sir Thomas Dick Lauder
NLS 15,974.186
              Bonaly, 24 October 1844
My Dear Sir Thos
      I wonder if you've come home yet. If you have, look at the last Town

1 HC had been reading Macaulay (on Barrère) in a recent *ER* (*CJ*, 237); his *Lays* (1842) and *Essays* (1843) had recently appeared.

Council proceedings, and you will see the *Provost*[1] *encouraging* an attempt to make the flat ground South of the Monument into *a market*!!! A beautiful and appropriate finish. D—m them. Our protectors will succeed in getting Edinr destroyed at last. It would make the monument absolutely absurd.

My impression is that the Statute ordains that whole valley, east of the Mound, to be kept as '*an ornamental garden*'. If this be the fact, what Black says about the possibility of having a market without buildings is immaterial.

But, besides, no market can be without buildings. Walls, and booths, are buildings.

Devil take these tasteless, yet presumptuous, beasts. It is only ten years since they wanted to have the gallows erected on the Calton Hill; and it is not thirty-five since the Town Council actually approved of a row of public Privies along the Northern slope of the Castle Hill, fronting Princes Street; from which truly magisterial decoration we were rescued solely by the energy of Mary, Lady Clerk.[2] The Provost's principle – and dangerous one for a magistracy – is utility. As if anything were more useful than public taste – i.e. the absence of brutality.

But are you at Grange, or still in Ultima Thule? If I thought there was any chance of getting you, I would ask you and Lady Lauder to dine here *tomorrow*. Nobody but my brother Robert and his spouse. *And I do ask you.* Why not? Short, no doubt, but a sark is easily turned. So I won't despair. Six, for mastication, but as soon as you like for a walk. I long to hear your log book.

Ever

H. Cockburn

To David Octavius Hill
Royal Scottish Academy
Bonaly, 23 August 1845

My Dear Sir

It seems to me that you have the best of it, both in facts and in spirit, in the correspondence.

But really it is distressing to see the Academy or the Arts obstructed and disturbed by such contemptible squabbles.[3] The Academy has been the

---

1 Adam Black (1784–1874), the publisher, Lord Provost 1843–8, and later Liberal MP for Edinburgh 1856–65.

2 Mary, Lady Clerk (d.1866), *née* Law, wife of Sir George Clerk of Penicuik, 6th Bt.

3 For the atrabilious row between the Academy and the Royal Institution see *Bic. Comm*, 66, and Esmé Gordon, *The Royal Scottish Academy* (1976).

injured, and attacked, and provoked party – as it appears to me; and it has done no more than its own defence required. But still, these are low matters for such a body to be degraded and pestered by. And it will never be out of them, so long as it depend solely on the Justice of the Managing Institutionists, who, I firmly believe, will never have any tolerance for any Artists who dare to breathe thro' their own nostrils.

You must appeal therefore to others – chiefly to the public.

For this purpose an Exposition of the rise, progress, present state, and prospects of the Academy ought to be made out, and circulated – an Exposition satisfactory to candid gentlemen, and therefore not unfit for Government. Not one that makes everything obscure – at least to idle readers – by accumulating all the little odds and ends of circumstances, but one that makes the Academy's claim on public protection clear by well selected simplicity. With no necessary accusation or refutation, but calm, relevant, and plain in its results.

There has been a good deal of this kind written and circulated already; but only in detached bits and for special objects. I am often asked by the well inclined where they can see the Case stated, and I feel that I can never refer them to any one thing. The power of such a reference is essential.

And I suspect that it ought to be made out by a person not an Academician. Simply because however able and well written the Academy manifestoes have been, they *necessarily* partake more of the little details than a careless public cares for.

You have willing workers in Moir, Logan and others. If I had my own way, I would have it done by Mr James Moncreiff Advocate – a safe and skilful hand. Give him a decent £10.10. fee, and get it done as a matter of business. It would *very* greatly aid the cause if you could get Mr Moir to give you an article in the Edinr or Quarterly Review; not on anything polemical, but on the Condition and Prospects of Scotch Art – with *intelligible allusions.*

If you could do without the public, all these courses might be disregarded. If you can't, then the public must be instructed. Anyhow, expect nothing from the Institution or the Trustees *left to themselves.*

Rutherfurd, who has read the recent printed correspondence, spoke to me of all this subject yesterday. He will do anything proper that can be required. But he too lamented that he could scarcely understand the matter, and wished that a clear statement existed.

Your appealing to the members of the Institution individually is a wise move.

I hope that the Provost and the Sherriff will stand firm. But, however firm, if they be merely passive, they will do [no] more good than the Castle Rock – which is quite firm. How is it passed over in such silence in the town council?

I go from home on Monday, and will be away almost all September.

Yours Faithfully

H. Cockburn

To William Sharpe
WS Library

Bonaly, by Colinton, 10 October 1845

Dear Sir

One good turn, they say, deserves another. And this too often means that when a man has done you one favour, you may ask him to do you a second.

It is now sixteen years since I took the liberty of asking you to find me a good gig horse, and said that I was so sensible of my own ignorance, and had such confidence in you, that I would not even look at [it] till after it was actually bought.[1] You sent me the *absolute perfection* of a steed, which has served me, without a headache, from that day to this. But time is at last doing him so fast, that I must have a successor.

Can you oblige me in the same way again?

What I want is not a showy, or a fine, horse – but a strong, practical beast. His chief business is to draw a family droskie. But he must also condescend occasionally to draw a plough, and even a cart, tho' these ought, *visibly*, to be beneath his dignity. He must be of the masculine gender, tho' deprived of certain masculine parts and partinents. The only colour I object to is *white*. The colour I would prefer is mixed black and grey – a mottled pepper and salt – because I have one of this colour already. The Age ought not to be above six.

But above all, don't send me an idiot. The last horse was a Type. Good sense, good manners, good temper, and good principles, a moderate Whig, attached to the Free church (tho' this last I have sometimes suspected was owing to the superiority of the Free to the Established Stable), never a moment ill, and always ready to eat.

In short you see what I want. A strong, practical, punch; with legs something like Lord Craigie's, and an understanding like Sir Harry Moncreiff's.

I am ready to receive him whenever you can find him; but am in no hurry

1 Cockburn's similar letter to Sharpe, [1829] is printed above, p. 102.

whatever. And I suppose that such an article might be got, at this season, for £20 or £30. The last one cost £30.

I scarcely know how to ask you to excuse this liberty. All I can say is that you have brought it on yourself by your past kindness.

Yours Faithfully

H. Cockburn

To Macvey Napier
BL Add.34,625.480; Napier *Corr.*, 1879, 511

Bonaly, Colinton, 22 October 1845

My Dear Napier

Can you spare me 25 or 30 pages of your next number, for an article written by myself?

The subject, like all mine in the Review, is Scotch, and practical. It is upon our criminal practice, including an estimate of David Hume's work. My chief object is to assail the Native Vigour.[1] And my bile has been raised against this extravagant pretension by the whole of my brethern having, some time ago, deliberately and solemnly re-asserted it.

I have been in communication with Plain John[2] upon this, to him incredible, point; and he swears another Session shall not pass without his introducing a Bill to declare it not law.

There are several other matters besides this in my contemplation – I mean for this article.

You may have it, if you wish it, soon after the court meets.

The only thing that grieves me is that Davie Bole will certainly go mad. For tho', to avoid this, I shall pay many undeserved compliments to his dearly beloved Justiciary, still I must expose and disdain much that he has all his life been idolising.

I heard of your late illness with great concern – I trust that all is right now, and that you are not ill prepared for the approaching campaign.

Ever

H. Cockburn

1 On this see also *Jnl,* ii, 146–7.
2 John Campbell (1779–1861), barrister 1806. MP for Edinburgh 1834–41; created Baron 1841; Lord Chancellor of Ireland 1841; Lord Chancellor 1859.

To Macvey Napier
BL Add.34,625.482; *loc. cit.,* 512
Bonaly, 25 October 1845

My Dear Napier

I fancy that I perceive a lurking aversion in you to have any concern with an article that may redden Davie's face when he looks at you.[1] If it be so, act on that feeling, which is a very natural one, and decline it. I do not suppose that I should have any difficulty in finding another vent.

For this discussion must take place. If Boyle be a man of sense, his sentiment ought to be one of gratitude for being, he and his court, so handsomely treated as they will be. If (as I suspect) nothing will please him, except that an abominable principle, and a dangerous evil, shall not be discussed or explained, because his court is the scene of it, then he must just be displeased. But it never occurred to me, or to your editorial prædecessor, that this was any reason why a public question should not be treated of, and even agitated.

As to myself, my feeling is that an abuse being in danger of being legalised in a Judge's own court only encreases the duty he is under to sound the Tock-fin.

If you be really dissuaded to receive the article, then I may say that *I don't expect it* to exceed thirty of your pages. But I can't calculate what my MSS. will print, and it *may* be more. But I don't think it.

So you don't know what the Native Vigour is? May you never feel it! The Review knows something of it however. *See* vol.39, pp.340, 368, 383. It is the power claimed, *and actually exercised,* by the Justiciary, of declaring any act that it pleases to be a crime – i.e. of indicting and transporting you for editing the Edinr Review, or me for having large nails in my shoes. But the explanation of this outrageous extravagance, the existance of which the public is not aware of, is only about a third of the article.

Let me hear from you, if you think it necessary, once more. And again, have no delicacy whatever with *me.*

Ever

H. Cockburn

Don't resign any thing rashly. Your giving up the class *may* be wise, but not now.

---

1 Napier was (from 1837) a Clerk of Session as well as editor of *ER.* Napier was authorised to make references to 'Davie' Boyle more flattering, so long as he was not attributed talents he conspicuously lacked, 'such as learning, manner, and talent' (BL Add. 34625, 521–3).

John Hill Burton[1]
NLS 3005.171
Bonaly, Colinton, 17 March 1846

My Dear Burton

I have just finished David – and cannot resist the pleasure of telling you how much I have been instructed and delighted.

The Collection of his letters, now, for the first time, put into order, would, of itself, make an invaluable book. But you have connected and explained them by most judicious observations; and have walked over the burning ploughshares which fanaticism and faction will for ever set in the way of any biographer of Hume, with great felicity. You may expect a scurrilous personal attack in the Quarterly, and sundry snarls from lesser teeth. Those who cannot be religious without being intollerant will never forgive you for being fair. And let them do their worst. The humane purety of David's life, and the almost divine tranquillity of his death, have done more in favour of true religion than all that his speculative doubts have ever done against it. The real question is whether, *religion and his speculations being properly understood,* these two be at all inconsistent.

Tho' the heathen therefore will certainly rage, and the bigots imagine vain things, they can do no harm to the biographer, who has performed his part with a more complete avoidance of offence than one would have thought possible.

It is so natural for an ill used man to retort violently that, to my mind, the great proof of Hume's real worth and magnanimity is to be found in the fact that he was never tempted to throw off all restraint, and to expose the intollerant, in the style of Swift or Voltaire.

Did you ever hear of this epitaph? I saw it once in a little, paltry, duodecimo, notice of great Scotchmen, in alphabetical order, and I have never found anyone who was aware of it –

Within this circular idea,
Called commonly a tomb,
Th'impressions and ideas lie,
That constituted Hume.

Rather a neat joke on his metaphysicks. It is more than probable that you know it already.

Yours Faithfully
H. Cockburn

---

1 John Hill Burton (1809–81); adv. 1831, historian and essayist, began his literary career with the two-volume *Life and Correspondence of David Hume* (1846). William Empson reviewed it in *ER*, January 1847, 1–72; W.C. Lake in the *Quarterly.*

To Francis Jeffrey
NLS Dep.235(1)
       Bonaly, 26 March 1846
My Dear Jeffrey

    My daughter Graham wants a letter of introduction for her Revd Spouse to Lord Holland, under whose British Ambassadorship they are at Leghorn.[1] I don't know anybody so likely to be easily able to get this – or to give it, if you know the Noble Lord – as you. So, I wish you would try it. The Introduced is the Revd Robert Stewart, Leghorn. Send any letter you may give, or get, here, and we shall forward it to him.

    I was glad to learn from Harriet Brown that you had made a successful journey. Are you going to Torquay, as I heard?

    Remember me to the Empsons. And to Jones.

    Eliza Maitland still lingers, but can't linger much longer now, tho' she may for a few weeks.

    Rutherfurd, and lady, left Edinr yesterday, and he means to be in the House tomorrow.

    I forget what day you went, but think it was before our four days of winter. These four days, beginning on the 17th, have settled our spring flowers. The water was frozen in my bason in the forenoon. Sir T. Brisbane's[2] Thermometer at Mackerston was at 6. Adie's in Edinr at 17. Our poor misled Ribeses are done for this year. And several of our rash Hyacinths, that had been tempted out into nearly full blossom, are stretched dead on the ground. Unluckily the sun melted the snow in the forenoon, and left the frost to do its worst at night. However, we are now green again, with plenty buds and mavises.

    I have been reading Burton's Hume – with great pleasure. The biographer's part of it, tho' dullish, is sensible, short, candid and temperate. All that worthy, but unpromising looking, man does, raises him. I am told that even his Bankrupt Law is excellent. What a poor botch young Macintosh has made of his father.[3] I have rarely seen a worse edited book, both from what it leaves out, and what it puts in.

    I am also overhead in the Reports of the English Criminal Law Com[missione]rs. What a complication of unnecessary distinctions and difficulties the

---

1 The 4th (and last) Lord Holland was then Secretary to the Embassy at Florence.
2 General Sir Thomas Makdougall Brisbane had his own laboratory at Makerstoun; Alexander James Adie (1775–1858) was a prominent Edinburgh maker of scientific instruments.
3 *Memoirs of the Life of Sir James Mackintosh*, edited by his son R.J.Mackintosh, 2 vols, 1828.

English law produces by the struggle of the courts to put nonsense upon rational grounds, instead of honestly discarding the nonsense altogether. For example, I see in the papers that, on a trial t'other day for theft, a witness having stated that the woman stolen from was married, Alderson immediately directed an acquital, because the 2/6 taken was not hers but her husband's. And there is page after page in these reports, in order to define, and expound, and qualify, the exact nature of the ownership, actual or constructive, in thefts. The *whole* of which would be avoided if they would simply tolerate the form of the Scotch Indictment, and charge everything stolen as having been 'The property *or in the lawful possession*' of the person from whom the article is taken. This 2/6 was certainly at least in the wife's lawful custody. This one change would save scores of fine distinctions and inconvenient rules. But what can be wondered at in a commercial system under which it was, until last year, *no theft at all* to steal *a dog or a cat* – and this, as I understand it, solely because they were not used for *food*; which seems to be John Bull's criterion of animal value. To steal [a] *bitch* no crime! I doubt if it be a crime, at least a *theft*, at this moment, to steal the whole of Pidcock's Menagerie.

What a strange story this is of George Drysdale, a son of the late Sir William.[1] The ablest and the most amiable boy I almost ever knew, he carried off all honours at our Academy four years ago, and afterwards at Glasgow. He went about two years ago to take a look at Germany, with a younger brother. His clothes were found by the edge of the Danube in, or close by, Vienna, and he himself could never be found. Of course, as the Police told the brother, he was drowned bathing. The poor survivor very nearly died in Vienna – unknown and not understood. The deceased's mother and friends were in the deepest distress; and one or two of our sympathising Academicians made the sad death of Geo. Drysdale the subject of our last prize poems. Well, about a week ago the defunct walks into his mother's house in Heriot Row, and explains that it was all a trick! He says he was in a state of grievous despair of fulfilling the kindly expectations he had excited, and thought it would be less grievous to his friends to lament his death than his failure; and that therefore he had combined this with avoiding suicide, by *pretending* to be drowned; and that he had all this while been teaching in some remote corner of Germany, but had now come to see things

1 George Drysdale (1826–1904) was a pupil at the Academy 1834–41, and *Dux* of each of his seven years there. He later qualified MD (Edinburgh) and became a general practitioner in London.

more correctly. The horror of his resurrection is, among his relations, perhaps greater than their grief for his death. Of course there must be a craze – a sudden Germanising of the noddle. But I never knew a youth apparently so secure, and this chiefly by affection, from such a disease. And the heartlessness of his conduct is the incomprehensible part of it. By his father's settlement his patrimony, in the event of his death, went to his two sisters; and they, on their recent marriages, have got it – which is rather funny – and I presume may keep it.

Tell me all news in your quarter. Except about potatoes – of which I'm tired. Is Rutherfurd to be Lord Advocate, as he supposes – in the summer Session?

Ever

H. Cockburn

To Thomas Cleghorn
NLS Dep.235(1)
Bonaly, 19 July 1846
My Dear Cleghorn

I have a letter from Stuart[1] today in which he says – 'There is not, so far as I know, any prospect of a vacancy among the Sub Inspectors, or of any addition to their numbers. The print works in Scotland are almost entirely in the Glasgow district, and the Sub Inspector for that district is quite competent to discharge the duty. I visited every one of the print works, when I was in Scotland in May.'

So this door seems be to closed against Fergusson. For which I am sorry. But not very. Because a Sub Inspectorship is a nasty avocation, implying constant manufacturing town residence, the odium of spying irregularities, and the great precariousness of everything depending on statutory crotchet, or the caprice of official superiors. I have always thought it below my notions of Fergusson. To be sure, anything is better than hunger or nakedness. But he is neither naked nor hungry. And I cannot doubt that, if he perseveres, something will turn up worthy of him. Tho' I am aware how sad it is to say to a young man, willing and able, 'Just wait', without being able to add, how long, or for what. But at his age, this is better than getting into a line that is unpleasant and uncertain, but conclusive. I do not know what he was

---

1 James Stuart (1775–1849), WS, and from 1836 an Inspector of Factories, who had been acquitted of the murder of Sir Alexander Boswell after the *Beacon* duel.

trained for; but I rarely see anything make up for the want of some of the known and regular avocations, in any of which merit is nearly certain to be at least tolerably successful. Can be preach? bleed? quibble? buy cheap and sell dear? speak Chinese? lay rails? act? teach? – or what? I know his merits as a person of general intelligence, talent, industry, worth, and good conduct and manner – and if I were a rich nobleman in search of a secretary, he would have a nice house within my park, and £500 a year, tomorrow. But these out of the way catches are very difficult to fall in with. Anything in one of the regular lines is much easier.

The present result of all which is, Nil. Only, I wish I could help him. Whenever you, or he, thinks that I can, I rely on your informing me.

Yours Faithfully

H. Cockburn

To Andrew Rutherfurd
NLS 9688.43

Bonaly, 20 August 1846

My Dear R.

It is said that the election to the vacant chair of Natural Philosophy in Glasgow will probably depend on my Lord Rector's vote.

I believe that there are only two placed horses – Thomson and Gray.[1]

Thomson I don't know, and never to my knowledge saw, but I have already heard him spoken of as a rising star in the Mathematical sky. In pure Mathematicks, I have no doubt that he is superior to Gray. But there are two misfortunes in him, in reference to this place. 1st: He has never been accustomed to teach, or even to lecture, 2nd: nor to apply his Mathematicks to the practical matters of such a class. At his age (about 21 or 22) these could scarcely be expected.

Gray I have known, well, for some years. I have stated certain *facts* about him in a certificate, of which I presume you have a copy, among others, which he got in reference to his present Aberdeen chair. I understand that he could obtain the highest attestation from Aberdeen, but thinks it useless, as he has only given one course there.

In the two respects in which Thomson may be doubtful, Gray is certainly liable to no doubt whatever.

1 Gray was already professor at Aberdeen. William Thomson (1824–1907), later Lord Kelvin, received the Glasgow appointment, which he held till 1899.

He is well manner'd, tho' in Society rather modest, properly dressed, sensible, an Established Churchman I believe, and *if* of any politics, gently liberal I should suppose, under forty, married, and has seen a little of the Nat. Phil. world, having once lectured to Mechanicks, then been a Proff. in New Brunswick, then Rector at Inverness, now Proff. in Aberdeen, and known to the scientific in England.

My sole interest in this matter is that Glasgow should get the best practical man.

Ever

H. Cockburn

P.S. But are you living or dead? I am keeping steady to my Bonaly August. And as tranquilly as the present system of nature admits of. Cursing the weather, which is all I do, would be pleasant enough, if it didn't get wearisome. Conceive a world without potatoes! I have not succeeded in getting the idea into my head yet. Think of a child born tomorrow, destined to know a potato only from books! Meanwhile I eat a double quantity, to keep me in mind of them, and that I may instruct the young.

I hope Mrs Rutherfurd is better.

Ever

H. C.

If you will come here on Sunday, you shall have a punch and a pig. Why should not you pick up Empson by the way? If you agree, send the enclosed to him. *If you don't agree, burn it.* But *let me know* in time for piggie.

To John Stuart Blackie[1]
NLS 2622.60

Edinr, 2 October 1846

My Dear Sir

Thanks for your Letter. I hope that the Citizens to whom it is addressed will read it as attentively as I have.

I agree with you in every point. Your two Universities is an absurdity, for the removal of which the Professors of both will never unite, and for quashing which disinterrested force should be applied. Untill you enable, and then compel, your lads to go to you better prepared, and revise your system, and

---

1 John Stuart Blackie (1809–95); adv. 1834, was then Professor of Humanity, Aberdeen; he became Professor of Greek at Edinburgh, 1852–82.

bake the poor crumbs of your paltry bursaries into a small number of substantial loaves, and have one field, and not two, for the academical races, you will do little good. The tree may not die, but it won't flourish.

But my veneration of antiquity, and my conviction of its academic uses, in so far as mere Temples of learning are concerned, are so strong that I should deplore not making what is now King's College the scene of your future glories. The sale of Marischall would put it into decent order.

Why the devil does not some rich heartless idiot, who means to beggar the kindred who have cherished him, since he will do this thing, leave his fortune to our colleges? He might easily be gratified by the adoption of his name, which is the vanity that raises pernicious hospitals.

Your statement that Glasgow is the most vigorous college in Scotland is only correct, in my opinion, in so far as relates to its Junior classes.

Yours Faithfully
H. Cockburn

To Mrs Leonard Horner
NLS 2214.19

Edinr, 25 November 1846

My Dear Mrs Horner

The box arrived today, and its various contents gave the utmost pleasure to the various donees. They are all excellent. I had a knife uplifted after dinner for the purpose of investigating the internal structure of the cheese, or what your Geological friends would call the Stiltonian System, when my arm was arrested by a written notice that it would be the better of being older, and this averted its doom – for the present. The best thing that the box contained however was the kindness that sent it. Many thanks, from us all.

We are all well, Jane as usual. All settled here till the 12th of March. I hope Horner is keeping well. Remember me to him, the Lyells, and everybody.

Do you remember the old Water Coy reservoirs, a little about Here Endeth the Second Lesson? Well these are going to be restored!

Do you remember Habbie's How? Well, that whole Glen, including the Fall (as I understand the scheme) is going to be made into a lake!!

And do you remember the Glen west of Bonaly ending in *The* Linn? Well – that's to be made into a lake – 90 feet deep!!!

And do you remember the wide open moor just to the west of that Linn – where we used to seek mushrooms. Well – two lakes are to be made there!!!!

All that the people of Edinr may get their faces better washed.

They engage not to diminish my burns, to give me a cascade 90 feet high, and to constitute me sole Admiral on the Lochs; and to do me no harm unless they burst, in which case they console me by assuring me that I, and the family, and the Tower, will all be rescued somewhere about Porto Bello.

As they don't actually take, or touch, my land or water, I have no right to object; and had I never known my Pentland world in its old state, probably the new state may be as good. But what will a man give in exchange for his old soul? It really often occurs to me as a great reconciler to death, that one shan't see many scene deforming changes, which towns, manufactures, rail ways, and other advancing abominations are destined to produce.

Meanwhile, let us enjoy our Quince Jelly, Pickled Walnuts, and Stilton Cheeses – to say nothing of old friends and old recollections.

Ever
H. Cockburn

To Andrew Rutherfurd
NLS 9688.49

Edinr, 14 February 1847

My dear R.

James Simpson wishes me to write to you in regard to the Vacant Clerkship, as a good reward for his educational services.[1] I have told him that he could indulge in no rational hope of an office which if not given to a W.S. would only be given to an Advocate, because this would be useful for issues – a mystery for which his better avocations had not prepared him; but that, since he wished it, I would write to you. Which I now do. I certainly wish that his old age could be cherished by some pot-boiler; but I fear that it is not to be found in the law.

Mrs Rutherfurd seems to be the very same John Taaffe. She dines here on Thursday, with Macready.[2]

We are all grieved for the Pundit; an Edinr change, and another of the old set disappearing.[3] When I saw him this day s'ennight, he was full of hopes and plans for summer. He died of the same thing that carried off, in two days, that nice lad William Macbean four years ago – an orifice in one of the pipes of the viscera, not, apparently, connected with his other complaints. Alex Duff[4] will

---

1 James Simpson (1781–1853); adv. 1801. Lecturer, author, phrenologist.
2 William (Charles) Macready (1793–1873), the actor.
3 Napier had died on 11 February.
4 Alexander Duff (1800–54); WS 1823; adv. 1848.

probably succeed him as Professorial Formulist. The Review, I fear, will, after distinguishing Edinr for forty-nine years, go, and die, in London. Murray is clear that it should be given to Burton – on the score of his *taste*!!! Others are positive that Edward Maitland is the man.[1] A capital man, but I should not have thought of him for this work.

All reasonable men are pleased with Gordon and Aberdeen.[2] I wished him and Wilson joy yesterday in the Exhibition; and do feel, cordially, for John, and for you. It is a great comfort; and now that he is a Mathewite, he will make an excellent sheriff.

Old Reed, Thomas's father in law, died a few days ago – aged near 90. About twelve hours before his death he asked for a glass of wine, and on getting it, smacked his lips and declared that he had never tasted better sherry. Soon after he took the Sacrament. Then played a rubber of Cribbage, then died. Worthy of Hermand.

Our friends the Artists have prefaced their Catalogue by a cursed discourse of eight pages, by Geo. Munro, which have nearly driven me mad. I had begged them to let me manage the reconciliation with the Institution, *quoad the lie*, in my own way. I was getting it beautifully settled for them; when, *pending the negociation*, the whole confidences are disclosed; the *proferred, but not yet accepted*, apology, and the result of the Report, *tho' not yet communicated*, except on injunctions of silence, are *published* for sixpence; and all this folly and perfidy, merely for the pleasure of insulting and degrading the very people who were holding out the hand of reconciliation, and saying forgive us – we were wrong. This is the conceited folly of Munro but the Academy homologated.

This only happened yesterday; and I have been raging ever since. I never gave man so contemptuous and savage a rebuke. Luckily they say nothing about the Trustees and higher matters. It is a beautiful Exhibition. The best, of the Provinces. They sold yesterday (their first day) about 600 season tickets. For every 20/- drawn last year by the London Academy the Scottish drew 7/-. A fact which shows the rising influence of Art here.

I wonder whether you be all out. I predict not; for who could come in? But Oh those bulls of Erin! Gore the beasts. Preach the expediency of a short Session.

---

1 Edward Maitland (1808–70); adv. 1831, 5th son of Lord Dundrennan; Solicitor-General 1855–8, 1859; SCJ (as Lord Barcaple) 1862–70.
2 John Thomson Gordon (1813–65); adv. 1835, Sheriff of Aberdeen 1847–8. He was John Wilson (Christopher North's) son-in-law.

We had a large convocation at Jeffrey's on Friday. He is delightfully well. His shrill sweet voice was heard over the general buz, like a lark's in the blue sky, above a rookery. And he is concupiscent anent a handmaid brought to town by the Browns.

Are your bills all ready to blossom? I rank and prefer them in this order: 1: The native vigour. 2: Lunatics. 3: Registration and consequently marriage. 4: The feudal system.

I am glad to hear that the Laird of Kirklands[1] has passed an eight, or a ten, hours' labour bill in his own favour. Mrs Maitland has the light in her bower, to guide her spouse, who she expects tonight. I have assured her that Ireland and Votes give her no chance. But Minerva, of course, speaks in vain to Love and Youth.

After a week of keen, blue frost, here is a bright April day; with a mild breeze softening every clod, as my gentle reasoning sometimes attempts to do to the hard head of an obstinate Lord Advocate. I dine at home. Sad, Unchristian fate. But dinners and I are done. Who the devil is to give them now? You, Goliah, Jeffrey, Thomas, The Pundit, The Body, the Friday, the New Club, and many others – cold is the kitchen range within thy bowers, the Cook, untold, forgets the hour. I had a pig and a splash of Champagne here yesterday.

Ever

H. Cockburn

To Mrs Andrew Rutherfurd
NLS 9688.55

Bonaly, 9 May 1847

My Dear Mrs Rutherfurd

I understand that, in spite of considerable dissipation, you are tolerably well. At which all good people must greatly gladden. Those in whom the genuine taste for vice is really constitutional can survive a great deal of it.

I have got a letter today which revives the old, and now strange like, time in which your husband and I used to walk about in military uniforms.[2] It is subscribed by '*Corporal* Dewar', and begins 'Dear Honorable Captain'. I remember him well; and if I could get his son made a Post Office *Stamper*, I would. I had also a delightful letter from Jeffrey two days ago. He seems well,

1 John Richardson.
2 See *Mems*, 180–3.

and writes, as he is, like an aged, philosophical Gentleman. It is difficult to keep one's temper at these idiots, Lords Peter and Duloch, scandalising us all by their low injudicial avocations. I trust, and expect, that they will stand a solitary pair in the Return.

Nothing is going on here except parturition. Mrs James Crawford,[1] Mrs Archd Davidson,[2] Mrs David Mure[3] – every Mrs that we know is at it. It's the Ether that sets them all agoing. I wonder who's not lying in. My son George's wife is to play her trump as soon as she lands. I hope his mother will have more sense. However, there's one good thing of the kind; our two cows have each got a son and heir – which has yellowed the cream already.

Detestible weather. However, today, tho' dull and rainy, we have a soft breeze from the west, and the Mavises, Cuckoos, Primroses, Hyacinths and Ribeses are spreading their palms to receive it; and the Planes are pushing out their fresh, fat, green leaves – as a noble Aristocrat used to push out his brood of young Tories, in the days when Sinecures were as thick as midges. You would despise our Hyacinths; but to us, poor contented bodies, they seem matchless.

I have not seen Ivory – who is at Castlecraig – but I hear that he is greatly felled. Nor have I seen Lauder; but tho' confined to the house, and mostly to his room, he is called better. With all his failings, I have a sincere affection for him, and would be very sad if I believed that his joyous laugh and kindly hilarity were over.[4]

Are you ever to get out of London? I suppose his Lordship won't till July. But as to you, remember that health at Lauriston is better than Sickness in Belgravia. So, if fragility comes over you, one way or another come down. I suppose the Maitlands will be weighing anchor, on their homeward voyage, soon. They seem to have been all very happy. Grahame's transplantation will be an immense loss to the family. It will take Helen much away, and leave the two old Hoodies on their dry branch. Yet the results of thse moves are often better, and very often different, from our speculations.

You would, no doubt, celebrate the nativity of old Richardson yesterday,

1 Mrs James Craufuird: Theodosia (1813–83), daughter of James Balfour, who m. 1834 James Craufuird yr of Ardmillan (1804–76); adv. 1829, Solicitor-General 1853–6.
2 Mrs Archibald Davidson: Margaret (d.1858), daughter of Sir Robert Dundas of Beechwood, who m.1836 HC's nephew Archibald Davidson (1805–66); adv. 1827, Sheriff of Midlothian 1865–6.
3 Mrs David Mure: Helen, daughter of John Tod of Kirkhill WS, who m. 1841 David Mure (1810–91); adv. 1831, SCJ 1865–89.
4 Lauder died on 29 May 1848.

with due jollity. Did the sight of such antiquity not make one grave, I should have liked to have been with you.[1] Do you never scent a quarry for Helen or Lizzy? I never once heard any body '*evened*', as we Scotch say, to either of them. Yet there's generally a fish looking at every set hook. He would be ill off without them. It is very odd, and very unfortunate, how few of my many girl friends and connections settle within reach of me. A new welcome door is the rarest of all props. But I fancy the young think us old Devils, Upas trees. Most unjust, so far as one Devil at least is concerned.

The Murrays went yesterday to Strachur. Even they would be invisible from Haar.

So God bless you

Ever

H. Cockburn

To Mrs Andrew Rutherfurd
NLS 9688.59

Bonaly, 1 June 1847

My Dear Mrs Rutherfurd

We are all struck, and saddened, by this unexpected death of Chalmers.[2] Who was a greater living Scotchman? Who has Scotland to boast of, as a Churchman, and on matters connected with the policy of religion, beyond him, since the Reformation? With his enthusiasm and eloquence, if he had lived in Knox's days, it may be doubted whether even Knox would have been owned by history as the leader. Every one else, even the Academic Robertson, would have withered in his furnace. And his walks have been so varied. Not confined to the commonplace, technical salvation of souls, he has enriched and enobled this pursuit by striking discussions of every kindred moral and political subject; and often leaves us to ask whether his pen or his tongue be the most powerful. He never wasted himself on little objects, nor tried to reach his ends in a little way; but aimed high, and sought

1 John Richardson was born on 9 May 1780.
2 Chalmers had died on 31 May. This private testimony was continued by a fully developed tribute in HC's *Jnl*, ii, 180–89. The general lamentation is shown in Jeffrey's tribute in a letter to William Empson: 'A great man is fallen in Israel! Poor Chalmers was found dead in bed yesterday morning. He had preached the day before, and sat up in bed preparing to make an important statement in Free Church General Assembly that very day. He was, I think, a great and good man; and the most simple, natural, and unassuming religionist I have ever known. I am very sorry that I shall hear his voice no more.' (*Life*, ii, 417–18).

no conquests but those that reason and enthusiasm, operating on the minds of masses, could achieve. That concentration of the mind on the object of present interest, which zeal always implies, sometimes made him forget what was due to other men or matters, and has exposed him to the only doubt – that of inconsistancy – to which he has ever been supposed to be liable. But this partiality of vehemence never made him long, or seriously, unjust. And thro'out a life of ardent practical conflict, he was uniformly simple, affectionate, and true. He was of incalculable use, both from what he did, and what he prevented being done. His name was a tower. His voice a thunderbolt. Many of his opponents will now rail, and many of his own party chatter, who were dumb before him. How thankful I am that I was familiar with the honest smile, and the quaint, picturesque oddities, of this most loveable original. He seems to have passed away almost as gently as Dr Black, for death had not made him even fall down on his bed, or relaxed his clasped hands from the apparent attitude of prayer. It is pleasant to think of his peculiarities, and his worth. The homage that he himself would prefer is that – very largely given – that proceeds from the hovels and the vennels.

Our ranks are thinning. I clouded myself today on my way out, sitting behind that faithful Geordie, by considering how the loss of two or three more would wreck me; and recalling the days in which – all at the gaiety of the bar, and not one of us dreaming of office – we closed a gay and not inglorious week, amidst the bowls, the claret, the talk, the boyishness, of Craigcrook. But these visions are all nonsense. They are not for practical man. The only wise conclusion is, let those who remain cling closer.

All well here. Jane as usual. George and his wife and weans very good. She is very well; and at present very round. But she will be slimmer soon. A nice, kind, natural, and very merry, creature. George sensible; deafish in the right ear; very happy; not so pious as I feared; and not more raw in matters British than most Indians are. I think you will like him.

Lauder called here yesterday. White, long, thin, all bones and eyes; but chearful, and recovering. Dean Medwyn too has been very unwell.[1] His tight trowsers have become wide ones, and flap over his poor Lent starved calf. But he is to be out tomorrow. There are worse fellows. Our weather is glorious. The ribes and the hyanciths and the primroses have had their benefits, and made their last appearances for this season. But the Hawthorn, the Laburnum,

1 i.e. the Judge rather than either of his two recently-ordained sons, who became distinguished
  Episcopalian clergymen.

the Rhododendrons, and the young soft tree leaves are all Hip! Hipping!! to nature. I have one scarlet rhododendron – my old one – with about 100 flowers on it – the pride of the parish. Lauriston! Artificial gimcrack!! This one transplant, direct from the sun, puts it utterly to shame. And oh! These long still warm night-days; when the blackbirds at last go to bed, and there is nothing living but Hesperus in the Sky and me on the Terrace. But I get poetical. Which to a lady who has wax lights kindling grand silk dresses in London drawing rooms, is rather absurd. God made every beast after its kind.

Therefore I give up to the lowness of your avocations. And I – proceed to dinner. Young neeps, gooseberry fool, cold punch, genuine grass-born cream, and other innocent ruralities, such as sheep's head and marrow bones. Would that Providence would be placed to take somebody I could name, to itself; so that lad Andrew Rutherfurd and I might once more have a few easy, self-proposed days e'er our pilgrimage be done.

The gong rings. Now for the marrow.

Ever

H. Cockburn

To Mrs Andrew Rutherfurd
NLS 9688.64

Bonaly, 24 June 1847

My dear Mrs Rutherfurd

Tell your affectionate spouse that I got his note this morning, and am delighted with Mrs Chalmers's pension. But tell him also not to let this act of Grace starve George Joseph's daughters. I grieve for the extinction of Sir William Hamilton's hopes. His direct public services are not equal to George Joseph's; but he is ill, and his house hungry. I see that there's nothing like dying suddenly. It got Andrew Thomson's family £6000 in a week. It made a great man of Perceval. It has greatly helped this pension to Mrs Chalmers.[1] I have a mind to electrify my numerous friends and the public by playing Pop on the bench, and seeing from the other world what it produces.

Jeffrey has been in bed two days from a feverish attack. But there is nothing bad in it. I found him last Monday evening frolicking, like Abraham, with his bairns and hinds, round a bone fire, in honor of a grand child's birthday. The

---

1 Professor Sir William Hamilton had suffered a paralytic stroke in 1844; George Joseph Bell had died on 23 September 1843; for Andrew Thomson, see *Jnl* i, 4, 5, 244, 294. Spencer Perceval's family received a substantial parliamentary grant after his assassination in 1812.

tea drinkings there are most agreeable; tho' but the ghosts of the old days. But in the kind and bright spirit of the man there is no change. Old Time will have a tough job before he makes Jeff. sour or dull.

Lauder is said to be better. But in my humble opinion he is very ill. I can't get them to take him to London; and indeed they have never seen a physician, except Christison *once*. I hope they are right. But my affection for Sir Thomas, and my fear that his death would sink the whole family, makes me fear that they are wrong.

George's lady has presented him with a fourth daughter. Don't say anything about it, but (entre nous) there is Hindoo blood in the babe. It is exactly the colour of dark gingerbread. But George, good natured fellow, is quite at ease.

Graham has sent us a small alabaster bust of her boy. It is very like, and very beautiful. But the material, especially in this land of smoke, is as fleeting in its purity as the infant features it tries to preserve.

Mrs Cockburn and Mrs Maitland were at Lauriston today. But I came out here, as usual, before dinner, and have not got their report. Goliah was to be put thro' his Catechism at Castle Douglas this very day. He did not seem at all comfortable about it – being obliged to have one side Catholic and one Protestant at the same moment. I trust that the fat weed that ro[o]ts itself at ease on Leith's wharf is to have no trouble. There is an outcry about his unscriptural habits. But then this is accounted for by many asserting positively that he *can't* write. A most useful mistake. For how can a man write who can't? I therefore never *show* any rare scrap I may get; but encourage the wonder who can do such much who has no pen.

Don't you taste the odour of the opening roses of Hermand? Surely you and July will meet there. Tell the Bodies to hold their gabs, and come away. *The days are shortening.*

So should speeches. If My Lord had been at home, he should have helped at a grand match at bowls here on Saturday. My only jollity for a fortnight. Yes, it is a fortnight since the juice of the grape stained these lips. Not even cyder, or perry, or ginger beer, or spruce – tho' they are all spouting round me. As to punch – it is what they call a dead letter with me, unless when Rutherfurd joins in 'the big draughts that make potation virtue'. No – I live at home at ease, a creamy and a flowery life. Our weather is not good. Not just cold, tho' to my taste not hot – and constant bursts of heavy rain, followed by hours of blue brightness, like Lord Robertson's Gleams.[1] This makes a heavy richness

1 Patrick Robertson (1794–1855); adv. 1815; SCJ 1843.

of vegetation, beyond what I have ever known.

And the evenings! The Terrace at ten at night! Last night the sky was loaded with dun calm clouds, except towards the west, where the long red streaks crossed the clear tops of the northern mountains, and brightened the sea. What a crash of birds, enjoying the warm moist softness, till one by one they ceased – tho' all within a few minutes – and left perfect, thoughtful, silence; except that behind the holly hedge there was the thick breathing of the sated cow, lying waiting for the morning dew to begin again; and in the fields below, the corn-craik, with its monotonous, but happy and ceaseless, cry – the nightingale of the clods; and then a twinkle, thro' the trees, from the drawing room window, saying that the candles were ready, and in, reluctantly, I came. It is delicious.

Do you ever see Helen Richardson? I am sorry to hear that she is not right. Johanna's holydays have begun. She is going to Ross, or to Brighton with her aunt, when she can; but in the mean time is at Dr Thomson's, 30 Welbeck Street. But I hope won't be there above a few days. N.B. I don't think Helen Maitland right.

What can I say more?

Yours Ever Respectedly
H. Cockburn

To Lord Curriehill[1]
WS Library (*SL* 58–9(–))
Bonaly, 22 July 1847
My Dear Marshall

Many thanks. But if I had known that your Kelly was reduced to three bottles, I should not have asked for one, or expected you to give it to me. Restitution however is now impossible, as the barrel has extinguished its identity confusions.

As to the prescription for making the delicate composition, it is very simple –

One lemon, about ten pieces of sugar in the ordinary tea size, and one *small* glass of rum, to a quart bottle of water. This is my rule. But something must be left to taste, as all lemons don't produce the same juice, nor all ten bits of sugar the same sweetness. But (with me at least) taste alone will not do without the rule. The chief thing is the rum, which should be as flavourless as

1 John Marshall (1794–1868); adv. 1818; SCJ (as Lord Curriehill [*primus*]) 1818. HC had pleaded for a bottle of special old rum from Marshall's cellar to 'recruit' his own barrel.

possible. The criterion of success is to have nothing sticking out in the broust. If there be a plain edge of sweetness, or of sourness, or of rumminess, quash it, and produce a vague, general, homogeneity, a gentle harmony, a steady, mild, well poised fusion of contrarieties, like the British Constitution – hit that, and you hit the thing. The general composition should resemble a calm temper, a soft sunset, a quiet conscience, a well-balanced, complete argument, an easy untroubled long vacation, a peaceful country holyday in the Summer Session, a gentle slumber under a roaracious sermon.

More water is the general corrective. Never spare the water, the great abater of edginess. It is the soft answer that turneth away wrath, whether of sugar, lemon or spirit, that may predominate. But if the rum be bad – above all if it be high flavoured – nothing will correct this all-infecting vice. It is like a one bad plea, which vitiates the whole record.

And to any elements and rules, must be added the exquisite tact, the delicate sensibility, the profound experience, of The Finished Punchifex Maximus. A rash, rough, ignorant and conceited hand may easily throw in the ingredients. A sow may mix, as a sow may drink. But it is not thus that the Poetry of Potation is to be produced. It is by nicety of hand, fine taste, deep thought, and long reflective practice.

These, *and Ice,* effect a result which exhibits chemistry in its brightest light. Cold is essential. And Cold must be a Genius of good taste; for no substance does he delight to settle so delicately as on this Nectar.

Iced Punch is the final end of the West Indies. What pious eye can avoid seeing that it was for this product that islands of rum, of sugar, and of lemons, are scattered over the ocean. It is the chief use of each. 'Spirits are not finely touched, but to fine Issues.'[1]

So, wishing you much success, and a great reputation, believe me
Yours Faithfully
H. Cockburn

To Sir William Liston-Foulis[2]
NLS 2257.169
Bonaly, 1 October 1847
My Dear Sir William
I beg you to excuse me for meddling with what you may think I have

---

1 *Measure for Measure*, I, i, 33.
2 8th Bt, of Woodhall, Colinton.

nothing to do with. My apology is that it is well meant and concerns you also.

You know the *Linn*, on your property, a little to the west of this. Much of our happiness here depends upon it; and its beauty depends much on the solitary elm that hangs over the cascade.

The Water Company[1] have begun their operations close beside it, not under their new, but under their old, Act, and are soon to have a great number of Paddies and other devils, who will be working there till the end of the year.

You are aware of an Irishman's love of shillela's. This love is so strong that nothing except warning and threatening can save a leaf of that tree.

I have spoken to the foreman, who *professes* fairly enough. But as he knows that the tree is not mine, of course he estimates all my threats at very little.

Now I take the liberty of submitting to you whether you should not write to the Manager of the Water Coy, admonishing him, at his peril, to touch that tree – or any thing about the Linn. No part of it is *on their line*, and except from carelessness or mischief, none of their people have any occasion to touch it.

Again, begging you to forgive this officiousness, believe me
Yours Faithfully
H. Cockburn

To James Ballantine[2]
NLS 1660.15
Bonaly, 28 October 1847
My Dear Sir

If you happen to be acquainted with a Gaberlunzie who goes about with a wallet full of scraps of meat and verse, I wish you would thank him, in my name, for some very good, and very complimentary, lines which he, or somebody in his person, has lately published about this humble spot and its humble master.

I am really grateful for the man's good opinion; especially as I am conscious that, to him at least, I have done very little to deserve it.

---

1 See, e.g., *Statistical Account*, I (1845), 757–8.

2 James Ballantine (1808–77), artist in stained glass, and author. HC approved of his *Gaberlunzie's Wallet*, first published in 1844, its name taken from the Scots word for a licensed beggar. This letter did little to keep the public at bay. On 9 September 1850 a further remonstration was issued: 'But don't forget the "Curse of Bonaly" – as a breakwater against the floods that your praise sends over this devoted and miserable place. I am thinking of keeping a regular Cholera at the gate, to warn them off.' (NLS, MS 1660.20.)

But I suspect that he feels that I have been negligent of him, and takes this method of punishing me, and an effectual punishment it is. Because from the moment he announced that my yett was open to all, I have been unable to call my own my own. There were successive hordes of roaming and roaring dogs out today – who positively took possession, and looked damnation to my eyes when I dared humbly to submit to them that property was property. One fellow's only answer was always by a loud stave of a song. The wee raggit laddies I don't object to, nor to any one male or female, who really enjoys the hills in decorum. But there is a species of riotous, devil may care, half and half genteel blackguards, that are very odious. Odious to others of their fellow creatures, to mavises, to burns, to roses, to cows, sunsets, lambs, and every thing reasonable. Therefore I mean to put up a placard saying 'No passage this way without leave from the Gaberlunzie!'. And if the Body can turn a penny, or fill his bag with heuk banes, for selling indulgences, like the Pope, I shall be very glad. Without some such check, a popular yett is a very inconvenient thing near a large town.

The Raggit Laddie is quite wrong, though, about Blackford. The first twenty-five years of my life were passed near – I may almost say upon – that Hill; and though, like other open ground, it was certainly roamed over freely enough, this was always understood to be by tolerance. All my boyish holydays were spent amidst the whins, the rocks and the views, of that delightful eminence; but I used to be often turned back, and the best thrashing I ever got in my life was for not instantly obeying. The move against shutters up is most meritorious, but nothing can be worse for their cause than their being defeated upon unjust claims. Nor would anything be better for it than their succeeding in a single claim that was just.

They will do no good however by merely resolving and roaring. They must subscribe. I read many heroic speeches, but never hear the clink of a guinea. Do they suppose that the silent, steady, constant tenacity of a Laird is to be relaxed by wind?

Excuse this long sermon, and the trouble of my commission – which last however won't torment you much, as I understand that the Gaberlunzie and you are much together. This season is done, and in few days I am a townsman again; but I shall look forward to the pleasure of seeing you both here as soon as 1848 will permit.

Yours faithfully
H. Cockburn

To John Lindsay[1]
NLS Acc.3521(20)

13 November 1847

State.

About 36 years ago, I married, *like a wise man*, on about £250 a year. From that day till this, the growth of, and attempts to output, an enormous family, combined with the too common want of fear about futurity, has, without much positive profligacy, kept me always from making money, except by keeping up two policies of Insurance. I never had a debt, however, till within these few years; since when they have grown, and are still growing, *alarmingly*. The result is that I must now set my house in order.

FIRST. My *income* is £3000. This will continue while I remain on the Bench. In two years I will have served fifteen years, and if then superannuated, I would have (as I understand) two-thirds or three-quarters (I forget which) of this £3000.

SECOND. My *substance*, supposing that I live till 1st January 1850, and were then to die, would be as follows:

An Equitable Policy dated 1813 for £5000. This I understand, will on 1st January 1850 be worth about	18,500
A Policy in the Scottish Widows dated 1836, for £5000, then worth	6,000
My House in Charlotte Square	2,000
My Books 1,000	
£ 27,500	

Bonaly – being burdened with a feu duty of about £100, I suppose is worth nothing but this may be a mistake.

---

1 John Lindsay, WS (1814). Cockburn had written the previous day to his old friend John Russell, WS (1803), breaking off a business relationship of long standing, on account of what he considered professional misconduct by Russell's son Alexander. Characteristically, he hoped that, though no longer client and agent, they could continue as friends. Russell replied, greatly relieved by the tone of HC's letter. HC thereupon sent Lindsay this full statement of his predicament.

Discreet management of reduced capital and income soon assisted partial recovery. By 1852 HC was able to send £1,500 to his son Henry, mining in Canada, who had sought help 'to put me out and assist me in Business', and a further £1,000 to settle debts. In February 1854 John Richardson elicited the information that the Equitable policy mentioned in the 1847 'State' was by then worth £16,900. 'It has made a renovated man of me,' HC wrote; 'I cannot tell you what a load it is off my heart.' (All in NLS Acc 3521(5). See also *Cockburn's Millennium*, 63–4.)

If my sister Jane, who is in very bad health, but much younger than me, dies before my brother John and me, then, by my father's settlement, I suppose my share of his estate would be about £2000, or £2500. If she survives us I suspect that it all goes, on her death, to the generation after us. But I set this chance down as nothing first because it is but a chance, second because £2000 of the fund stands now advanced to me in loan, and therefore, to this extent, my interest in the estate consists merely in my not being required to *repay*.

THIRD. My *debts* are these:

This £2,000 to my father's Trust Estate; against which however is to be set my spes successionis	2,000
By personal bond to Captain Stirling – for which my son Laurence is also bound	1,200
Loan from Mr Waugh, secured on my house	1,400
Loan, on the security of my Scottish Widows Policy	900
Debt as at last June to British Linen Coy secured on my Equitable Policy	4,700
Contracted lately for my son Henry by per. bond	1,000
My *proportion* of a loan in 1844 for my son Archd. The whole of this bond, quoad the lender, is £1,600	1,000
Sundry debts for my sons James and Laurence, etc. – say	1,000
£	13,000

Unless I be called upon, by the failure of the other obligants, to pay more than my portion of No 7 [re Archibald], the above is the outside of every thing. And if my son Archd sells his business, as he talks of, and leaves Ross, even the £800 may not be required.

The last £1000 – in No 8 [re James and Laurence] – is not yet borrowed, but I don't see how it can be avoided. My intention was to borrow it, in addition to the £900 on my Scottish Widows policy.

FOURTH. My *fixed annual burdens* are:

Interest on debt	650
Premiums on Policies	412
£	1062
This, deducted from Salary, leaves	£ 1938

The Problem is, to make this do for decent respectability, and to save something for contingencies.

Two things are certain, viz. 1. That there cannot be another shilling of debt. 2. That I can be plucked by sons no more.

I should like to be protected against all future plucks by some sort of a real or a quasi trust, which, without appearing, might act as a Break-water.

If Mrs Cockburn's shop debts exceed about £300, the excess is unknown to me.

H. C.

To William Empson
NLS Dep.235(1)
                    Edinburgh, 22 November 1847
My Dear Empson

I am requested to ask you whether ten or twelve pages of your next Number could be allowed for an Article on Art – chiefly Calotype. The author is to be Dr John Brown,[1] Physician here, the son of a very excellent and very eminent Dissenting clergyman. I don't know him, never even saw him; but his character both moral and literary is good, and he is reputed to be a good thinker and writer on Art. He is author of what is held to be a respectable review in the *North British* of last February, on *Modern Painters*, by a Graduate of Oxford.

This application proceeds from certain Artists here, who hold that this is the Paradise of Calotype – an opinion on which they are supported, I believe, by Landseer, Stanfield, Eastlake, and other competent Judges; and no doubt (but this is only my suspicion) they want their own glorification, incorporated into a general Art Article. The Article is not written, but can be ready in a fortnight.

And so my mission is ended.

Remember me to Mrs Empson.

The Bear, and Rutherfurd and I were with Jeffrey last night. He is delightfully well.

                            Ever
                            H. Cockburn

1 No article by Dr John Brown (1810–82), author of *Horae Subsecivae* (1858–82) and *Rab and His Friends* (1859) is recorded, either in *Ed. Rev.* or in the *North British Review*, for which Brown had reviewed John Ruskin's *Modern Painters*.

To William Gibson-Craig[1]
HWUA: 2/E/24a
Edinburgh, 16 December 1847
My Dear Craig

When a man of my sense or delicacy gets into trouble, the thing that he regrets most is the necessity of tormenting his friends. No one ever felt this more deeply than I do.

You have (no doubt) heard of a whole shower of great, and unexpected, calamities which have recently fallen on me. In so far as I myself, or Mrs Cockburn, or my daughters, or George, or Frank, are concerned, these are unworthy of a thought. But the position of some other of my sons is dreadful; and it is they who have cast a cloud over us, much darker and colder than any one that has ever yet come over my singularly sunny life. This house can know no comfort till these *men* are out of it, in a decently creditable way.

Maitland has told me of your kindly disposition towards James. Henry – poor ruined creature – I at present contemplate sending to Canada, in a situation I had intended for James, but for which I now fear he is not qualified. How James is to be disposed of, I don't yet see. The one I now pester you about is Laurence.

He is the youngest, and has got less done for him than any of the others. He has had the sense to stick to New South Wales, tho' for the last two years he has scarcely been above destitution.

I received a letter from him two days ago, in which he *mentions you* in reference to a request he makes, which has at least the advantage of being specific. He wants Government employment in the Colony, of which, he says, there is a great deal – chiefly in the form of Commissionerships, many of which require nothing beyond 'simple arithmetic and a knowledge of Bush Law'. The most certain way of obtaining this, he says, and the most usual, is by a letter *from the Colonial Office to the Governor, mentioning the party, and recommending him.* And what he implores for is a letter to this effect.

Can you do anything to get one? This is the Short and the Long of all I have to say.

It is proper to explain that some months (eight or so) ago, I wrote to Mr Ed. Ellice[2] to the same effect, only in favour of *James* as at *Ceylon.* Mr Ellice sent

1 HC corresponded frequently with (Sir) William Gibson-Craig, 2nd Bt. (1797–1878; succ. 1850), MP for Midlothian 1837–42, then for Edinburgh 1842–52, on civic and other matters. He kept strictly separate this multiple patronage request.
2 Probably the elder Edward Ellice (1781–1863), MP for Coventry 1831–63 and previously, a celebrated Whig intermediary.

me a very kind answer, with a note from Lord Grey to him saying that he had little in his power, but would do what he could. But soon after this, as James wrote that the Ceylon fever was to drive him out of the country, I was obliged to write to Ellice to stop Lord Grey from doing anything.

Whether his Lordship will, or can, do for Laurence in New South Wales what he was willing to do for James in Ceylon, is the question.

Having told you my story, I must leave you to work upon it. Whatever you do – or if you decline doing anything – I shall be equally certain of your cordial *desire* to assist me.

Your colleague was elected today, amidst the cold and wet applause of about 300 damp patriots.

Lauder is wonderfully chearful; but I don't suppose that he is substantially any better. Macbean is doing well, and will weather this gale. I hope you are to reappear during the recess. We shall be here. I doubt if Jane will ever see Bonaly again. A dreadful attack on Sunday; tho' Chloroform assuaged it.

Be *prompt* about the Artists. And the *four* rooms.

Ever

H. Cockburn

To William Gibson-Craig
HWUA: 2/E/30
Bonaly, 26 December 1847
My Dear Craig

Poor Speirs! I don't wonder at your agitation, for he was indeed a person of rare excellence; both of head and of heart.[1] The unexpected termination of his usefulness has made a great impression here; not merely among his friends, but among multitudes who knew him only by character. His is one of the voids that cannot be supplied, either publickly or privately.

I have read the part of your letter about the Artists to Hill.[2] They are all quite pleased with the report – as well they may. Your anticipations of the working of the new system are probably sounder than mine. To encrease their chance of being so, my old objection to go into the Board is now laid aside;

1 The advocate Alexander Speirs of Culcreuch had died on 24 December, recalled by HC for his solid (and solemn) support of the Free Kirk ('their weightiest layman') in *Jnl*, ii, 205–7.
2 David Octavius Hill (1802–70), artist and photographer, much involved with the Academy of Arts.

and as the Academy now needs no Extra-Board Tribune (and should not have one), I am ready to become a member.

I am sorry to learn that Hamilton the Architect[1] has prepared a rival design to Playfair's for the proposed building. I have told a friend of his to let him know: 1: That the Treasury must decide on the plan it is to pay for. 2: That by Statute Playfair has been named as the only safe Mound Architect. 3: That having had the doing of the north end, and also of the south, it would be unjust to take the intermediate and connecting part from him. But whoever designs, you of the Treasury must at last come down with £10,000 more.

I really cannot express to you what relief you give me by your kindness about Laurence. I suppose that the Boyds you are about to be in communication with are connected with (if not the same with) certain people of that name who are friends of James Stuart, who got me some *letters* from them for him about a year ago. They were good *letters*, but contained mere general recommendations to his people abroad, and therefore they won't, I fear, produce anything practical.

There are some Boyds in Australia of whom James gives no very favourable account as likely to be of substantial use to any young man. He says they have *scores* of *under-paid* clerks, and servants – with whom they are constantly parting. But these are perhaps not the Boyds on whose trail you are.

No want of applicants already for the Midlothian Sherriffship. *Bobby Hunter* is one![2] So is Alex. Dunlop,[3] a person I love and admire. But bad for this place. Too Free; inconveniently Anti-Catholic; and probably not likely to be popular with the country gentlemen.

It seems to me that there are only two fit men – Davidson and Gordon.[4] And of these I am clear, and have told Rutherfurd so, that he should take Gordon. A patron should not job for his relations; but to overlook the fair claims of relations is a miserable infirmity, often resorted to by weak patrons for the vanity of being praised for candour. Gordon is able, agreeable, popular, and now quite steady; in so much that were he not the Lord Advocate's nephew he would probably be promoted at once. The late Crown Agent tells me that he found him as attentive and able as any Depute he had to deal with. So, if you can put a word in the right place, do it. I should really be sorry if

1 Thomas Hamilton (1784–1858)
2 Robert Hunter (1791–1871); adv. 1814. Sheriff of Bute 1838–71; and of Dunbarton (1853–71).
3 Alexander Dunlop of Corsock, later MP for Greenock.
4 Archibald Davidson (1805–86); adv. 1827. Sheriff of Kincardine 1847, Aberdeen 1848–65, Midlothian 1865–86.; probably Edward Strathearn Gordon (1814–79), Sheriff of Perth 1858–68, Lord of Appeal in Ordinary as Baron Gordon of Drumearn.

Rutherfurd should be prevented by unjust delicacy from making his nephew independant for life. Davidson may get Aberdeen, I suppose; but, whether he goes or not, Gordon should get Edinr. Jeffrey will be for Cosmo Innes – in vain; and I fear that Maule may have a hankering after Dunlop.[1]

Then there is a Proff. in lieu of Syme.[2] No difficulty here. Both Duncan and Miller – the only two candidates – are 'ill principled', but if Miller be moved, then: 1: There is nobody fit to take the Surgical chair which he will vacate. 2: And the Town Council, who are the surgical patrons, would put in *Lizars*!! I would give Syme's chair to Duncan. The only misfortune of this would be missing another opportunity of excluding a good teacher by the Test – which Millar, who is Free, can't take.

And then (never rains without pouring) old Jeffry, the Glasgow Anatomist, is dying, aged about 90, and Alan Thomson wants this. Five Thomsons there already.

Ever

H. Cockburn

To Adam Black
NLS 3713.204
14 Charlotte Square, 15 January 1848
My Dear Lord

I have only today understood the damnable projects of the Railway Coy for extinguishing Princes Street, by new roads, tunnels, Station Houses, etc., on the Eastern Division of the North Loch.[3] If these designs be carried, no further thought need be given, by the real friends of Edinr, about the preservation of that beauty which is its only wealth.

There is no one on whom such of the people of this place as are not railway mad are so much entitled to look for protection as your Lordship. For it was chiefly your evidence that accomplished what I had always predicted was the fatal step of letting these beasts set their hoof on that valley. You meant them to have a mere right of *transit*. But you see all that the inch ends in.

The present scheme is *absolutely destructive*; and I don't think that Playfair's correction of it is much better.

1 Comso Innes (1798–1874); adv. 1822; Sheriff of Elgin 1840–52. Maule probably Fox Maule-Ramsay MP, later 2nd Earl of Dalhousie.
2 James Syme (1799–1870), surgeon.
3 See HC's commentary in early April, *Jnl*, ii, 213. Gibson Craig, who 'baffled' the project, is quoted at 214n.

The only remedy is to resist *all further encroachment.* The instant that they are allowed, on any pretence, to come west of the Little Mound, it is all over. So long as they have their Dalry Station they have, or may make, room enough for their goods. And if not – then this only shows the more what must be the result of letting them in upon the new ground east of the Mound. In a few years it must all be covered with buildings and roads.

I do trust therefore that you will not lose this opportunity of raising yourself still higher with the rational portion of the public, by a vigorous resistance, and a marked separation of yourself from whatever portion of the Council, or of the Lunaticks, may be favourable to *any part* of the proposed scheme.

So many people are interested in this railway, and so many more are crazy about furious communication, that I fear that any public meeting that could be called would be favourable to any accommodation to any railway. But I cannot doubt that a strong remonstrance might be obtained from a great number of the disinterested and the sane. Do you only lead them.

Excuse this from one who is mad on the other side, and who – *deliberately* – would rather see all the railways in Scotland bankrupt, than that one fragment of this projected Hunnism should be perpetrated.

Yours Faithfully
H. Cockburn

[Addressed]: To the Lord Provost

To Thomas Cleghorn[1]
NLS Dep 235(1)

Aviemore, 17 April 1848

My Dear Cleghorn

I got your letter – at Aberdeen. And one, to the same effect, from the Rector. All right.

But I execrate the leather; and am satisfied it does us great harm. Calvert should be instructed to give our masters the right reading of Shakespeare. They say 'It is honoured in the *breech*', which is a mistake. I assure you there is deeper feeling against us on this subject, *particularly among former pupils,* than you are aware of. I have taken the liberty of giving the Rector a hint on the subject.[2] An ardent friend SAW a master teaching, t'other day, with the

1 Thomas Cleghorn (1818–74); adv. 1839, soon to become HC's son-in-law.
2 John Williams (1792–1858) was Rector of the Edinburgh Academy 1824–8, 1829–47.

tangles of a leathern implement *hanging out from between the leaves of the book* that the man was using – displaying to all visitors that it was too often needed to admit of its being laid aside, and that there was no delicacy about it, in this school, which was set up partly to avoid the cruel, boy debasing, and pedagogue corrupting, barbarity.

We are wending homewards; but still have several days of Perth.

Ever

H. Cockburn

To Mrs Andrew Rutherfurd
NLS 9688.84

Bonaly, 21 June 1848

My dear Mrs Rutherfurd

There is only one L in Bonaly. It rhymes to daily. It's only Bonally, that rhymes to Dally.

And this is your husband's birthday. Which, no doubt, you have celebrated by a copious goblet of that delicious chalybeate which cherishes the wizened gebbies of the old dowagers who frequent Buxton. Depend upon it, he has had a good wacht to his own health, in a better liquid. Many nativities may he see. But I begin to be impatient for his getting into a good harbour berth, and being done with the turmoil of the political sea. But alas! we all look beautifully healthy. John Hope is the best seasoned of us all for Heaven, and the one of whom this world is the least worthy – so he had better not waste himself here any more. But I fear that compassion for our follies will keep him here as long as he can stay.[1]

So you are in Buxton! I passed August and September there, in the year of our Lord 1799!!! My father, who went there often, for gout, took me, and I did not dislike it at all. I was twenty, had a horse, flirted egregiously with a strapping bright eyed Buckinghamshire Miss Bailly, and was one of the two who secured a warm plunge bath while it was yet pure, by going to it at seven in the morning – the other, my swimming rival, being a Bishop, or Archbishop – I think of York. Then here were merry public dinners, and plenty dancing, and scampering round a covered ride, and always with Miss Baillie. I have never heard of her since. Hech! She's probably a queer composition by this time. We lodged in your Great Hotel, the other one being called St Anne's, and the gentlemen's public

1 John Hope died in 1854, outliving Rutherfurd by four years.

breakfasting room was nearly below your parlour, at the very end of left curve of the building.

As to being melancholy, surely anything is chearful after illness under the hot roar of that devils' drawing room you have got out of. If your Castalia do you good, I shall expect to hear of your appearing as the matron of the next rhumatic dance, or the Duenna of the gout whist club. Do try and get well. You have no notion how much it concerns your friends.

Sir Wm Newbiging says to me that he is under no alarm whatever about Mrs Jeffrey; and even Jeffrey speaks very chearfully about her. Nobody has seen her, because while under a course of mercury she is almost always in her own room. Mrs Cockburn has gone out twice, but has only seen Mrs Empson – who, when I saw ten days ago, was looking red and scurffy, and altogther foul, in the face. Jeffry himself, tho' thin, wee and grey, is quite well – singing in the court like a bird in its cage.

The Lauders are all behaving naturally and sensibly.[1] I have not seen the poor widow, but she is quite composed, and all the girls quiet and reasonable. I don't know any particulars; but I understand that the ladies are all left comfortably, and that Sir John is the only one who is probably growling. But he too has at least £1500 a year, and when his mother dies will have £2500 – and £3000 when the girls are paid off. This last may not be soon; but the mother can't cumber him long, and in the mean while £1500 is fully equal to his deserts. But all this may be wrong.

We got Jane here a fortnight ago, and she has not been the worse of it. Mrs Cockburn and Elgin have had a dreadful work clearing us out from dear old No 14, and getting us into No 2 Manor Place. How trash, and dirt, do accumulate! In one closet there was found an entire, and rather handsome *Skeleton* – a relic of the Doctor. No 2 is far off, small, and in all the back rooms abominable; but I call it Chambers, and mean not to be in it above three months yearly – so it must do. The worst of it is, that we must give up the dining room to Jane, and must dine in one of the abominables. However, eight or nine months of the year in this spot, which is now in the perfection of its glowing hills an opening roses, is enough for any reasonable man.

Mrs Fullerton, who has been dwable (i.e. debile) is recruiting at Carstairs. The Maitlands are well. *I believe* that Graham ceases to be one of us in July.[2]

---

1 Sir Thomas Dick Lauder had died on 29 May; his son John succeeded as 8th Baronet. Charlotte Lady Dick Lauder lived until 1864.
2 When she married Robert Stewart.

Meanwhile she has performed the curious operation that is called 'taking off her marriage clothes'. An odd proceeding a month before the wedding.

Think of Bouverie Primrose's happiness in succeeding Sir Thomas.[1] £700 instead of £400; less work; his own hours; sun light in place of gas light; *and a cutter!* He being a yacht man.

Farewell. Bowls and iced punch here on Saturday. How your poor spouse's parched jaws would splash themselves in the simple nectar. *Get well.*

Ever

H. Cockburn

Mrs C. wrote you a long letter ten days ago – which somebody stole. I suspect that the Housemaid, kindling a fire, made a flaming epistle of it.

To Mrs Andrew Rutherfurd
NLS 9688.88

Bonaly, 25 June 1848

My Dear Mrs Rutherfurd

I saw Newbiging yesterday. Mrs Jeffrey doing well; but still not cured, tho' curing.

Jeffrey told me on Friday that Simpson[2] had seen her, and concurred with Sir William.

As the newspapers make Brougham get £50,000 by the death of that horrid old hunks James Watt,[3] I was in hopes that his far truer friend Jeffrey was to have got at least £100,000, and then the long review about Watt's father would not have been written in vain. But the truth is that the Evil's legacy consists of a copy of some of Piranesi's engravings, and Jeffrey's to something less. Old beast. He is supposed to have left half a million, and has given it all to distant Watts; few of which he ever saw and none of whom he could endure. His relation Pat. Muirhead, Advocate – his friend, secretary and associate, and the translator into English of Arrago's eloge on the Steam Engine improver – is made ridiculous by a bequest of £1,000![4] Surely the devil is blowing up the coals below him by one of his own engines.

Dreadful weather – cold, raw, thick, easterly haarr. Positively December

1 Bouverie Primrose (1813–98) CB, 2nd son of 4th Earl of Rosebery.
2 J.Y.Simpson (1811–70), Professor of Midwifery.
3 James Watt (1769–1848), partner in Boulton & Watt; son of James Watt (1736–1819).
4 James Patrick Muirhead (1813–98), adv. 1838, had in 1844 married a daughter of Matthew Boulton of Tew Park, Oxfordshire.

would be insulted by it. There was a bowling party here yesterday, and we never saw the hill. A crawl, in greatcoats, was all that could be accomplished. The very iced punch had a raw, haarry edge. (But it seemed to get over tolerably well.) But today, tho' cold, it is bright.

I wish our friends up stairs were less shaky. But the West Indies and Reform are enough to haul down anybody. I am not quite clear that they are right about the West Indies, and as to reform, *in itself* it is mere nonsense. But *it will come* – and in the form of what is called a republic. It is a republic already, *in effect*. But it will have the *form* of it in time; tho' not, probably, in our day. Poverty, National Debt, Sectarianism, the freedom that we have, even education – all tend that way. We are better as we are, I fancy. But you and I shall only look down on it.

I hope your bath is doing its duty. If it be, stay longer. And if it does you good, is not that a hint of a call towards Germany?

An English stranger who has lately been cast a good deal in Boyle's way described him t'other day as 'a stiff trump'. Which I think rather happy. I dined at a great sixteen party at Ivory's on Friday, in honour of Handyside and his old giantess.[1] And had I not the delights of meeting Provost Amos! – who would attend to no mortal but me, and spoke loud out to, and laughed outright at my Amosian jests, and declared he had not been so happy since he 'gave the Lord Advocate up'. The only change is that from want of being fed with powder his wig has become as yellow as a daffodil. But wait till we see it snowed over, and with the gold chain sparkling below it, in October.

Now do get strong. Why should you not stump with me, after all, to the top of Arthurs Seat and Cape Law. It requires nothing but a resolute will. Think of Jack Tar and the baby.[2]

Ever

H. Cockburn

Two not bad things.

At some meeting lately, Joseph Hume was sneering at the Torries for mean submission to their leaders, and called them a parcel of '*well bred Spaniels*'. On which Sibthorp rose in vast wrath, and among other things said that 'he would rather be a well bred spaniel *than an ill bred cur*'.[3]

The minister of Dolphington (on the other side of the Pentlands) lately

---

1 Robert Handyside (1798–1881); adv. 1822. Solicitor-General 1853; SCJ 1853.
2 A legendary sailor, mentioned elsewhere, who had himself breast-fed an orphaned baby.
3 The Radical Joseph Hume and the ultra-Tory Charles Waldo Sibthorp.

rebuked a poor fellow, by name, for sleeping in church. Mr Richard
Mackenzie, the Patron and great parish Graaff, was foolish enough to interfere
on the spot, from his pew, and told the parson, aloud, that he was quite wrong
in rebuking anybody in public – and that all censure should be in private. To
which replies the reverend censor, 'Well then Sir, I wish you would follow
your own rule'.[1]

Each Sea

Thus is your Sunday's order obeyed. But you have kept me from the Free.
Candlish be merciful to me, a sinner.

To Thomas Cleghorn
NLS Dep 235(1)
Bonaly, 9 July 1848
My Dear Cleghorn

I have nothing more to say; but lest you think that your letter to me of
the 3rd Inst should be answered, I have merely to repeat, in substance, what
you have already said – which was this.

Considering your admitted present incapacity to maintain a family, the
long time that must confessedly pass before it can be known if you will be able
to do so even then, and the extreme dangers of all long, understood,
engagements, I can give the scheme *no encouragement*. No man of sense
could expect me to do so. If these were matters that depended on mere reason,
it would clearly be better that it was abandoned.

But, on the other hand, considering that these are *not* matters that depend
on mere reason, that I have always had a sincere regard for you, that an
attachment has arisen, and that your prospects are by no means hopeless, I am
as little disposed to give the plan any *obstruction*.

The practical result is that you two must settle it for yourselves. You are
both old enough to decide, on your own responsibility.

If you resolve to go on, I suspect that concealment of what is in truth the
engagement cannot be long possible – and I am not at all sure that it is
desireable.

Your intercourse in the mean time must be regulated by your own good
sense and good taste. As I have said that I do not obstruct, this implies an
understanding that you have the usual honorable intercourse of your situation. There is nothing so disagreeable and wearisome in a house as a perpetual

1 John Aiton (1797–1863), Minister of Dolphinton from 1825.

flirtation; and I, in particular, scunner cordially. Still, I can submit to whatever is reasonable.

On the whole, therefore, I leave it to yourselves. I shall trust that it may end well, *if you resolve to proceed*; but as it has not been my doing, I shall not consider myself responsible for its turning out ill.

I shall send both your letter to me, and this answer, to Elizabeth.

Yours Faithfully

H. Cockburn

To Elizabeth Cockburn
NLS Dep 235(1)(*SL*,62–3)
Bonaly, 9 July 1848

My very Dearest Liz

As to *the* affair, I send you a letter from Mr Cleghorn to me of the 3rd inst, and a copy of my answer to him.

My answer explains my views and feelings sincerely and plainly; and what I have said to him, I say to you. I don't know what more I could say, or think. I formerly [*sc.* formally] explained to him that I had nothing better to desire as to his family; that for himself I have always had a great regard; and that I have not one sixpence to give.

So it just depends on your two selves. My advice, since it cannot be for a long while, *if then*, and all engagements are dangerous, is to give it up. But this is not an advice which I feel it to be my duty to try to enforce. If, therefore, having got my advice, you chuse to take your own way, I, without incurring any responsibility, can only hope your own way may turn out the best one. I have no object but for your happiness.

Meanwhile, if you resolve to proceed, I trust that you will try to avoid the usual bad tendencies of being long under engagement. These arise from indifference to everything except the engagement – idleness, manœuvering, unsociableness, and that odious and most wearisome eternal flirtation. Two years of this! It may be very pleasant to the pair. But for me, I would rather have two years sea sickness or jaundice than witness it. At the same time, I certainly cannot expect, or wish, that my new son (if he is to be one) should not come to his father's house, or be dealt with as one of the family. I only don't want the Terrace be called Flirtation Row.

What can I say more? If anything, tell me what it is, and I shall say it.[1]

1 Elizabeth Cockburn married Thomas Cleghorn on 27 December.

I have settled with Marion Thomson that she is to be here on, or before, the last day of July.[1] I have suggested her reaching us, *if she comes by sea*, on Friday the 28th. If she comes by land, she can take any day. They want you to go to Welbeck Street for a fortnight; for which they promise *a ball*!! I have said *No. Poz. Quite Poz.* Not an hour. It would cost money. It would make the Ross visit useless. London heat, and noise, and racket, would wither you. *No. Poz.* If Marion comes by land, per[haps] you may arrange to meet.

Remember me kindly to the Miss Ainsworths. I am grateful to them for giving you so much good pleasure. I envy you seeing these picturesque haunts. It is a beautiful country, and should have been ours. I wonder why our ancestors gave it to the English. It must have been because the poor flatt bodies would not otherwise have known what a loch or a hill were.

But I envy your scene-seeing less than your seeing Mrs Fletcher.[2] That's a woman for you! Go to her once more – fall on your stumps – hit your contemptible noddle in the dust before her, and say, 'Oh, Dear Mrs Fletcher! Give me some of your talent, more of your enthusiasm, and most of that glowing and boundless benevolence, which makes your aged face and grey hairs more beautiful than all the charms of even your beautiful youth'. Off with you! What are you sitting there for! When an ass said at Lord Jeffrey's, two years ago, that he could not conceive any one having more respect for a human creature than for St Paul, I did not *truly* say that I had more for Mrs Fletcher – the woman sitting, with her bright eye, by the ass's side. Down on your horrid, stiff stumps.

Jane well – for her. Mary well. Bairn ugly.[3] Oh, if you saw my roses. Paradise had not more, or better, before the Fall. Uncle Thom came yesterday. Sent for and up again today.

Ever

H. Cockburn

Send me back Cleghorn's letter. Be sure, and my answer. And be sure that you and Marion be here *in July. Short* visit at Ross if you only go there on the 18th.

---

1 Marion Thomson, second daughter of Dr Anthony Tod Thomson and sister of Lizzie Thomson who had been on a previous Circuit with HC. Her journal of the Summer 1848 tour is now NLS Acc 7372.

2 Now 78 and living in the Lake District.

3 Archibald Cockburn's wife, née Balfour. Their bairn, HC's eldest grandson, was Henry (1848–1936), later a prominent London actuary, and a mountaineer.

To William Gibson-Craig
HWUA: 2/P/13

Bonaly, 13 August 1848

My Dear Craig

It appears by a letter I had yesterday from Rutherfurd that even for the Commissariat James is too old.[1] So there goes that chance!

Mr Tuffnell suggests, or rather offers, what Rutherfurd calls 'an Australian Clerkship' – worth '*about* £200 a year' – in the gift of the Treasury.

I have written to him (by this post) that I cannot determine about it till I know something more of it, especially as James's Australian experience gives him no notion what it is, but that he ought to secure it, conditionally, before he leaves London.

What I want to know is – what is the nature of the situation? Clerk to whom? or to what? Does *about* mean £200 – or £300 – or £100 – or £50? *Above all,* does it naturally lead to anything better, or is it for ever the same?

Can you tell me anything about it?

Lest Rutherfurd should think it safer to do it all himself, you can leave him to enquire and report, if, after seeing him, you think this best. I have told him that you will do either.

It begins to look desperate. He may exist upon me, so long as I live; but I shudder when I think of his position when I shall be gone. I got Rutherfurd's intimation last night, and, after going to bed, I first dreamed that I was legally hanged; and then that I threw myself off the top of Black's shop down to the Railway – where I saw myself lying flat and all broken; and now that I am awake, I begin to suspect that either quietus would be better than this cursed living state. I sometimes derive an odd comfort from patriotism. For since a long life of Whiggery, aided by the most attached and zealous possible friends, in positions of influence, can't procure a bare subsistance of any kind, or in any place upon earth, for a son, my conclusion is that there is not one thousandth part so much power of bribing and corrupting as the uninitiated suppose – which really does comfort me.

But nevertheless my baseness would prefer being comforted by a small job for myself.

So Oh Lord deliver me. D—m. I really do not want to sell all my books and send him back to Australia on his account – yet I should not wonder at it.

You see what your kindness subjects you to.

Ever

H. Cockburn

1 James Cockburn (1816–85) had had no success in business in Syria, New South Wales, or Ceylon. He became a stipendiary magistrate at Mauritius.

To Jane Cockburn
NLS Dep 235(1) (*SL* 64(–))

Ballachellish [*sic*], Wednesday 6 September 1848, noon[1]

My Dearest Jane

The only thing that has troubled me since our departure has been hearing that you have been ill again. I trust that you are easier before now.

Joe, I dare say, tells you all our proceedings. So I need not. Till today, our weather has been most beautiful. But this day is conscientiously making up for it. We dined yesterday with the Laird – in a little Eden, close by.[2] All very natural and kind. A very pretty, well coloured, slender, long necked, wife; but timid, sad looking, thin-lippet, and to appearance (but obs[erve] only to appearance) not over soft in the temper. We meant to have sailed up (a boat the only road) to his brother's cottage; but catch me committing my back to the good ship Lumbago, for a ten mile voyage, in such a day. The only misfortune is that, escaping the deep sea, we are catched by the devil; for I want no more of the loud talking laird and the long necked, sad lady; but if we be here he will be sure to force us there.

9 p.m. But he did not. On the contrary, he regretted he could not; as some people had come upon him we would not like to meet. Very true. Among the rest, including himself, there are four Stewarts with excellent titles, viz. Fasnacloich, Ardvoirlich, Culdares[3], and Ballachullish. George and John Steuart, who once dined at Bonaly, went a-fishing up Glenco, and returned, as usual with fishers, with all the fish in the water, at half past six. Marion and I made out a two mile walk, splashing tho' it was. We *mean* to try our sail tomorrow; but, thinks I, humph. At any rate on Friday we proceed to Oban; and the sea stomachs to Staffa on Saturday. And to Loch Ettive on Monday. But by Jingo how it does pour. Humph.

They are all behaving very well. Joe does not trouble the beauties of nature much; but eats and laughs well – and sleeps excellently. Charlotte is somewhat stinted in food by every ten mile stage, but gets thro' by the aid of sandwiches, and is very handy, and very good natured. Marion is in constant extacies – with everything. A most agreeable, intelligent and yet unobtrusive companion.

---

1 HC, with a family party including Marion Thomson, was on the West Circuit: see *CJ*, 343–50.

2 They were visiting the laird of Ballachulish ('a hospitable, kind but vulgar man', wrote Miss Thomson), elder brother of HC's friend John Stuart, MP and Chancery barrister,

3 Stuart Menzies of Culdares, 'a bad specimen of Highland gentry', reported the sharply observant Miss Thomson (MS Acc.7372), after a dinner that 'was long and tedious – the drawing room adjournment worse'.

The young laird of Ballachellish is a strong boy, with rough red cheeks, a mop of flaxen hair, stumps of legs, a kilt, and speaks Gaelic; but tho' eight years old does not know the letters of the alphabet. They seemed horrified, and not over pleased, at my admonitions about a distant school. I have renewed my acquaintance with Miss Stewart, the said John's daughter, who was here a long while this forenoon, and then she and I had a walk. A very clever, kind, nice person – not ill looking, aged about twenty-four, and a linguist. She is now teaching herself Danish. She is in Mrs James Craig's style. She had on the very model of a wet country dress – a sort of India rubbered straw bonnet, an India rubbered cloak, as light as guaze [*sic*], a pair of shoes with cork soles that make mine seem like pumps, and thin water proof upper leather, nice *red* worsted socks – all put off and on as such things were of yore at Niddrie. Now, none of your sneering, for she is neither a fool nor a fantastic, but a very sensible young woman – and very fond of me.

Love to everybody – Mama, Lizzie, James, the bairns, Stewart if he has reappeared, and Thom.

Ever

H. Cockburn

To John Marshall (Junior)[1]
WS Library

Kirklands, 12 October 1848

My Dear Sir

I have written to your father, regretting that the necessity of being here, and the difficulty of being in two places at once, prevents me from attending the launch which I am told is to take place on Saturday at Curriehill, and giving the good ship a cheer as it goes off.

But I send my benediction. May its voyage be prosperous, and its final anchorage secure.

But whither bound? I surely have heard this; but if I ever have, I have forgot it, and I don't at present know what sea you are to plough.

How then can I admonish you? But warning being the great duty of age to youth, I lay three rules for you in each of the lines into which it is likely that inclination or Fate may lead you.

Are you going to be *Mercantile*? Then:

---

1 John Marshall (1827–81), eldest son of Lord Curriehill, chose a career at the bar, becoming Lord Curriehill (*secundus*) in 1874.

1. Having ascertained that the Head of the House has feathered his nest, marry his daughter Peggy.
2. Whenever you are Insolvent, sequestrate at once; and eschew the quiet charms of a private trust.
3. Convince yourself, as soon as you can, that £100 a year saved, accumulated, and secured, for fifty years, leaves more in the end than £30,000 a year for a hundred years, all hanging on what is called a safe speculation.

Or *Medical*? Then:

1. Dress well, avoid eating your brethern, even when there is no other cheap food to be got, and never be out of the way.
2. Invent, or discover – or at least pretend to invent or discover – something. No matter what, so as it can bear your name. Dr Glauber made a fortune by his salt. Let Marshall's Pill immortalise you.

Clerical? Then:

1. Whatever ordination may put into you, don't let it squeeze all charity out of you. Do unto others as you would *not* be done unto, is the prevailing Sectarian maxim.
2. Don't become, practically, an idiot.
3. In the pulpit, try to be powerful calmly. Few ministers know it, but there is really no necessary connection between eloquence and sweat.

A *W.S.*? Then:

1. Don't fancy that general ignorance is a proof of professional knowledge.
2. Deal with every employer on the anticipation that whenever his folly shall drive him into bad hands, he will quarrel with you, and contest everything.
3. Don't, except as a last resource, appropriate your client's money – detectably.

An *Advocate*? Then:

1. Never forget that want of law is not so fatal as want of character. Even if cheating were your object, nothing facilitates it more than the reputation of honesty.
2. Avoid the common extremes of being all law and no literature, or all literature and no law. High practice – which is always a thing to be aimed at – requires both.
3. Reverence the Lords. So that when it is convenient to insult them, it may be done the more safely, and the more effectually.

These should surely steer you; and I need box the compass no more.

I have only to add, therefore, that you may safely come to me, whenever you think that I can give you a lift. I must have become much changed, if I can ever so far forget my long regard for your father – to say nothing of his son – as to be indifferent to what interests him.

Yours Faithfully

H. Cockburn

To Aeneas Macbean[1]

MS. Private

Bonaly, 14 January 1849

My Dear Macbean

In the first place, I wish you a good new year. Better late than never. In the next place, how are you? A ridiculous question to put to a man in 1849, who was examined in the Scotch Privy Councel in 1687. But still he has many friends who rejoice in his prolonged welfare and youth; and are always glad to hear about him.

We are all as well as can be while No 11 is closed. Much more virtuous. As for me, I don't know what a bottle of Champagne is; and coveys of young ladies are in danger of forgetting the forms of a Polka, and the nature of flirtation. Some people think there should be a committee to inspect (mere inspection) the cellar; because wine long unused is apt to take neglect amiss, and become sour – like friends.

Scotland stands just where it did, as in Macbeth's days. Edinr has had a great flight of marriages. Lizzie's to the nephew of Douce Davie, I hope you approve of.[2] They dined here yesterday, with the Maitlands, and James Moncreiff. The said James is rising steadily in his craft – as he well deserves; for he has a sound, quick intellect, a plain, vigorous power of speech, a warm heart, and a taste for high principle. Jeffrey is under an attack of his Trachaea, as I am told, for Mrs Cockburn and I have been in these solitudes for ten days, and only know city tidings by rumour. Duloch when I saw him, three weeks ago, was quite well, tho' old like. Murray's musical evenings continue; but my poor contemptible ears have been unworthy of them all. Timotheus is in great vigour. Timothea colded all winter. Pillans strong as a bull, gay as a lark, voracious as a wolf. The College is up in

---

1 Known to HC as 'The Damned Body'. He (1776–1857) became WS 1807; his nephew (also Aeneas Macbean) lived 1820–99 and became WS 1848.

2 Probably David Cleghorn (1775–1840), WS 1800; Crown Agent 1833–40.

numbers, and all the Proffs are in high feather. I see in the papers that Dr Christison's wife is dead. Poor fellow – he had just got settled in a grand Moray Place castle. And Fully is turned out of 27 Melville St; and is wandering about for new dry ground for the sole of his foot. Our tabernacle in Manor Place is abominable, and too far off. But the horror of another movement will, I suspect, keep me where I am.

James is to be a Mauritius Stipendiary. For which – that being a French island – he is labouring away with Senellier at Parlez vous etc. He will not leave us till April. George's wife's wi' bairn again. What an ass. However he has been very successful hitherto in avoiding the masculine gender; and his girls are very nice. Robert Stewart who has been in Britain four months goes back to Leghorn in a few weeks. And, to my sorrow, takes away his child – an absolute angel.

I see the Lauders now and then. John has set up a large hot house, and been cutting trees. Lady Lauder and the girls are well put up at Greenhill, but I suspect it will be made too dear for them to continue there after May. They are all as well as a tree can be without its leaves.

Goliah is as large as the life. And my Lord Advocate full of force and society. Ten or twelve days carry these poor Senators back to what they call Town again. Miserable beasts. The wretches are waiting impatiently for one or two of us Lords of Session to get out of the way. Dogs! I shall stick on, just to disappoint them. I never hear anything of Kirky;[1] but I fear that his household is not [in] so good a way as one would wish.

William Ayton is going to espouse Prof. Wilson's daughter.[2] Ugly monster. I suppose the Prof. will be driven into second matrimony. So I recommended Susan Rutherfurd t'other day to attend to her interest. And – never despair – Allan Thomson's lawful spouse, after taking 12 years to deliberate about it, is going to give the earth a young Allan! Well done the Glasgow air.

The said Glasgow has been sorely stricken, like Edinr, by Cholera. But Typhus and Influenza killed *above double*, in the same period, last year.

My dear Macbean, take care of yourself; and come back to us as soon as it may be good for you – but not a moment sooner. Tho' we don't write, we all often, often, think, and speak of you – and always with affection. The best way you can testify your regard for us is by attending to yourself.

---

1 Probably John Macfarlan of Kirkton rather than Richardson of Kirklands.

2 William Edmondstoune Aytoun (1813–65); adv. 1840, Profesor of Rhetoric and Belles-Lettres, Edinburgh 1845–65; Sheriff of Orkney 1852–65, married Jane Emily Wilson (d.1853) the following April.

Give my heartiest love to your nieces. To whom I beg you to attend too. Each of you owe much to the other.

And so farewell – and may God bless you.

Yours ever and faithfully

H. Cockburn

Elgin has been very ill – and long; but he is getting better. This is her 38th.

[*Addressed*:] Aeneas Macbean Esq., 19 Brock Street, Bath

To George Thomson[1]

Huntington Library, 10022, p.17

Bonaly, 8 June 1849

My Dear Sir

A thousand thanks for your kind letter. It shows that there are hearts which no time can chill.

I trust, and believe, that my son has made a fortunate conjugal selection. There is no want of the Poortith[2] which is said to make love warmer; but the island of Paul and Virginia needs no coal – or dress – and so I hope they will get thro'. It was an attachment nearly as old as themselves.

I am sorry for your Colonel. I have never known him; but sympathised with any one so near to you, under such an affliction.

I am glad to hear that you think so favourably of Macbean. I fear he can never be the D——d Body again – for that implies, liquor, and laughter, and profligacy – but it is a great pleasure to hope that one who has been the cause of so much happiness may still enjoy some of it himself.

Edinr has made two great steps within these few days. The railways have been obliged to pay £4000 to the Town for their brutal mangling of the valley east of the Mound. Of this sum £2000 to be laid out in decorating – which means cleaning – the valley and its adjuncts; and the other £2000 are to be laid aside in order to produce a permanent annual fund for keeping it in repair. So we shall soon have the Monument, and the whole place, put into as good order as the presence of these cursed, grunting, belshing, whistling, and altogether infernal, trains, with the more infernal beasts that own and guide them, admits of.

And then the Mound – the Mound! We have got a Government grant for

1 The friend of Burns and collector of music, then aged 92.
2 Poverty; Bernardin de St Pierre's *Paul et Virginie* (1788) is a sentimental tale of Mauritius.

the execution of Playfair's beautiful Design for a Gallery etc for the Artists. There's a step for you! The Mound, no doubt, had better be left free; but this it would not have long been; and therefore the securing of that long, low, elegant, colonade makes my very Middriff quiver with delight.

I have been urging and manoeuvering about it for two years; but it is to our member William Craig that we truly owe it.

I have been amidst my hills since the 20th of March. A bitter, bitter Spring. That old ruffian Haarr coated our lungs, and iced our very marrow, by his damp heartless breath, till about three weeks ago. But since June began to get the upper hand, we have had dry, bright days, and these delicious northern nights that are truly but days softened. I have five grandchildren crawling round me – all, mercifully, of the feminine gender. But two, if not three, of them will, with their father and mother, be in Calcutta this year.

I fear you are right in not risking the Caledonian climate – since cough adheres to you even in the South. But, by Jingo, if the Colonade be up, down shall you come to see it, cough as you like. Meanwhile gratify us all by taking care of yourself. The affection of your Edinburgh friends is unabated. They remember the old times, and they love the old man. No one does so more warmly than I do.

My God bless you
Yours Faithfully
H. Cockburn

To John F. Macfarlan[1]
Cockburn Association. (NLS Dep 245)
Bonaly, Colinton, 1 August 1849
Dear Sir

Amidst such Edinr barbarities, or rather brutalities, as the extinction of Trinity Church[2] and of Knox's house,[3] it is consolatory to find one man who, whether he be right or not, at least *takes an interest* in the preservation of that beauty on which the reputation of Edinr chiefly depends.

I agree with you *so far* as to think that the removal, or even the narrowing,

1 Chemist and druggist, North Bridge; also from 1835 Secretary of the Edinburgh Chamber of Commerce.
2 Dismantled 1848 when the North British railway bought the site; a re-erection between High St and Jeffrey St was begun in 1872, by which time many stones had been lost.
3 Restored by Handysyde Ritchie in 1850 (Ballantine did the Knox window).

of the screen – especially for such a contemptible object as the gaining of a few feet of width for the horses of Leith Street – would be atrocious.[1] Yet there are hundreds who roar in behalf of this atrocity. I have done all I could to prevent it, and successfully.

But I do not anticipate the injury which you dread from the Statue. Work is never to be judged of half done. My belief is that when the Statue is erected, the general result will be to improve the whole edifice.

But my opinion on such a matter is worthless. It is an architectural question. Now I understand, and have not the very slightest doubt, that Mr Playfair, whose taste is now the just pride of the city, *approves of what is doing.* If this be *not* the fact, then I agree that there is ground for great alarm. But my conviction that it *is* the fact, makes me confident that the result will be satisfactory.

All the substitute sites proceed on the idea that the *Statue itself* is not to be considered, but only *the ground.* Almost all Statues ought to face the South; and this one was made on this principle. This one fact disposes of every scheme for placing it to any other than a Southern exposure. But so foolish are some people about this purely artistical question, that there is one man who is at the pains to publish a proposal – in the sense of which he is quite positive, for mounting this Statue between two of the Columns on the Calton Hill!!!

But tho' I don't agree with you on this matter, I do rejoice in every symptom that such a matter is cared about at all. The Calton Hill, or part of it, is at this moment getting itself converted into a *public washing green*!!!!! with iron poles, and ropes, and wells, and streaks of worn grass – i.e. mud – and yellow, ragged blankets, and tubs, and stones, and bitches. All this on the Calton Hill! And not from right, or old usage; but by a voluntary magisterial act, cursed by a few, but applauded by many!!

Do keep your eye on all such pieces of Hunnism. And do not imagine, because I differ from you about the Statue, or because I cannot now agitate, that I am regardless of them.

Yours truly
H. Cockburn

[*Addressed*:] Mr John F. Macfarlan, 17 North Bridge

---

1 The stone screen in front of Register House, later narrowed, was an object of discussion from the start.

To John F. Macfarlan
Cockburn Association. (NLS Dep 245)

PRIVATE
                    Bonaly, 7 August 1849
Dear Sir

I have not forgotten you at all. I only was uncertain of your identity with the person I was writing to. No man is entitled to expect to be recognised, who does not mark himself by giving his full Habitat.

As you still doubt Mr Playfair's opinion, I shall try to get it in writing.

I repeat that my zeal for the preservation of Edinburgh is as intense as ever it was.[1] But I cannot now agitate. If I could, the very causeway stones should rise up against certain most accursed projects. But why are others, with whom agitation would not be improper, so silent? The last Edinr papers report the dirt that issued from the mouths of certain presumptuous idiots who lately held a meeting in favour of *destroying* the screen. *I see, and hear of, no counter meeting.* Not that the thing will depend on such opinions either way – any more than a surgical operation would, or should. It is an architectural question. But it is scarcely fair, or safe, to expose those who must decide to hear roaring only one way. They should know that the wrong minded by no means represent the whole community.

But it must be confessed that the general apathy of Edinr on such matters is most discouraging and humiliating. I know well, by experience, how difficult it is to get even half a dozen of people to take the slightest trouble for any, even the most important, object of decoration, or of preventing abomination. The prevailing feeling is indifference – or rather a paltry preference for any piece of mean utility, when it comes into competition with the noblest public adornment. Everything dignified and beautiful must be sacrificed to the lowest bodily conveniences of what is called '*the working man*' – as if Judges and Druggists did not work, and were not entitled to have their tastes too. These people would have thought the garden of Eden wasted if it had not a distillery upon it, if one had been wanted.

                    Yours Faithfully
                    H. Cockburn

---

1 As shown most prominently in HC's *A Letter to the Lord Provost on the Best Ways of Spoiling the Beauty of Edinburgh, 1849,* and eventually the foundation of the Cockburn Association in 1875 (on which see George Bruce, *Some Practical Good,* 1975).

To William Gibson-Craig
HWUA: 2/F/28
                        Forres, 15 September 1849
My Dear Craig
        I have just got your note.
        I greatly rejoice; and now only hope that Playfair won't delay till I be dead. You have never – or at least not often – done such good service to Edinr, and so far as my explanations can, you shall not lose your reward.
        I shall not be home for a fortnight. Four murders at Aberdeen. An Inverness Jury has given a recommendation to mercy in the case of a North Uist Clearing which will ring thro' the country – and through the world.[1] *Between you and me*, it is quite just. An *acquittal* would have been wrong and done great mischief; but the conviction, which vindicates the law, and the recommendation which condemns the provocation to violate it, was founded on most scandalous facts. The people who had sown, and were entitled to reap, their corn, had their houses pulled down, with *no other houses to go to*, no *poor house*, no *ship*, nothing but the bare beach to ly upon. My regret is for Lord Macdonald,[2] against whom, because his *name* appears, it all operates; but who personally was quite innocent. It was his doers and creditors.
                                        Ever
                                        H. Cockburn

To W. A. Parker[3]
NLS 588.1330
                        Bonaly, Colinton, 24 October 1849
Dear Sir
        I have been from home, and only received your letter of the 15th inst three days ago, near Kirkcudbright.
        I am glad that you take an interest in preserving, and extending, the beauty of Edinr. The friends of this cause need all the aid they can get.
        The propriety of some sort of Association for the promotion of this object has often occurred to me also.

1 The 'Inverness Criminal Business' finished on 12 September: see *CJ* 354–6 (and *Jnl* 247–8); also John Pinkerton 'Cockburn and the Law', *Bic. Commem.* 118.
2 4th Baron Macdonald of Slate (1809–1863).
3 Name of addressee has been cut away but supplied in another hand. An Edinburgh architectural association was founded in 1858, then only the fourth such body in the UK. On HC's *Letter to the Lord Provost* see note above on letter to Macfarlan, 7 Aug 1849.

But it is a matter that would do more harm than good, if it were not organised, and conducted, very cautiously.

And it is clear (to me at least) that any Judge taking a lead in it would be objectionable.

But these are all points requiring consideration, and therefore, and as it is not convenient to discuss them in writing, I shall be glad to have an opportunity of conferring with you about them when the court meets.

Yours Faithfully
H. Cockburn

[Addressed:] To W. A. Parker, Esq., @ Architectural Association

To T. F. Kennedy
LAS 535

Edinburgh, 27 January 1850

My dear Kennedy

The greatest possible calamity has, suddenly, befallen us. Jeffrey died yesterday evening. [1]

He was in Court last Tuesday – quite well and in his usual mental energy, next day he staid at home colded, but on Thursday and Friday he was thought to be quite recovering. But he grew much worse during the night, and on Saturday (yesterday) forenoon was pronounced to be in great and immediate danger. He lived however till about six in the evening, when he passed away from us, in perfect tranquillity and without suffering.

You know what he was to this place, and to his friends. It is difficult to fancy either without him. Nor is it possible to estimate, or almost to exaggerate, his value in literature, and in the promotion of public spirit and of sound opinions.

But, as yet, it is the personal loss of the friend that is bitter.

Mrs Jeffrey is quite composed. I fear she will settle with her daughter in England, and thus remove the last trace of Jeffrey here.

Maitland, *I suppose*, will be the Judge,[2] and James Moncreiff the

---

1 On Jeffrey's death see *Jnl*, ii, 253, with obituary remarks at 254–9; see also, on possible monument, *ibid.*, 263–4.

2 So it happened. He was elevated on 6 February: see *Jnl*, 259–60 where HC remarks that with himself and Fullerton there was a probably unprecedented trio of brothers-in-law simultaneously on the bench. HC disapproved ('—— nonsense!') of Maitland's taking a territorial name (Dundrennan) rather than a family one. Maitland died in June 1851.

Solicitor.[1] But this must depend on Rutherfurd's own views – which I don't know.

I am not sure that you know Moncreiff. An excellent lawyer, a powerful speaker, an admirable writer, and a generous, spirited fellow, he is worthy both of his father and of Sir Harry.

Edinburgh without Jeffrey! – and his Court! He was its light and its pride.

I trust that you are all well. I beg to be remembered to Mrs Kennedy.

Ever

H. Cockburn

To Mrs Sydney Smith
NCO Arch. 4429

2 Manor Place, Edinburgh, 7 February 1850

Dear Mrs Smith

I received your packet today – and thank you very sincerely for it.

The Sermon on the utility of meditating upon Death, in the first of the vols you have been so kind as to send me, is *not* the one I referred to, however – beautiful tho' it be. The one I referred to – and which I still hear – was preached, in Edinr, some years after the death of Horner, in 1817; for I remember a passage which we all thought alluded to that event.[2] I dined with Mr Smith that day at Mr Thomson's, where there was some discussion about the discourse.

Jeffrey's death has put every heart into mourning. To his friends it is irreparable. There is no other Jeffrey – and nothing like him. I never knew such sorrow.

Mrs Jeffrey has been, and is, very unwell, and will be left here till she can be moved, by the Empsons, who go to Haileybury on Monday. She will follow, I hope soon. But then comes the second, and last, cloud – for she will part with Craigcrook, and we shall see her no more.

1 James Moncreiff (1811–95); adv. 1833, son of the judge, became Solicitor-General and then (intermittently) Lord Advocate. He was MP for Leith 1851–9, for Edinburgh 1859–68, then for Glasgow University 1868–9. Lord Justice-Clerk 1869–95; created Baron Moncreiff of Tulliebole 1874. See also *Jnl*, ii, 261.

2 HC had in May 1849 praised Smith's finely *read* sermon, in contrast to the United Presbyterian Synod's prohibition of *reading* from the pulpit, in *Jnl*, i, 242–5. Sydney Smith, an *ER* colleague of Jeffrey's, had died in 1845.

Again, thanking you, believe me,

Yours Faithfully
H. Cockburn

I remember the text of the Sermon I heard – viz: 'There is but a step between me and death', 1 Samuel, 20 chap., 3rd verse.

To [the Revd] John Mackenzie[1]
MS. Frackleton

Bonaly, 24 May 1850

My Dear Sir

I shall do anything you like, either in June or in July – but upon the condition that I have the pleasure of seeing you and Dr Hanna here.

If Jeffrey professed infidelity to Chalmers, nothing can ever convince me that he did so as a sincere expression of his true opinions. Because tho' he was not a religious man, or rather not what is commonly considered so, *most unquestionably* he was not an infidel. He must have been trying an experiment on Chalmers's charity or forbearance; or, possibly, protecting himself from the imputation, to his own mind and the mind of his friend, of courting Chalmers by the profession of those religious feelings by which he knew that he was most easily attracted, and which, in the Doctor's sense, Jeffrey did not possess. But he might have wanted these, and not been an infidel.

However I am very glad that any letter bearing such a construction is destroyed.

I shall be very glad to see any others of Jeffrey to Chalmers; and am very anxious to have any of Chalmers to him – unless Dr Hanna[2] means to publish them.

But of all this when we meet.

Yours Faithfully
H. Cockburn

1 Minister of Dunkeld and husband of Thomas Chalmers's daughter Elizabeth.
2 William Hanna, Minister of Skirling, also a Chalmers son-in-law and author of the principal biography (1849–52).

To Mrs Leonard Horner
NLS 2214.102
Bonaly, 2 June 1850
My dear Mrs Horner

I am very sensible of the kindness that invites me to join your projected rustic festivity. Seeing your scenery would, of itself, be delightful; but still more seeing the various chickens collected under the maternal wing (tho' by the bye old Power is rather a full grown chick). But I *cannot*. This is the very heigh day of our courts, which work on till about the end of July. So, unless you will come here, you won't see me this year. But express my benediction and love, at least twenty times, to the whole assembled clan. And don't kill yourselves, either by walking, or laughing, or stuffing, or quaffing. To the Powers, who I see seldomest, you may extend the twenty to twenty-five times.

I had a nice letter from my friend Frances t'other day. She is a nice creature, and I hope will rise into gigantic strength. Take care of Catherine. Doing that job ill becomes a habit. The person I am sorriest for is Sir C. Lyell.[1] But time and his good sense will soothe the irritation natural to one so ill used, and the circumstances, so [long] as he keeps himself out of new mischief, are good enough for a moderate man. To Mary you may go to the length of fifty – or infinity. Tell Susan I shall write to her soon. I trust that Leo's legs have been giving him a prudential hint.

Jane is certainly better. The hooping cough gone. The two children are my hourly delight. I had a walk with them a little ago, along the terrace. Many a daisy did they pull, many a cuckoo imitate, many a bee chase. It is a calm, hot, grey, heavy, lurid day; and I have four bottles of punch in ice for four burgh cronies who promised to come out to dinner.

Craigcrook!! I shall never see it more! I heard the funeral service read over Mrs Jeffrey, in the once happy drawing room there, last Wednesday. Jeffrey, Mrs Jeffrey, Craigcrook, and 24 Moray Place, all extinguished within four months! An obliteration that darkens the brightest scenes of my life.

May the survivors cherish each other the more.

Ever

H. Cockburn

---

1 Sir Charles Lyell of Kinnordy (1797–1875), Kt 1848, Bt 1864, the geologist, had in 1832 married Mary Elizabeth, eldest of Leonard Horner's six daughters.

To Mrs Andrew Rutherfurd
NLS 9688.120

Bonaly, 8 August 1850

My Dear Mrs Rutherfurd

Are you all alive? If you be, tell me what you are doing, or are about to do; for these long gaps in our acquaintance are frightful, and, as they seem always to occur at this season, are, I suppose, unavoidable. You have a cargo, I fancy, of these learned boys, and of other unlearned Suthrons. And I heard it whispered, by a bird in the air, that you are going to the Gem of the Ocean. But of course you will wait on Her Majesty on the 30th, and help Albert to lay the Stone;[1] when the Provost, and Pluffy, and all the Board of Trustees who have no other titles, and all the Scotch Academy, are to be knighted – about eighty – all at once.

Tell me all about every thing.

I am, and have been, living here in glorious tranquillity – amidst roses, and peas, and black currants, and cream, and hourly strolls, and conscientious sleeps, and an absolute rejection of the town. Jane is on the whole, for her, well. Archd's wife and bairn are here – as their present home. He is in Sutherland, visiting a friend – seemingly quite well – a recovery absolutely miraculous – and goes in a few days, at least so he plans, to London, where he thinks he has made an arrangement with a retiring doctor at Kensington. A Miss Evans – one of the best families in Herefordshire, and to whose kindness he has all along owed more than to anybody even in that, to him, kind shire, especially during his late illness – has been here about a month. Middle aged, not at all pretty, but ladylike, chearful, sensible, natural, and not at all chatteratious. Johanna has had sundry toothy jobs, but is well. The two children, the two cows, and the two pigs – all delightful. And so you have a full bulletin of the whole house.

Poor Tarly![2] What a storm has passed, in about five months, over that house! But I never anticipated that the leaves of Spring were to be laid low as well as those of Autumn. It is really severe upon Charlotte; and still more on the feebler constitution and, I fancy, more sensitive heart, of Empson.

I am busy with Jeffrey's papers, of which I got a great mass a month ago. I mean his youthful ones. And they are indeed very curious. I never knew him till now. What a student! And what a wise, precocious, spirited, self training, little amiable devil! One single poem alone – *On Dreaming* – is as long as the *Essay on Man* and *The Pleasures of Hope* joined. It is very nearly 2000 lines!

1 The foundation stone of the Academy's new gallery. See Esmé Gordon, *RSA*, ch. 6.
2 The Jeffreys' daughter Charlotte.

And it is only one of many! One Greek translation of about 5000 lines. Hech! The reading of them is kittle. Indeed I don't do it. All I can do is torture my poor dimming eyes sufficiently to be able to conjecture what his long folio pages are about, ill written, on paper now brown, ink now pale, no punctuation, seldom a title, and never any division into paragraphs. The misfortune is that with all the talent, and all the virtue, and all the industry, and all the usefulness of the man, there is so very little to tell, biographically.

Mrs Cockburn and I and the Hereford lady are going to visit, for two or three days, in Stirlingshire on Monday. And then I suppose I must renew my acquaintance with Kirklands – which however Helen's absence, who is trying to soften Hallam,[1] tho' beyond his Middle Age, on the continent, will diminish the sunniness of.

And thus the broken thread of our intercourse is reunited; as much as a letter can reunite it. Splice your end of it.

I hope his Lordship is keeping sober, and idle. Remember me to him. We are too far asunder, locally. But November – heartless brute – is hobbling on. My next town engagement is on the 11th of that month. After that I am disengaged – and entirely at your service.

Ever

H. Cockburn

If I did not think it was in vain to expect you here, I would say Saturday or Sunday. If you can, let me know soon for the calf's sake.

To Sophia Rutherfurd
NLS 9688.124
Bonaly, 31 August 1850
My Dear Mrs Rutherfurd

Hearing your spouse was dwabble, I went to see him yesterday, and dined with him, with Sir James Stewart, Playfair, and And. Clerk. He is pale a little, and thin a little, and very weak; and consequently neither with the mutton, nor the bottle, was he the old Saint. But those who had seen him before said he was much better than he was a few days ago; and tho' not himself, he was by no means utterly bad. He drank, and ate, and laughed reasonably, and talked pretty fully. On the whole, I came away better pleased than I expected. We are so little accustomed to see him ill, that we can't see a

1 Henry Hallam (1777–1859), the historian.

single feather ruffled without fancying that the whole bird is moulting. And as he neither went to the Orion, nor to dine royally, it has been a smartish touch; but I have no doubt he will soon be the same John Taaffe.

Think of Pluffy's felicity yesterday! At one o'clock Albert laid the foundation of his Galleries, and at four The Queen went over his Hospital, *speaking very much to the architect himself,* and admiring everything. It was his great day. And delighted, modest, and amiable he was – in spite of all the laughter, and bad jokes, and parodies that I could exhaust myself in pouring out on him. Her Majesty was charmed by the *scite* of the Hospital; but, poor royal Creature, she had never heard of the Pentland Hills! – on which she gazed with especial admiration. Think of a crowned head never having heard of the Pentland Hills! But her admiration shows that the head was not unworthy of the crown.

She has had beautiful weather. When she arrived, she went slowly, in an open carriage, past Parsons Green, to the Abbey; with, it is supposed, 100,000 cheering people on Arthur Seat. Yesterday morning she went round The Drive, and walked from Loch Sappy to the *Top of the Hill,* under a splendid, calm sun, and with not 100 people on the hill to disturb her.

I suppose she is the only sovereign to have been there since the days of Arthur himself; and when were his days?

The Founding was beautiful. The Orators were His Reverence Principal Lee,[1] who prayed a good prayer, only the sun blinded him, and he was not heard five yards off; Davie Bole, the handsomest and youngest man there; and Albert, whose address – whosoever composed it – was excellent, and excellently spoken. All we – I mean of the Board of Trustees etc. – were introduced to him in the Gallery of the Royal Institution, thro' which he walked. He particularly admired my shoes. Everybody was in some sort of uniform, or decent private dress; except three noble Lords, who chose to show their superiority, and their familiarity with royalty, by appearing as scurvy as possible. These were Rosebery – a scrul, who always pretends to be ill when he is required to lay out a penny; Bucchan – who used to remind us by his elegance and sprightliness of the aerial Henry Erskine, but always a fool, now a broken down beggar; and Belhaven, who gets £2000 a year for upholding the Kirk by dressing himself ten days yearly – yet yesterday had positively robbed a scare crow for his dirty raggs.[2]

After this ceremony Her Majesty went, in an open carriage, thro' both new

1 John Lee (1779–1859), Principal of Edinburgh University 1840–59.
2 4th Earl of Rosebery (1783–1868), KT 1840, here a scruff, grandfather of the Prime Minister; 12th Earl of Buchan (1783–1857), nephew of the eccentric antiquary; 8th Lord Belhaven (1793–1876), KT 1861, frequently High Commissioner.

and old towns, and again round the drive. Even the severe Dunphy says that the Apartments in Holyrood are magnificent.

She is off this morning; and in seven hours hears the murmur, and sees the liquid crystal, of the Dee.

The Foundation stone is the great event. It greatly adorns Edinr – and saves it from a fatal danger, which nothing except the ornamental appropriation of the ground could have averted; it marks, and promotes, the progress of Art; it gives the Artists a dignity, and a permanency, of station, which nothing but a connection with Government could have given; and it refines and elevates the local taste, and the local objects. I hope the artists will show, by their works, that they deserve it. Paton, I hear, is pretty far on with a beautiful conception.

Sir John Watson Gordon, their President, was the most picturesque gentleman in the ceremony.[1] A full suit of black velvet – lace frills and ruffles; silver buckles – and a very handsome gold medal hung from his neck. He was exactly like an English nobleman, 250 years ago, going forth to get his head taken off. What can I say more?

When do you mean to come back? I have no idea that Rutherfurd needs you; and I am so affraid of the Autumnal strangers exhausting him, that I would rather he was with you. Anyhow, take care of yourself. There are fewer pearls on the string now than when we first knew it. Let none that remain drop off unnecessarily.

Miss Elphinstone is dead – mercifully, for she could never have moved. We are all wellish. Tho' Joe disturbs us, with her back and her weakness. I asked little Charlotte t'other day, if she has a spine? To which she said 'No, but I've a spade'. A much better thing, certainly.

Ever

H. Cockburn[2]

To Mrs Andrew Rutherfurd
NLS 9688.133

Bonaly, 31 March 1851

My Dear Mrs Rutherfurd

Thanks for your letter.

I am sorry that Rutherfurd has not gone on gaining weight as he was doing,

1 John Watson Gordon (b.1788, as Watson, added Gordon 1828), PRA and Kt 1850, d.1864.
2 It was soon after this, in mid-September, that HC, on the South Circuit, was struck down by illness and 'in great torture and great danger'. He lay at the King's Arms for some three weeks, remarking when he recovered that the attack might have been caused by railways. (*CJ* 367).

last week. He ought never to cease remembering that he is in the stage which requires most active care, and that gained strength is too apt to tempt to rashness.

Poor, dear Moncreiff.[1] How kind, and how true a heart. How steady and honest a life. In intellect how narrow a range, but what force within it. Unchanged, from the day he held up the candle to exhibit Henry Erskine in 1796, to the day he *presided* at a similar meeting, in the same place, in 1820 – and from that till he died yesterday. Too true to affect knowledge, and too sincere to try to conceal ignorance, and too recluse to acquire tact, his simplicity, which some thought idiocy, tho' it often made him ridiculous, was one of the charms of his character. I have no doubt that I shall often laugh, as I ever have done, at his diverting dotages; but as I never ceased, so I never shall, to venerate his nature.

I go towards Inverary next Monday. But I shall be here all this week; and if you can catch a good day with you, and think it not too far, I shall be delighted to see you both here. But not to even [consider] the risk of any injury.

I have seen, in the distance, that you have been under a long cloud shower both at Edinr and Lauriston. We have had no rain here, except, I mean, the spring showers, thro' which the sun shines, and larks sing (when they can). We are all well. Graham leaves us, to my great grief, on Thursday morning.

I wish I had the disposal of the vacant gown; as to which I have three very decided opinions.

I am beginning to be angry at little Lord Johnnie.[2] Has the body no mind of his own at all? If he has, why not stick to it? You will see that his dropt clauses (as they call them) will be restored in spite of his teeth. And what then?

Ever
H. Cockburn

To Mrs Andrew Rutherfurd
NLS 9688.137
Bonaly, 8 May 1851
My Dear Mrs Rutherfurd

We have all been delighted to hear of your easy journey, and untired

---

1 Sir James Wellwood Moncreiff (1776–1851) SCJ 1829, died on 30 March.
2 Lord John Russell. On him and his Reform proposals of 1852 see *CJ*, ii, 270–73.

arrival. Don't let the seductions of the Devil's drawing room lead you into fatigue and relapse. And so you are Right Honourabled.[1] Whatever it may be, now as ever, I rejoice in every thing that contributes to your happiness. There is a rumour here of a still further honor – but I don't believe it. Does not your return only on the 17th give Rutherfurd rather little time to recruit, if the journey should happen to fatigue him?

I have never been so anxious for any Judge's success. On our other chairs, a deserving man is independant and safe, and his merits get fair play. But in our Outer House, and the best Judge in the world is subject to be past [sic] by if enemies or idiots chuse. There was no *good* reason why Murray should be absolutely left dry on the beach; nor why Wood should be careering full sail over everybody.[2] But it does not depend on desert, but on *popularity*; and without this precarious virtue no Lord Ordinary – not even Andrew Rutherfurd – will succeed, no, not altho' he had Solomon, and Lycurgus, and Minerva, and John Hope, all within his waistcoat. So he must avoid Benchy Slumber, and harshness, and impatience, and over-bearingness, and over-blandness, and all overs – but especially the strange over-Ivorian infirmity of an ambition to be so immensely perfect in his judgements, that the egg was never laid till the intending eaters were all dead. For the parties, a bad judgement on Monday is preferable to a better one on Saturday. So if Rutherfurd becomes Murray the Second, it is not my fault.

The change makes a great, and, I think a merciful, odds on your future life. Less money than you had; but less need of it, repose, self possession, and secured health. There need be no great abatement of jollity; I mean of that temperate and moral jollity that becomes old men, and owls of the law. Indeed, amidst all your past scenes of social profligacy, have not I – yea I alone – preached and practised to you that the moral part of the banquet was the only part that would survive, or that pleased *me* even while the Folly was loudest, and when, to avoid the appearance of meanness, I *seemed* to join in it.

Do what little you can to introduce the new fledged chick of a Lord Advocate favourably. I shall never be indifferent to that which represents the virtues and the vigour of Lord Moncreiff and old Sir Henry.

1 Rutherfurd had been appointed Lord Ordinary 7 April, Privy Counsellor 5 May, and took his seat as SCJ 23 May 1851. (He died at his St Colme Street house on 13 December 1854.)
2 Murray had been on the Bench since May 1839; Alexander Wood of Woodcote (d.1864; adv.1811), after a year as Dean, had gone onto the Bench in November 1842.

I hear nothing of Mackenzie,[1] and nothing of his resignation. I do trust that his successor will be McNeill. I grudge our adversaries the fact that seventeen years of Whigism have not made one Tory Judge, whereas the seventeen preceding years of Toryism made seven Whig ones.

Torquay has done Helen Maitland much good. Fully is enlivening his dullness at Craigie. Goliah is peopling the colonies from Perth. He has insisted on having the glory of the whole North Circuit to himself.

We have been living here, till within three days, under zephirs direct and fresh from the North Pole. But for these three, the air has come, mildly and gently, from the South West; and vegetable life seems to be starting with surprize. Our vernalities have been beautiful; at least to our eyes and noses, trained to what Scotch nature can give. And I always delight in the weedlessness of this season. And the Blackbirds and Mavises! I flatter myself that they know me, for they never think either of flight or of silence, how near so ever I get to them. I know the very branches where, at evening, they are sure to be perched; and no doubt for every songster there is an incubating mate close at hand. These faithful husbands always remind me of Rutherfurd and myself, who spend our time piping to a couple of yawmmersome wives. (Delicate ground, so I get off it.)

Richardson is off tomorrow to his trouts. Would I was with him; for I have not forgotten the beauty of the place, nor the (Lady-loved) Ayle, nor the note of my first heard Nightingale. Then, it is a shame not to see the great Glasshouse. Tho', after all, it has an air of contemptuous dignity to be able to say No, I did not go to see a thing so common.

I have got a delightful letter of Jeffrey's, in 1819, offering £500 to relieve Moore of some pecuniary embarrassment.

Love to Rutherfurd – whom I do love as cordially as ever man loved man.

Ever

H. Cockburn

To James Rutherfurd
NLS 9688.225

Bonaly, Colinton, Edinburgh, 21 June 1851

My Dear Colonel

On entering the drawing room of Lauriston last Thursday I was met by a youth, who looked in my face, and said with an innocent gaiety, 'You'l be

1 Joshua Henry Mackenzie (1777–1851; adv.1799). SCJ, 1822. McNeill became SCJ 1851.

surprised to see me here'. I was very glad to find my friend Andrew again. He has grown tall, and is still an affectionate and sensible boy.[1]

The elder Andrew is getting on steadily. He is still pale and thin; but his voice is strong and the general man strengthening. From his position, he luckily can have very little to do in court till November, by which time he may be the same John Taaffe. She is well, and the place beautiful, tho', to my taste, too urnified

This loss of poor Maitland[2] is a very severe calamity on us all. And it is but a bitter consolation, that had he lived, it could only have been in deplorable infirmity both of body and of mind. You, who know our social and domestic habits, can appreciate the blank of his closed door, and crushed household. They are all well – including Mrs Maitland – for their situation. She is going, we hope, to Hermand for the summer.

And Moncrieff!! But there is no use in counting the fallen leaves. Let us enjoy the end of the Autumn that remains to us.

We are all well here. I mean as well as the coldest and stormiest of Mays and Junes admits of. Your Sherbornian gales are mere sighs, compared to our Caledonian zephyrs.

Pluffy is beautiful. And his Mound will be glorious. The new road by the west side is finished and is most admirable. The look down into the West Garden is the finest *internal* town scene in this island. I called on poor Mrs Clark a few days [ago]. Not the first call, but the first time I had seen her since her son's loss. I have a great regard for her, and she, I believe, for me; and so we had a comfortable greet, which, after all, is all that human consolation comes to.

Our little new tiny Lord Advocate has already earned Parliamentary Laurels even from the most fastidious judges.[3] I never expected anything else; tho' I did not expect it so soon. He is a very fine, spirited creature. His Depute Andrew Clark is doing well. A clever fellow, and not nearly so offensive to some as he once thought it became his dignity to be. He has lowered his English a peg, and is more quiet and modest. This steady and affectionate

1 James Rutherfurd's only son, Andrew Rutherfurd (1835–1906); adv.1857; Sheriff of Lothians (and Peebles) 1882–1904.

   His sister, Margaret Anne (1836–1902) married in 1854 Andrew Rutherford Clark (1828–99); adv. 1849; Solicitor-General 1869–74; Dean of Faculty 1874–5; SCJ (as Lord Rutherford Clark) 1875–96.
2 Thomas Maitland had died on 10 June.
3 James Moncreiff (1811–1895) was beginning the first of four spells as Lord Advocate between 1851 and 1869.

conduct towards his uncle during the late long illness sets him high up in my eye. He'll do very well.

Give my love, with all possible affection, to Mrs Rutherfurd; and with more than possible to her once called Corbie. And take it to yourself. Were not the recollections of old men, tottering into dotage, apt to become childish, I could say much about our past days. But it would be useless. While our sun is up, let us work — in any field of activity, or kindness, or duty, or enjoyment, that is still open to us. Therefore if you will come and spend some time here, you [will] find plenty present delight in the Tower and on the Pentlands — and may even have the 'pleasant vices' of your youth all revived; and, I doubt not, ditto if you could get me to Sherborne, which however never can be — apparently. I had a characteristic and excellent letter from Tom Erskine three days ago about Maitland. No one else could have written it. Full of all his heart, all his piety, a good deal his metaphysical Theology, and some of his German wildness. But delightful in its affection, and talent.

And so, my dear James, for this bout Farewell. I hope you've given up Gout now. Andrew gives a bad account of the Sherborne water; which I hope does not drive you into Ale or Cyder. Your true remedy, for everything, is to come here, and daily mount Cape Law.

But if you won't, at least remember us — as we do you. Mrs Cockburn sends you all her love. And so do I again. And may God send his.

Ever

H. Cockburn

To John Richardson
NLS Dep 235(1) (*SL* 67–9 (–))
Bonaly, 17 October 1851
My Dear John

Your personal kindness makes you partial to the red book.[1] But indeed, tho' I have eiked notes occasionally on passing occurrences, I have not read the vol. you have for twenty years at the least. Since you are willing to wade on, and have got into the stream, I do not see why you should not be indulged. But in 1830 it ceases to be a narrative, and becomes entries of things as they

---

1 On the Red Book as the origin of what became *Memorials of His Time*, see *Bic. Commem.*, 166–80. This letter indicates the suspension of the *Mems* around 1830 and the inauguration of the *Journal* at the start of 1831. The *Circuit Journeys* begins in 1838.

arose; a far more valuable form both for the truth of facts and of impressions, but less agreeable to a person reading straight thro'; and, among other plagues, it is more blotted and illegible. But the second volume too would now be pretty new to myself.

I meditate being with you on Friday next, the 24th, and home on the following Monday. But any time the week after would do just as well for me. I can't assist at your Divan tomorrow because Robert Stewart,[1] a most capital fellow, from Leghorn, is to be here tomorrow for 1 days!!!

But I am clear both about Education, and Parliamentary Reform.

The true, and the *ultimately* prevailing, principle is to proceed as if secular ignorance was a crime, or a pestilent disease: and therefore to put it down; and that untill all Sectarians shall agree (which they never will) what religion is to be bound up with it, there must be no religion bound up with it except such as Government, or the District, or *some power external to Clergy*, may approve of. The case of Scotland is peculiar, in so far as the whole country is nearly Protestant, and nearly Presbyterian; and therefore I am for abating the strict application of this general principle to this country, so far as to accept of a system that may require *General Protestantism* to be joined to secular education. But if, as I anticipate, different Protestant Sects will not concur in this, and each shall want the people only to see thro' its spectacles, then I think the people ought to be secularly educated, and each sect left to knead its own dough. The great thing for Melgund, or for any wise and firm man taking up this subject, is *to insist on the right principle*, viz. education without state-taught Creed – and not to *begin* by sacrificing this principle in order to conciliate Priests, who, do what you may, will not be conciliated; but, on the other hand, to *end* by making concessions *provided* these will really let the people be educated thoroughly.

As to the Reform with which Government has let the radicals make it pregnant, I am short, and clear, and *poz.* –

I am for all that Extension of franchise that does not imply *lowering* it. It is low enough. Experience has proved that the large constituencies like the worst members – that is, members likest themselves. Bringing in more of these electors is bad for the peace of the country, and hurtful to the characters of Members; who instead of forming a Wittenagemote, or an assembly of wise men, become the mere delegates or attorneys, not merely of the interests and opinions of their masters, but of their follies and passions. But many a thousand good man who is a ten-pounder in reality, is

1 Cockburn's son-in-law since 1839.

now excluded. Let them all in, but keep all else out, particularly the fictitious, or rather the fraudulent, voters. We live under a Monarchical Republic already, and I am not for admitting a mob sufficient to sweep the monarchical element away.

I am terrified about the coming Delivery from this pregnancy. My anticipations are that the bantling will be either too small for the people to lift, or too large for the Aristocracy to rear, and that between the two stools Government drops; that after this, a Tory Government will bid still higher for popular favour; that a dangerous measure will thus be carried, and after this, who would become security for the throne?

Moral – Extension without Degradation.

Ever

H. Cockburn

I have not become a Tory; but no Whigism I ever had required me to make members slaves of the low multitude, any more than of the high aristocracy.

Rutherfurd has just been here. Remarkably well. Palish – but walked all over the place, drank claret, ate minced collops, laughed, and talked, excellently.

To Thomas Cleghorn
NLS Dep 235(1)(*SL* 71–2)
9 March 1852
My Dear Cleghorn

I shall write to Richardson tonight. There can be no doubt of his being well disposed towards you; but his potentiality is quite a different matter. *Any* Scotch Counsel who does one appeal well, and is handy at making common sense perceptible to English legal brains, is nearly sure of employment if Scotch causes be much gone into. James Keay went up on chance for two years, and returned, *each* time, at least £2500 plus. But Keay had mental eyes that saw thro' the thickest fog, and a tongue the wagging of which dispersed all obscurity. Why should not yours?

Ever

H. Cockburn

To Mrs Fletcher
Autobiography, 303

Edinburgh, 12 March 1852

A copy of Jeffrey's Life, which is to be published on Tuesday, leaves this tomorrow morning addressed to you.[1]

There are some things in it which you will miss; but I found it absolutely necessary to confine it to purely personal matter, and there are some things in it which I hope you will like.

My object has solely been to unfold the character of our late lamented friend, and by doing so, to give the public better reasons for loving him than it had before.

How little so ever may be thought of the first volume, I cannot doubt that the second, written entirely by Jeffrey, must impart undivided delight. If there be better letters in the English language, I have never seen them.

I wish I had an hour's dialogue with you on the state of the world. The general opinion in this Northern region, deducting Radicals and Tories, is strongly against the new Reform Bill, and seems to all good Whigs to introduce what is practically universal suffrage, and this they think a thing only to be liked by County Tories and Town Radicals.

A terrible retribution surely awaits, and sooner than they think, the tyrants of the Continent. I, knowing the ever young benevolence of your heart, talk of these things to you, because I know they interest you.

Farewell. Though absent, be assured of the respect and affection in which you are held by all your Edinburgh friends, and by none more sincerely than me.

Yours faithfully
H. Cockburn

1 Text from Mary Richardson (ed.) *Autobiography of Mrs Fletcher* (3rd edn, 1876), 303. This contains a number of appreciative comments on HC, including her report of a meeting with Lord John Russell: 'When I told him Lord Cockburn's son-in-law, Mr Cleghorn, had lately told me Lord Cockburn had left an historical account of Scotland, in what might be called the reign of terror, his face lighted up with a radiant smile, and he said, "Yes, even Dugald Stewart was afraid", adding "No man but Cockburn could have done it; we sent for him to consult him about the Reform Bill for Scotland".'

To Robert Carruthers[1]
NLS 10,997.94

12 March 1852

You formerly rendered me valuable, and very kindly, assistance when I first began to contemplate a Life of Lord Jeffrey. That rash undertaking has come to a close, and will be formally published next Tuesday. A copy leaves this for you by some rail way or other tomorrow morning. There are a few words of MSS. upon it, and therefore I could not send it by post. Be as merciful as your conscience will allow, to the only two volumes – or rather the only one – of which I have ever been guilty; especially as I am not likely ever to transgress in this way again.

My sole object has been to unfold the personal nature of Jeffrey. The life of a man who, thro'out the thirty years of his manhood, did little except by writing anonymous pamphlets (called Reviews) and by bamboozling Courts, is necessarily devoid of incidents. But thro' this atmosphere his friends knew, and felt, that there ever gleamed a bright ray of goodness, of which strangers could see little. If, without adulation or invention, I have imparted this truth, and good grounds for it, to the public, my end is attained.

Whatever may be thought of the first volume, I shall be mortified and surprized if the second, which is all Jeffrey's own, do not afford general delight.

I intend to be in Inverness at the circuit in April, when I trust I shall have the pleasure of seeing you.

To John Richardson
NLS Dep.235(1) (*SL*.69–70(–))

Bonaly, 19 March 1852

My Dear John

We came here today – all safely. Mrs C. got down the stair, and through the drive, and up the stair – all well – and is very cheery now at 8 p.m.[2] My dorsal district was cupped into something like a raw beef stake yesterday; and as it is still obstinate, I have sentenced it to a blister tomorrow.

A Bannatyne Notice which I presume you have got will show you that I

---

1 Robert Carruthers (1799–1878), editor (1828) and from 1831 proprietor of the *Inverness Courier*; his writings included a contribution on Jeffrey to the 8th edition of *Encyclopaedia Britannica*.

2 Mrs Cockburn had suffered a 'paralytic attack' (stroke) in mid-November 1851.

have not neglected your commission about the Marquis of Lothian. The Reverend gentleman I never heard of, and think we will be the more comfortable priestless. So I don't X him.

I am very much gratified by your approbation of the Life; not the less that I ascribe part of your liking of your book to your liking of the author. There is one part of it which I anticipated was to incur the displeasure of you and of George Dundas.[1] It has incurred Dundas's, and therefore I am the more comfortable from your silence about it: *Cranstoun*. I never liked him, and thought him exposed to some deep objections; but I meant to give him high praise in departments where it was due; and on the whole was conscious that, *with my opinions*, the praise was fully high. But Dundas says it is very coldly done, as much as if I had simply said in a note referable to George Cranstoun, '*The Late Lord Corehouse'. This is nonsense. Mere Dundas-ism. But I don't know that you don't inwardly disapprove of that passage.

I really wish that you and Rutherfurd would instruct me about the Red [Book].[2] He has seen only the first vol. but I suspect has not had time, during Session, to read it all. To divert his wife, I made her welcome, and she has read it all, but is so charmed with old Esky, that he half supersedes everything else. The sole question is, ought I to attempt to make a continuous history out of it; or ought [I] just to go on recording, and leave the mass to be put into shape by others after I shall be sodded? The chief objections to my doing it are: 1. That it would be done so near the persons and the events, that it must be dilluted into insipidity. 2. That an unbroken narrative necessarily loses the freshness of immediate memoranda. The objections of its being left to descendants are: 1. That it may be thought not worth meddling with. 2.That it may be selected and worked up ill. Perhaps a safe middle course would be for me to do it, but to leave it unknown and unseen till distance and my removal made its publication not indelicate. And there is another safe and simple course – present conflagration. By my settlement, as it at present stands, my trustees are *allowed* to do as they like with it – even to burn it – but are *advised* to be guided by you and Rutherfurd if you survive me.

---

1 George Dundas (1802–69) adv. 1826. Sheriff of Selkirk 1844–68; SCJ (Lord Manor) 1868. The passage on Cranstoun referred to is in *Jeff.*, i, 209–12.

2 Having completed his work on Jeffrey, to which they had made a considerable contribution, HC was becoming increasingly concerned with his own literary records. On 3 April he prepared Directions to his trustees, setting out plans on which posthumous publications were to be based.

I hope you did not think, in the Life, I have been penurious in praise of our old friends Grahame and John Macfarlane.[1]

Lord John does *not* appear to me to have backed out of his self-wrecking reform; but on the contrary to have backed into it; for he says he only gives it *while he is out*, as it is only when *in* that he can carry it.

Plain John was quite right in rejecting the cunning Priest. But not in *rebuking* him of the High Sherif, *if it be true* that other Judges had homologated.

If Alex. Blair be the thin, pensive looking, gentle, and rather humble, long necked, scribe who you and I know, and is still on the Edinr earth, the biographer of Gregory Wat[t] should be referred to him.

Ever

H. Cockburn

To Elizabeth Cleghorn
NLS Dep.235(1) *(SL 72)*
Inverness, Court,[2] 13 April 1852
My Dearest Lizzie

Ivory is now under the luxury of a competition of Celtic lies (called a trial), so I may as well tell you that we are all well. Johanna's cold is better today, seemingly gone. She and the other three ladies are in court, enjoying the beauties of Gaelic exaggeration. I have rebuked the Ivorys for giggling; at which they, very sensibly, only giggle the more. I commanded the presence of the thoughtful and lady like Susan this morning at 8, and she and I had nearly an hour's walk of discourse and admiration, amidst the most glorious of days, and of objects. We were at Relugas yesterday, and I never saw the Findhorn in greater beauty. I was against Susan's giving herself the pain of revisiting their lost Paradise. But she wished it, and, tho' moved, was pleased that she had done so. We left Knockomie after dinner at 5, and were here by half past 8.

I am very glad to hear of your mother's wheeling and walking out, and am most thankful that you and Thom are with her. I feel the kindness of your being so.

But the neck? Strange things, bumps. All from the other side of the house,

---

1 For Grahame, see *Jeff.*, i, 111–13. For Macfarlane (of Kirkton) (1767–1846), adv. 1789; *ibid.*, i, 113–14.
2 On the North Circuit, April 1852 (*CJ*, 373–86).

mind. I am very sorry for your continued suffering; but cannot doubt that it will, in time, be recompensed by recovered health.

I am grieved, and alarmed, about Fullerton. But their silence makes it seem worse than it really may be.

Hech! It's het! And oh these Celtic idiots! However, not understanding them leads my fancy home – and I please myself by seeing you all in your various employments, and all happy, in all helping each other. But query – have you punched the gentleman's ribs today?

He won't get the turnip field ready, unless a gentle admonition of this kind be administered daily (or hourly).

Love to everybody.

Auntie Jeanie was looking at our grand procession today from her window.

Ever

H. Cockburn

To James Ballantine
NLS 1660.22

Perth[1], 26 April 1852

My Dear Sir

Your excellent, because native, epistle has this moment caught me here; and tho' actually in court, I hasten to beg you *not* to dedicate the song to me. I have the greatest respect for him of the Gut, and the greatest regard for the Author of the Song; but the devil take them both, and the theatre, and all the Audience, and the whole human race, that adds to the publicity of Bonaly.[2] The short and the long of it just is that I must either acquire the character of an inhospitable brute, or leave that place. If the curious public will *pay the Rent,* that would be a different affair. But I never hear any word of this.

I am glad that your eyes, at least, feast upon the Pentlands; for some of my friends have had little other feasting there for a long while. However I hope to

1 Again 'in Court', at the end of 'the most murderous Circuit I have known', which had several capital sentences (some with grounds for leniency) to be reported: see *CJ*, 372–84 for a detailed account of legal business as well as the reminiscences that in the later *Journeys* often take the place of topographical narrative.

2 Cockburn's courteous antipathy to Ballantine's continued verse tributes was unabated. 'Bonnie Bonaly's wee fairy led stream / Murmurs and sobs like a child in a dream' cannot have been welcome. For the hordes of strolling intruders, see e.g. the letter of 14 August 1852 below.

have done with this Transporting work soon, when I shall endeavour to show them something more substantial.

Yours Faithfully

H. Cockburn

To Andrew Rutherfurd
NLS 9688.159

Bonaly, 14 May 1852

My Dear Rutherfurd

Well, the apple will sometimes fall on the wrong side of the wall, and it has done so conspicuously on this occasion.[1] I am sorry for the public, and sorry for the person into whose bonnet this Presidential fruit ought to have dropt. But he has too much spirit and sense to repine or be angry at the fate of war. There is time enough, if he takes care of his health, for the wheel to take another turn some unexpected day, and to put things into their right places.

So the prayers of the Just do not always avail, and I have worn a hole in my best trowsers in vain. I do still think that my dear friend John Hope would have done less mischief as President than he does as Justice Clerk – not in reference to the Session, but to the Criminal Practice, as spread Circuitously over the country, where his approach seems to be to be anticipated by a gloomy shadow, and his departure followed by bright sunshine. The general satisfaction which his not being made President seems to give, is merely the popular homage to his unpopularity. However I must resign myself to his mild and reasonable sway during the remainder of my judicial pilgrimage. And I submit, as the soft and silent worm does to the ten ton roller that crushes its guts out. Oh Lord! Oh Lord! Some people say that there is hope of his drinking himself to death within two years. My Dear Rutherfurd, you are one of the persons who deal in fine wines. Do send him adequate supplies – as kindly gifts. Don't be scrubby. Grudge not. And the stronger the better.

Since I came into the world there have been President Dundas, President Miller, President Campbell, President Blair, President Hope, and President Boyle; and now we are to have President Duncan McNeill!!!!!!! I hope he'll always (as in Colonsay) wear a kilt, and give forth Gaelic Interlocutors. The

---

1 HC's hopes for Rutherfurd were dished by the change of Government. It was McNeill who accordingly went to the head of the Court. (See Walker, *Legal History of Scotland*, VI (2001), 270.) He continued Boyle's preference to be known as Lord Justice-General rather than Lord President, which HC would have greatly preferred. See *Jnl* ii.281.

Small Isles will certainly rejoice. Having a taste for soft voices like his own, he ought to have a vacational gathering in his Hebridean retreat of Hope, Anderson, and Aytoun, and then 'The wild beast of the desart shall meet with the wild beast of the Island, and the Satyr shall cry to his fellow, and the Screech Owl also shall rest there.' I hope it will not be true that 'The Isles shall *wait* for his Law'.

The Historian's[1] mounting the Bench would, I must confess, be rather ludicrous, considering the Hibernianism of the legal section of his brain. But still I hope he will mount. First, because I have always agreed with the public in thinking that, in spite of its many absurdities, [it] has considerable merit. Second, because I love him personally; and thirdly, and especially, because I don't see how he can at present be kept out of the Justiciary – which will *certainly* drive his old friend our chief even madder than he is.

All this for yourself.

I heard from Fully, I believe for the first time in my life, two days ago. Not by any means well, but better. He had then got no answer to his application for leave, and said nothing about his motions.[2]

Love to Mrs Rutherfurd, who I must go to see in the floral beauty of Lauriston.

Ever

H. Cockburn

To Elizabeth Cleghorn
NLS Dep.235(1)

Kirklands, 14 August 1852

My Dearest Lizzie

Were the waters tasty this morning? Tom surely means to leave you and to see continental sights. Heidelburgh *at least* he *must* see – not two days off, according to my *accurate* Geography.

I came here three days ago; where they are all well, social, and in great beauty – from the clouds downwards. We explore ten miles of the Jed today; and The Right Reverend Principal Lee preaches at Ancrum tomorrow; and on Monday I sink into my bowers again. I left your mother at Nasmyth's, trying another cobble at the tusks – which I understand has been somewhat successful. She was distressed by a desponding letter from Graham, faint

---

1 Archibald Alison (1792–1867); adv. 1814, Sheriff of Lanark since 1834. He was created Baronet 25 June 1852.

2 He had some three years still to live.

hearted on the anticipation of the coming job. I wish it was well over; and wish they were all out of that horrid country, from which I predict more evil now than ever. But the fear of the responsibility of urging any change keeps me passive and dumbish.

Think of Bonaly now – with shut gates, and debarring and denouncing placards, and self enjoyed internal solitude! But the intruders' numbers and impudence aroused my wrath. Fancy the impudence of a band of silked ladies and gentlemen descending from an open barouche, with a gorgeous hammer-cloth, and brilliant lacqueys, and, without saying by your leave, or with your leave, *putting their horses into the Stable*, and filling the racks with my hay, and then proceeding to flaunt and giggle thro' my borders and over the hills. Philip Brodie called them 'Besoms' – just the very word.

We had a nice day on the 10th with D.O. Hill, The Gaberlunzie, McLea, etc., and much mountain expatiation. Johanna Richardson, after being long talked of as Neuralgic, has been quite cured by getting a tooth extracted. And, by the bye, as she and her maid were going to Edinr for the pluck, she happened to ask a person in the railway carriage if he could tell her if there was a hotel near Mr Nasmyth the dentist's. On this another person she had never seen before, interfered and said that if she was going to get a tooth drawn, she ought to go to no hotel but (putting his card into her hand) to his house, hard by. She, not liking the idea of a hotel, agreed; and, having got the pull, went to him, found a room, a kind family, and a good lunch – and was here again that evening. The Sammaritan was Dean Ramsay.[1] And it was an act of Sammaritanism which I envy. What more could a Free Kirker have done? By the bye again, it would have done you, and many others who are ignorant of my merits, good, to have heard Candy's eloge on giving *my health* at the Academy dinner.[2] Just, and delicious. Dear Candy.

Write and tell me all about yourself, your neck, your strength – everything – and say that you are better than quite well, and mean to continue so. I expect the Horners next week. We had a day of the Miss Farquharsons, and of Agnes and Mrs Thomson lately. All well and pleasant. Mrs Thomson, like you all, too fleshless. Farewell – a while. Do oblige me by getting strong. Love to Tom.

Ever

H. Cockburn

1 Edward Bannerman Ramsay (1793–1872), Dean of Edinburgh 1841–72, known for his *Reminiscences of Scottish Life and Character* (1858).
2 Robert Smith Candlish (1806–1873), Minister of Free St George's and later (1862) Principal of the Free Church College.

To Sophia Rutherfurd
NLS 9688.165

Bonaly, 7 October 1852

Yes, My Dear Mrs Rutherfurd, you are quite right in your recollection of my identity. I am still a tall man, with bushy black hair, and fierce moustaches. But as I begin to fear that the old man gets tiresome to his friends, I mean, when I reappear, to come forth in a new form. I have already got my pate shaved, and the moustaches singed, and I practicing a venerable bend to diminish my stature. So don't pretend not to know me – for I warn you it is me. All that you will find unchanged is my attachment to my old friends.

I was glad to learn of your visiting, as it seemed to show that you was able for it. I trust that you have not done too much, and are now moored for the season. You are feeble, I am aware, and sometimes worse – but you are perhaps the only one not aware how much happiness, to how many friends, depends on your preserving the stock even of imperfect health that you have.

Rutherfurd, from what I saw t'other day, and from the life he is leading, seems to be truly the identical John Taaffe.

This has been an awful break in our intercourse. But, in our vocations, it was unavoidable. I recollect no summer when I was so much at home – not, I think, a fortnight away at all, circuit included.[1] It has been delicious. Your worthy spouse wanted me to dine at Lauriston on the 12th, and I half engaged. But I doubt – or rather don't doubt – my not fulfilling, for various reasons – one of which is that I suspect I shall be in the shire of Roxburgh. At present I am so shilpetish [*sc.* pinched] with cold that I shrink from shivering in the funeral ceremony of tomorrow.

What an enviable release Thomson had![2] Few powerful men escaped more shipwrecks than he did during life; but this last one beats them all. What a thing it is to live above eighty years of unchecked enjoyment, with nearly uninterrupted good health; and then, when Time was beginning to do his worst, to jink him, and the Druggist, and the Doctor, without leaving his chair, by a death so gentle that it consisted in merely ceasing to live.

He was an admirable man, in many respects, but with great defects – but these of habit rather than of nature. I anticipate great comfort to you from the presence of James's boy and your interest in him.

Ever

H. Cockburn

1 Cf *CJ*, 385–6.
2 Thomas Thomson died at Shrubhill, Edinburgh, on 2 October; he had resigned his Clerkship the previous February.

To Sir William Gibson-Craig
HWUA: 2/J/2

2 Manor Place, 6 January 1853

My Dear Sir William

If I knew what the objections to the re-appointment of Mr Deas[1] to the Solicitorship were, I might be in a condition to judge of them. But I don't, and therefore can only speak in general.

But I can at least do this candidly, for tho' I have known him, personally and professionally, for several years, I have never had any particular or domestic intimacy with him.

The only objection I ever heard to him on his *first* appointment was that some people thought him rather vulgar. I was one of these myself. But, in reference to a working public officer, this is sheer nonsense, and not worth talking about.

His conduct, and rise, since then, more than justifies the promotion he then met with. His purely professional position now is among the very highest at our bar; in so much that, with the exception only of the late, and of the present, Lord Advocate, I doubt if, for general professional ability, he has another rival. Certainly he has not two. He is unquestionably an able, and most honourable, counsel. And his personal character, in all the relations of life, has always been excellent.

If there be any good, or even plausible, objection to his reappointment, I have not even a suspicion what it is – unless it resolves into mere party spirit, or to partiality to some other person.

He sacrificed the permanent place of a sherriff for his first Solicitorship, and did the duties of both offices well; and could not be now passed over without what the public would consider as degradation.

Still if a man *deserves* degradation, he must submit to it. All I mean to say is, that if you ask me *whether* he deserves it, I answer that, so far as I know, he not only does not, but would be most worthy of still higher promotion. If he be refused to be re-placed, I have not a doubt that it must proceed from some misapprehension of what he is, or some misrepresentation by, or for, some competitor for the office.

Yours Faithfully
H. Cockburn

1 George Deas (1804–87); adv. 1828, Sheriff of Ross 1850–51, Solicitor-General 1851–2, SCJ May 1853; Kt 1858.

To Andrew Rutherfurd
NLS 9688.171
Bonaly, 11 April 1853
My Dear R.

Nothing to say, except that we are all well – and trust that you are so too. Your trip has been a great pleasure to us, for we think that you needed it. She who has been in sole possession of your memory ought to live, and will live, there, for ever.[1] But moping, most adverse to her chearful nature, does not tend to retain her. She must still be an associate of your happy and your useful hours. So I am glad that you have been in Paris, and still more that you are with our old friends (but not the *oldest*, observe) in London, and that you are to return to us in mental, as well as bodily, leige poustie [sound health].

Go and dine with Kirklands on a Sunday. You will find only his nice daughters and that everlasting rose Lady Bell, and you and he may, and should, crack a bottle of Bourdeaux over much quiet talk. And do instruct our excellent Lord Advocate *de rebus scotticis*. Give evidence to the Sherriff Committee.[2] If I could – as I certainly can not – be there, I should like to propound, and to prove, that there *never can be* a good *resident* local Judge. Consider the collaterals which promote and uphold the English Supreme Judges – the check and inspiration of each other, an able and powerful bar, the open ear of parliament, a large and varied society, ignorance of who parties are, the glory of justice. Well, remove all these spurs and bulwarks, by setting each of these Supremes down for life in a remote sphere, where their removal is aggravated by the presence of all the *opposite* attractions – in what state will these now excellent judges be in a few years? If this be true of high men, how much truer of low?

Lord John's Education scheme is sneered at here for what people call its nothingness. But they are probably wrong. The conceited give the Government no credit for want of power, and the last thing that the upholder of an abstract principle can tolerate is anything less abstract. But I hope our Scotch scheme will be something more universal. Scotland has often before now proved a good experimental garden for England, which scunners at Exotics.

Poor Duloch is said to be very ill – some say dying.[3] I have not seen Fully,

1 Mrs Rutherfurd had died on 10 October 1852.
2 Its deliberations led to the Sheriff Court Act of 1853, on which see HC in *CJ*, 296–8, continuing his argument against the 'ignorance and particularities of constant provincial residence' that would result from Sheriffs being obliged to live within their jurisdictions.
3 Cunninghame resigned later in the year, dying in 1854.

but his wife is pleased about him. Henderland got quite well at Riccarton – and keeps so. They are all in Edinr, but for how long I can't say. I had three days of Steell – eight hours each – and never thought anyone's back so beautiful.[1] On the day after tomorrow I perform Jethart Justice; leaving Dumfries to Ivory, whom I meet at Ayr.[2] We had two nice Saturdays and Sundays here of your nephew. A very sensible, trusty fellow, with one of the few manners going that are at once simple and well bred. And then the clear natural voice! It is a voice that reminds me of a burn in a wild glen. His friend *Willie* is very well.

Don't kill yourself in London. You should take at least three weeks of May at Lauriston before yoking for the Session. Our weather has been good and bad – but on the whole good. Too much wind – the most teizing of all the elements. I had Deas here again. He improves on acquaintance, but is awkwardly timid, and not a very good discusser.

Ever

H. Cockburn

If, as I anticipate, Duloch makes a vacancy, I hope Moncreiff won't bite, or be allowed to bite, the bait. If he does, then there will be an offence; for a Tory will either be made Advocate, or if this falls to Handyside, Solicitor. Such compositions seem inevitable in a composite government.

To Mrs Trotter of Dreghorn
NLS 20,263.14
2 Manor Place, 13 December 1853
My dear Mrs Trotter

Mrs Cockburn is as well as usual. She drives out on alternate days, and has not, in health, suffered from the recent event. Her chief inward regret, I suspect, is that her infirmity renders her so incapable of being actively useful. In such a scene formerly, she would have been the chief adviser, and the chief soother.[3]

---

1 Steell's bust is now in the Parliament Hall.
2 The April South Circuit is recounted in *CJ*, 389–94.
3 Mrs Cockburn ('she who for above forty-three years has been, and still is, my second and better self') was 'no longer able for journeys beyond her own flowers', and HC did the Spring Circuit alone.

Lord Fullerton was 77.[1] I hoped that resignation and repose would have given him some period for renewed health. But he sank rapidly in a few days, and died after only a few hours of gentle unconsciousness.

The family are all as well [as] can be in the dreadful circumstances. For they are left *in absolute destitution.* Some debt will not be paid – for which I care very little. If creditors will lend foolishly, that is their affair. But the widow and four daughters have, literally, not one farthing. *Not bread.* How this has happened, it is not easy to explain, or to comprehend. There must have been very considerable, and long continued, imprudence; and the public imputation of this it is very bitter to be obliged to submit to.

An attempt is making made to raise among relations and friends what may give them £300 or £400 a year; but the success of this effort is very doubtful. At the best, they are certain to be crushed into a position new and painful to them. Mrs Fullerton, in the meanwhile, and a daughter, are going to Hermand, we take the only son, who goes to India in summer, and the rest go to Fullerton's sister Mrs Monteith of Carstairs. Poor Mary, the Roman – and except in her Romanism a sensible young woman, and very dutiful – has raised herself greatly in my sight, by announcing that she means to go out as a Governess (I suppose) and that she is already in communication with a family – Papistical of course – which she thinks will be glad to have her.

Sad! Sad! Less on account of present degradation, than on account of the self blame of now irrecoverable error. That the family was kept ignorant, only adds to our wonder of the folly of the able, agreeable, and amiable person who is gone. The spectacle of this ruined household ought to reconcile others to their smaller privations.

Coutts' success delights me.[2] Really delights me. It proves his talent and industry, and his health, and will send him on his eastern destination strong in character and in hope.

1 On 16 November 1853 HC wrote an account of his recently retired brother-in-law's public career for *Jnl,* ii, 302–4.

   The wider family busied itself on behalf of the widow and daughters, as HC reported to Thomas Cleghorn at the end of the year: '£400 a year has been obtained, without resorting to any stranger, or going beyond 6 or 8 of the nearest relations; besides about £1000 for setting whatever permanent system of living may be adopted agoing. This is as much as the family needs, or ought to need.'

2 Coutts Trotter was second in his year at the East India College, with medals in political economy and history, and prizes in classics and Hindustani.

Make Mary's skin and cold water intimate acquaintances, and the Bath air won't weaken her. And don't overwork *the Governess*. Remember that the progress of life, with its natural acquisitions, is the true teacher; tho', no doubt, the ultimate fruit is connected with the culture of the soil.

I never see the Pentlands now nearer than from this street. They look very chearless – when seen – for our fogs are so thick that last Friday John Dundas and a sober cabman could not find the way to Riccarton, and he had to come back undined. Incredible I admit, but, like many other incredibilities quite true.

And so, God bless you, and yours. Love to Louisa, and every body.

You will understand how this unexpected calamity clouds us. Mrs Maitland and Helen are in town – both well.

Ever

H. Cockburn

To Coutts Trotter
NLS 20,263.18

Edinburgh, 13 December 1853

My Dear Coutts

Your mother has told me of your success, and no one can be more heartily gratified by it than I have been. These early, and just, triumphs are honorable and elevating to youth; but they derive their chief value from their effects in a later stage. They confer consideration and character upon occasions when these things produce important results, and raise the possessor in his own sight, and keep his views on higher objects. I do cordially sympathise with you. But I have even a deeper sympathy with your mother, whose gratification is a reward to a right minded son, beyond all that medals and glory can confer.

So, My Dear Coutts, just take these few advices. Get strong. Go eastward. Reap there the harvest that you have sown here. Don't marry a Hindoo. And in due time return, with unalienated heart, and pouches heavy with rupees, to dear old Colinton, and make Dreghorn ring with life, hospitality, and kindness.[1] A certain person will be disposed of long before that; but age can anticipate the prosperity of young friends, and cheer itself by doing so.

I hope that we shall see you before your Asiatic flight. I wish I could

---

1 HC continued these injunctions on 1 April the following year, bidding him Farewell: 'If you keep your health, I have no doubt of your rising high in your profession, and proving "a seamark" to many friends, saving him that eyes it. You are secured by age and sense, from the too generally fatal rise of early debt. It is a noble field, and will be more so yearly. It will probably not be in your time that we will need to resist, in India, the rapacity of that Imperial Theif the Czar. Horrid impudent beast.'

[268]

overhear my son George's first colloquy with you on the subject of the Pentlands – their prospects, and their new lakes.

Ever

H. Cockburn

To John Hill Burton
NLS 9395.156

Bonaly, Colinton, 25 March 1854

My Dear Burton

It is the duty of a good *Scotsman* always to proclaim, when it can be done truly, the superiority of the law of Scotland to that of England. If we don't keep our own, they will stuff us with theirs.

You see the denials by some of their sages, and the doubts of others, as to its being a crime in England when you sell compressed, and therefore not very examinable, hay, to give the package a false weight buy stuffing its inside with rotten sheep, dirt, or any other heavy thing *not hay*. I have seen too many of the oddities of English Law to wonder at any thing absurd that it may be said to contain. But our exemption from them should always be shown.

Now I don't remember the date or the name, and I have no Law books here; but the Criminal Reports will show you that within these three years or so, a worthy contractor who engaged to furnish meal for the poor in the Hebrides was tried, convicted, and punished, for this very offence at Glasgow. He mixed his meal with sand and other refuse not meal; and was convicted of this as a Fraud by our common law.

It seems to me that you might be worse employed for five minutes, than in compounding a paragraph on this subject. Besides illustrating the particular case, it might afford another to the thousand similar instances, of the folly of some of our countrymen who are ambitious of swamping our sense under the flood of English nonsense.

The Lord has laid his hand on me – in the form of a cold – ever since I came here.[1]

Ever

H. Cockburn

1 The South Circuit, at Ayr in Spring 1854, provided material for one final descriptive passage in the *Circuit Journeys* (pp.404–5). He dealt with a murder case and sentenced the panel to be hanged. On 21 April Cockburn returned to Edinburgh, made his last *Journal* entry on the 22nd, was 'seized with a serious illness' (a bowel complaint) the following day, and died on 26 April 1854, in his seventy-fifth year.

To Elizabeth Cleghorn
NLS Dep.235(1)
> Bonaly, [undated]

My Dearest Liz.

Tell Miss Cleghorn that there is only one good way of knowing how to rumble eggs – which is to come here and see me rumble them.

In so far as *description* can go, here it is.

Take a smallish pan – a *clean* one inside if possible, else the eggs will lick up all the dirt, of which they are very fond. Put the pan on the fire, till the butter melts, and then shake the butter over the inside of the pan. The object of this is to get the sides of the pan sweetly greased (like an Advocate Depute's purse by salary) and thus to prevent the eggy matter from sticking to the pan; if it does which, then, like a good Episcopalian minister who sticks to his church, it gets Bishoped.[1]

Then break the eggs by a neat pap of their sides on the sharp edge of the pan, and let their whole insides fall into the pan. Four, six, or eight make a good mouthful for two, three or four persons. Egg by itself an egg, won't rumble. N.B. Don't put in the shells.

When they are in, put the pan on the fire. In a minute, or less, they begin to show their delight by puffing out and singing.

Instantly begin to lift them off the bottom, and the sides of the pan, and keep always turning them, with a spoon. This is the agitating moment! If you don't scrape them off the pan, they will stick to it, burn, Bishop – and all is over. And don't awkwardly cut, and smash, and bruise their delicacy. It is a process of scraping the sides and bottom, lifting, and *turning*. To prevent the operator from being burned himself, the pan may be *often* taken off the fire – and then the scraping, lifting, and turning goes on sweetly, and leisurely.

In about two minutes, or less, the whites of the eggs disappear, like snowdrops, and the yokes rise in burnished yellow, like red crocuses. The whole slobbery consistancy is gone, like the primitive mud of this earth, and there is a secondary formation of beautiful little dryish knolls.

It is done!

He was buried, simply as he had requested, on 1 May 1854, in the Dean Cemetery, near Jeffrey, Rutherfurd and Thomson. James Gibson Craig told George Combe, who had it from one of Cockburn's daughters, that Henry Cockburn's last words were 'This is death, and a strange feeling it is.'

1 burnt in the cooking (*OED*).

Turn these churny hillocks out into the *Oval* plate, with the spoon. Eat while they are hot, and you will have ate eggs in their best form.

But *Take Notice* that the eggs had better be fresh. At least for ordinary palates and noses. But if rotten ones be preferred, this process brings out their flavour delightfully. And it is not a bad way of doing even the chickens.

But the true way is to come here and see it. Which I hope your Aunts will soon be able to do. Or if you chuse to give an egg party in town, my services are to be got upon reasonable terms.

Ever

H. Cockburn

Appendix: Cockburn's Children

Cockburn and his wife had eleven children, most of whom married and produced grandchildren. The two unmarried daughters were *Margaret,* who died in infancy in 1818, and *Jane,* who died in 1878. Jane was an invalid even in her father's lifetime, but survived to be the final life-rentrix of Cockburn's Trust, of which a distribution was arranged following her death. The other sons and daughters were:

Archibald William (1814–62). At Edinburgh Academy 1824–30, then medical training: MD (Edin.), FRCSE. In practice, then a Government Inspector of Lunatic Asylums. Married 1844 Mary (d.1903), daughter of James Balfour of Pilrig.

James (1816–85). At Edinburgh Academy 1824–30. In a Syria merchant's office for two years, then in a New South Wales commercial house, which failed; then for two years in Ceylon, planting coffee. Became, through Lord Grey's influence, a stipendiary magistrate in Mauritius.

Graham [daughter] (1817–97). Married 1839, the Revd Robert Walker Stewart (1812–87), Protestant evangelist of the Waldensian Alps.

George Fergusson (1818–66). Edinburgh Academy 1825–7; East India College, Haileybury 1834–6. HEICS, Bengal 1836–66, latterly Commissioner at Patna; retired 1866. Married 1842, Sarah Charlotte Bishop (d.1903). (Evelyn Waugh was descended from George Cockburn's daughter Lily, later Raban.)

Henry G. Day (1820–67). Edinburgh Academy 1828–34. With a Liverpool merchant 1836, later in Canada. Married Anne (Annie) Weatheley

Laurence (1822–71). Edinburgh Academy 1831–7. Married 1856, Annie Maria Smith.

Francis Jeffrey (1825–93). Edinburgh Academy 1833–9; East India College, Haileybury 1843–5. Married Eliza A. Pitcairn. HEICS Bengal 1845–73, latterly as judge of Dacca, and later of Sylhet. (Claud Cockburn was descended from Francis son Henry, of the Chinese Consular Service.)

Elizabeth ('Wifie'), d. 1908. Married 1848, Thomas Cleghorn (1818–1874), advocate; Sheriff of Argyll 1855.

Johanna (1831–88). Married Archibald David Cockburn (1826–86), and was mother of Harry A[rchie] Cockburn, the family historian.

Index